SPECULATIONS ON AMERICAN HISTORY

SPECULATIONS ON AMERICAN HISTORY

MORTON BORDEN
OTIS L. GRAHAM, Jr.

University of California, Santa Barbara

D. C. HEATH AND COMPANY

LEXINGTON, MASSACHUSETTS / TORONTO

ACKNOWLEDGMENTS

Stewart Alsop, "War, Not Politics," *Newsweek,* 14 May 1973, p. 132. Copyright © 1973 by Newsweek Inc. All rights reserved. Reprinted by permission.

Daniel Ellsberg, *Papers on the War* (New York: Simon and Schuster, 1972), p. 28. Reprinted by permission.

Herbert Feis, *From Trust to Terror* (New York: W. W. Norton, 1970), p. 92.

David Halberstam, *The Best and the Brightest* (New York: Random House, 1972), p. 301.

David Halberstam, "Roots of a Tragedy," *Santa Barbara News Press,* 22 April 1973. Reprinted by permission.

John F. Kennedy, Foreword to *Decision-Making in the White House,* by Theodore C. Sorensen (New York: Columbia University Press, 1963).

Ernest R. May, *Lessons of the Past* (New York: Oxford University Press, 1973), pp. 22–23. Reprinted by permission.

Daniel P. Moynihan, *Coping* (New York: Random House, 1973), p. 33.

Richard P. Nathan, *The Plot That Failed: Nixon and the Administrative Presidency* (New York: John Wiley and Sons, 1975), p. 92. Reprinted by permission.

Kenneth P. O'Donnell, David F. Powers, and Joseph McCarthy, *"Johnny, We Hardly Knew Ye": Memories of John Fitzgerald Kennedy* (Boston: Little, Brown & Co., 1972).

Preface

The authors, as teachers of history, have always led their students in some speculation about "what might have been." We recall that our own teachers frequently did so, as have historians in their writing from the earliest times. In careless hands, such speculation can range from diversionary flights of fancy all the way to flogging the dead for not having done what we would have done. But properly handled, the investigation of options not taken is a marvelously illuminating method of inquiry. It refreshes interest in sometimes jaded events by suggesting that they were not inevitable. It revives actors and options long forgotten, enabling them to be taken seriously again as they once were in a fluid historical context. It helps us to reconstruct historical episodes with greater fidelity to the actual ordering and weighting of events and factors by removing somewhat from our minds the overwhelming knowledge of who the winners turned out to be. One asks: How might the thrust of history have been changed if a certain event or decision had gone another way? Could things have turned out very differently and, if so, how differently? Such speculation sharpens one's sense of how change occurs. It was with this in mind that Sir Lewis Namier liked to say that history could not tell us what would happen in the future, but that it did suggest the sorts of things that were *not* likely to happen.

Some historians, impressed with the possibilities of taking seriously what might have been, have conducted entire studies which project likely historical outcomes from some altered factor. Such is, for example, the "counterfactual" economic history pioneered by Robert Fogel and others. In this book we propose nothing quite so formal, although we build upon the same conviction that the serious study of alternatives is a promising tool of analysis. Speculation of this sort brings us immediately and repeatedly to one of the fundamental questions: the role of individuals as against historical forces. We have frequently focussed on just this issue in these essays, asking how things might conceivably have turned out had one person's decision been altered or a decisive presence been removed. A few of the essays deal with more impersonal conjunctions of events. Occasionally, we conclude that things would probably have been very different if some pivotal moment in history were even slightly altered. History sometimes seems to us full of diverse possibilities. Sometimes we cannot escape the judgment that those who hoped for a different path, indeed, contemporaries who would criticize our predecessors for some error or folly, failed to perceive the irresistible convergence of events toward one outcome.

We do not expect everyone to agree with our conclusions. Quite the contrary, our purpose will be served if they engender discussion, dissent, and renewed inquiry. Our hope is that, by reflecting upon what might have happened, the reader will better understand what did happen. We would like to think that these essays may dispel somewhat that deadening and misleading sense of fatalism which so strongly pervades contemporary life, and which led the aging John L. Lewis to say: "The doors of history swing on tiny hinges. Nothing is more barren and futile than speculation on what might have been." This sentiment suffocates history, for it rejects the numerous exciting options whose import and interaction it is the task of the historical imagination to revive.

Morton Borden is the author of the first six essays; Otis L. Graham, Jr., of the last six. We owe a special debt to Rexford G. Tugwell, as well as to our colleagues, W. Elliot Brownlee, Carl V. Harris, and Donald Hickey, who had the patience to read and to criticize some of these essays. What mistakes remain are ours, but there would have been more without their perceptive comments. Our debt to Penn and Ann, our partners these many years, is measured by a different scale which only the four of us understand. We dedicate this book to them.

MORTON BORDEN
OTIS L. GRAHAM, Jr.

Table of Contents

1 1759: What If Canada Had Remained French?   3

2 1784: What If Slavery Had Been Geographically Confined?   17

3 1789: Could the Articles of Confederation Have Worked?   29

4 1801: Would Aaron Burr Have Been a Great President?   43

5 1832: What If the Second Bank Had Been Rechartered?   57

6 1850: What If the Compromise of 1850 Had Been Defeated?   71

7 1887: Whites and Indians—Was There a Better Way?   85

8 1917: What If the United States Had Remained Neutral?   103

9 1933: What Would the 1930s Have Been Like Without Franklin Roosevelt?   119

10 1945: The United States, Russia, and the Cold War—What If Franklin Roosevelt Had Lived?   139

11 1963: The United States and Vietnam—What If John F. Kennedy Had Lived?   163

12 1974: What If There Had Been No Watergate?   183

Index   197

SPECULATIONS ON AMERICAN HISTORY

What If Canada Had Remained French?

Conventional wisdom has it that tremendous historical consequences were at stake in the summer of 1759, when the English general, James Wolfe, appeared with his army before the walls of Quebec. Had he lost to the French defenders led by the Marquis de Montcalm, so it is argued, the American Revolution would not have taken place. English colonists would never have risked a rebellion while the French menace remained. Moreover, the French would have controlled the great Mississippi basin and would have imposed their own cultural patterns and political forms which, in time, would have expanded to the Pacific Ocean. Instead of inheriting from the English "the boon of rational and ordered liberty," North America would have absorbed its institutions from a corrupt and despotic regime. Thus the battle of Quebec pitted freedom against feudalism, individualism and self-reliance against obedience and uniformity, an open society against a closed society, and religious liberty against Catholicism. This Anglo-Saxon interpretation is at the core of nineteenth-century scholarship and continues as the dominant theme in many texts. The following essay offers a somewhat different speculation.

Quebec was a difficult but not an impregnable target. Located on a steep granite cliff fronting on the St. Lawrence River, it was vulnerable to attack from the landed side. But all summer long the repeated skirmishes and bombardments had not advanced Wolfe's goal. Quite the contrary, the English field hospitals overflowed with the wounded, and Wolfe ordered the graveyards camouflaged to mask his losses from the enemy. Only once had a French force ventured from Quebec in a farcical night-time raid of utter confusion, which resulted in their firing upon one another. Thereafter Montcalm stayed within Quebec in a distinctly defensive posture. If he could hold out long enough, the Canadian winter would lift the siege of Quebec. Ice skim was already reported in September, and the English fleet had to leave the St. Lawrence or risk being trapped by a freeze which would doom the entire squadron.

With courage born of desperation, Wolfe decided to attempt a final maneuver. Ships and men were rowed upstream and then, on a dark night, drifted down in silence to Anse au Foulon (now known as Wolfe's Cove), a mile from Quebec, where a narrow trail zigzagged up the rock cliff. "The difficulty of gaining the top of the hill is scarcely credible," Admiral Charles Saunders reported. "It was very steep in its ascent, and high, and had no path where two could go abreast, but they were obliged to pull themselves up by the stumps and boughs of trees that covered the declivity." One by one, a handful of English soldiers scrambled to the top and quickly routed a small force of French defenders. By dawn an English army of 4,800, arrayed for battle, stood on the Plains of Abraham against a French force of comparable size. With his supply lines cut and with no reserves of food in Quebec, Montcalm's options were limited. He could wait a brief time for reinforcements of troops and artillery, which were available, or he could march on the English immediately. Impulsively, Montcalm chose the latter. "Etes-vous preparés, mes enfants?" Montcalm asked his troops, who roared their affirmative. But the French soldiers were amateurs compared to the skilled, professional English legions.

On the morning of September 13, 1759, under a withering and accurate fire at close range—an English historian called it the "most perfect volley ever fired on a battlefield"—the French broke and fled. Both generals were mortally wounded, with Montcalm in retreat and Wolfe dying in the happy knowledge of an impending victory. Montreal fell after Quebec and, by the peace treaty signed in Paris in 1763, half a continent changed hands.

Military history is particularly susceptible to speculations of what might have been. Chance and circumstance weigh heavily in battle. Napoleon Bonaparte once remarked that a wise strategist must calculate the odds with mathematical certainty lest "an overlooked fraction" alter the results. Had the little cove at Anse au Foulon been better defended, had Quebec been better provisioned, had Montcalm not attacked prematurely, had the English been forced to leave because of winter, Canada might still be French.

So many contemporaries predicted that the English victory at Quebec would generate a revolution in the colonies that it became virtually a self-fulfilling prophecy. Scarcely two months after Quebec fell, an English officer stationed in New York wrote home advising against the annexation of all of Canada. "Another advantage of a French neighborhood," he warned, "would be a good pretext to oblige each colony to support a certain quota of troops, apparently for their own defense, but also to keep them in proper subjection to the Mother Country."

From 1760 to 1763, the question of whether England should annex Canada or the sugar island of Guadeloupe was widely debated in the press, in pamphlets, and on the floor of Parliament. Once England opted for Canada as the spoils of war, a number of French statesmen voiced their delight. The French ambassador serving in Constantinople remarked to an English acquaintance: "You are happy in the cession of Canada; we, perhaps, ought to think ourselves happy that you have acquired it. Delivered from a neighbour whom they have always feared, your other colonies will soon discover that they stand no longer in need of your protection. You will call on them to contribute toward supporting the burden which they have helped to bring on you; they will answer you by shaking off all dependence." Ten years later, when the colonies were in fact in the throes of rebellion, the governor of Massachusetts, Thomas Hutchinson, noted that had Canada "remained to the French none of the spirit of opposition would have yet appeared." There would have been no colonial surge for Western lands, no imperial parliamentary legislation to antagonize the colonists, no reexamination of their position within the British empire, no consciousness of their separate identity, and no revolutionary motive. The scholar Francis Parkman put the matter most succinctly: "With the fall of Quebec began the history of the United States."

Such logic seems to ignore the entire direction of American colonial history which, almost from the beginning, pointed toward self-determination. As early as 1656, James Harrington wrote in *Oceana* that, while the colonies "are yet babes" in need of a parent, they would "wean themselves . . . when they come of age." Lord Cornbury, who served as governor of New York, said essentially the same thing: "If once they [the colonists] can see they can clothe themselves without the help of England, they—who are already not very fond of submitting to government—would soon think of putting into execution designs they have long harbored in their breasts." No one in America spoke of revolution, but decades before the Seven Years War there was a growing awareness of the colonies' distinct interests, which the English government chose to ignore. "The last and greatest unhappiness the Plantations labor under," an anonymous pamphleteer wrote in 1701, "is that the King and Court are altogether strangers to the true state of affairs in America, for that is the true cause why their grievances have not been long since redressed." In 1736 Sir Robert Brown complained to the Earl of Egmont "that there was a spirit in all the colonies to throw off their dependency on the Crown of England."

Year by year, colonial legislatures were assuming greater powers. They had control over taxes and appropriations, and the power of the purse gave these assemblies a major voice in military and judicial matters, in the appointments of public officers, in Indian relations, and in ecclesiastical policies. The fact is that—whether or not Canada remained French—England and its colonies were on a political collision course. "The assembly," warned William Shirley, governor of Massachusetts, in 1748, "seems to have left scarcely any part of His Majesty's prerogative untouched, and they have gone great lengths towards getting the government, military as well as civil, into their hands." The governor of New York, George Clinton, agreed. It is "high time," he informed his superiors in England, "to put a stop to these perpetually growing encroachments of the assemblies."

The English government intended to do just that, but the Seven Years War temporarily interrupted their determination to tighten imperial controls. Nevertheless, articulated colonial dissent was common throughout the war years. When English officials imposed an embargo on colonial shipping from Virginia northward in 1757, the Pennsylvania legislature remonstrated with these words: "A people cannot be said to be free, nor in the possession of their rights and properties, when their Rulers shall by their sole authority even during the sitting of their assemblies, stop the circulation of their commerce, discourage the labor and industry of the people, and reduce the province to the greatest distress." Still other portents of later struggle began to surface with increased frequency. Patrick Henry in 1759 argued that the Privy Council's disallowance of a Virginia law was a violation of the original compact. In 1761 James Otis, as counsel for Boston merchants, argued that parliamentary writs of assistance, which permitted royal officers to search private property for smuggled goods, were null and void. An English vicar, traveling through Virginia in 1759, noted that the people were "haughty and jealous of their liberties, impatient of restraint, and can scarcely bear the thought of being controlled by any superior power."

One could find many indicators of loyalty to England throughout the colonies: the Union Jack displayed, oaths of fidelity, toasts to the empire, prayers for the health and long life of the monarchy, and appeals to fight against the French. A poem published in a Philadelphia magazine in 1757 contained the following couplets:

> Reason's sovereign empire, *Britons,* O maintain,
> While Deamons yell, and Monks blaspheme in vain. . . .
>
> Thy Country calls! Rise, with recovered force
> To curb the insulting *Gaul's* impetuous course!

Benjamin Franklin testified that, before 1763, the colonists "had not only a respect, but an affection, for Great Britain, for its laws, its customs and manners, and even a fondness for its fashions. . . . Natives of Great Britain were always treated with particular regard." Yet the colonials gradually were becoming conscious of their separate identity. Third- and fourth-generation inhabitants spoke and thought differently than the English did. Moreover, hundreds of thousands of non-English immigrants had decisively broken English ethnic homogeneity in the colonies. A sense of continental community began to emerge. They published *American* magazines, boasted of the superiority of *American* arms, and spoke of a unique *American* destiny. Clearly they considered themselves more virtuous than the English, whose electoral corruptions were common knowledge. They resented the discriminations practiced by English officials, and bridled at the cultural condescensions of English visitors. " 'Tis true we in America are little inferior things in comparison of you great folks in London," James Logan noted sarcastically. Colonial patriotism received an enormous spur from the English victory at Quebec. Even then, while genuine, it was limited, fragile, grounded in self-interest, and laced with a thousand jealousies.

Let us assume that Montcalm had defeated Wolfe, and that Canada had remained French. How would that have altered conditions? *First,* England still would have had an enormous public debt, the accumulated costs of four major wars fought in 70 years. King George III still would have complained about "this bloody and expensive war." Englishmen still would have rioted against the heavy tax burden, and pressured Parliament for relief. They still would have had the cost of maintaining garrisons in the West Indies, Gibraltar, Minorca, and the thirteen colonies. Under these circumstances, Parliament would have enacted tax measures against the colonies, and those laws would have been resisted.

Second, during the Seven Years War the English government was angry at the large number of colonists who, with no consciousness of guilt, traded with the French and Spanish. "This dangerous and ignominious trade," William Pitt called it, "was subversive of all law, and highly subversive of the honor and well-being of this Kingdom." Healthy commercial relations with its colonies was an economic sacrament of English mercantilism. Yet, in 1760 the total indebtedness of the colonists to English merchants amounted to £2 million, and that figure would soon double. Does one suppose that, with such a deterioration in the American balance of trade and with the French nearby, England would have permitted the colonials to continue their easy evasions of Parliament's navigation acts? Does one suppose that the colonials, who were economically dependent upon this trade, would have willingly relinquished it?

Third, Wolfe's defeat at Quebec would have confirmed colonial doubts about the competence of English generals and the fighting qualities of English soldiers—a scorn that was reciprocated by the English. It should be remembered that Wolfe's contemptuous regard for colonial soldiers was overlooked because of his victory and would not have been overlooked in case of his defeat. Colonials, at times with more faith than evidence, regarded their militia as superior marksmen, strategists, and guerrillas, who could assemble quickly, knew the forests, and possessed the determination that professional soldiers lacked. Their distrust of standing armies—leeches whom they had to house, feed, and pay taxes to support, and who could not fight very well—antedated the Revolution. Wolfe's defeat would have spurred colonial self-reliance and a movement for intercolonial cooperation.

As for the French, colonials hated but did not really fear them. A hint of their attitude was revealed in a notation that Benjamin Franklin inked into the margin of his pamphlet: "The Interest of Great Britain considered with Regard to her Colonies and the Acquisitions of Canada and Guadaloupe." Franklin had argued for Britain's retention of Canada so that the American colonies would feel secure from the French menace. His later marginal comment read: "Never were apprehensive of the Indians, nor much of the French." In 1760 the Americans outnumbered the Canadians by a ratio of twenty to one in total population, and at least three to one in the Northwest.

Historians reason that the removal of the French, and the problems of governing an empire, necessitated laws and policies which terminated in revolution. They sometimes comment upon the overwhelming colonial reaction after 1763, the sudden sprouting of rebellion which seemed out of proportion to the stimulus. But the seeds had been planted years earlier, and those seeds had taken root and would have flowered in due course. One might argue, of course, that French retention of Canada would have bound England and its colonies closer than ever before, and that they would have sought and found workable political solutions to imperial problems. Such an argument presumes that the English government was wiser, and that the colonials were prepared to make greater economic sacrifices than was actually the case. Of necessity, there would have been new revenue laws, quartering acts, stricter controls on illegal trade and smuggling, and curtailment of provincial legislative encroachments upon royal authority—with appropriate colonial reactions.

One can more reasonably speculate that the divergent concepts of power of the English and colonials, their quarrels over rights, their potential for economic rivalry, and their separate visions of the future, had to end in separation.

If Montcalm had won at Quebec, according to the implications of Anglo-Saxon texts, legions of nuns and priests would have descended upon North America. The spirit of the Enlightenment would have been crushed, and religious uniformity enforced from the St. Lawrence to the Mississippi. Every aspect of government would have been rigidly controlled by the old regime through its corrupt bureaucracy. The growth of capitalism would have been retarded. Soldiers would have kept a craven and inferior people in check. Thus the assumption of many scholars is that, while English colonials were transformed by the New World, the French were not. The former were "much more susceptible to the wonderful leavening effect of the frontier," writes Howard H. Peckham. "The democratizing influence, the nationalizing impact, the demands of resourcefulness, the experience in establishing governments, the rich rewards of individual work—all these factors infused Englishmen in America with much more ardor than Frenchmen and gave them strength." French colonials were saddled with a feudal inheritance, and four authorities—monarchy, clergy, aristocracy, and monopoly—drained their vitality and initiative. "New France . . . was truly an extension of the Old World," Peckham concludes, "and therein lay its failing."

The fact is that France in the seventeenth century tried but was unable to impose a feudal system upon Canada. A society was planned in which the vast majority would be peasants firmly fixed to the land, living peaceably in their villages, and responding obediently to the lay and ecclesiastical *seigneurs* whose rights, privileges, and duties were spelled out in meticulous detail. But in Canada, as in the English colonies, the realities of the New World altered the blueprints of European planners. Both societies were short of labor. Both were forced to make concessions to attract immigrants, and valued workers rather than gentlemen. Both used indentured servants, many of whom fled into the wilderness. In Canada, as in the English colonies, there was a degree of social egalitarianism unknown in Europe. "Everyone is *monsieur* or *madame*" in Canada, the traveler Peter Kalm noted in the 1740s, "the peasant as well as the gentleman, the peasant lady as well as their greatest lady." Another observer, Baron La Hontan, remarked: "The peasants are at their ease. What, did I say peasants? . . . They do not pay the salt tax nor the poll tax; they hunt and fish freely, in a word they are rich. How can you compare them with our wretched peasants? How many nobles and gentlemen would throw their old parchments into the fire at that price?" The peasant had been transformed by North America into an independent freeman who might be influenced or gulled but never driven.

And what of their character? The Canadians also shared a sense of alienation from the motherland. French and Canadian officers quarreled bitterly. "We seem to belong to another, almost an enemy, nation," complained Montcalm's aide, Colonel Louis-Antoine de Bougainville. Montcalm himself commented that Canadians recognized "neither rule nor regulation," though he complimented their "intelligence and courage." Certainly the English victory embittered the French Canadians, and as a conquered people they have maintained and even intensified their cultural heritage.

But even before 1759 the Canadians formed a remarkably homogeneous bloc. Like the English colonists, they frequently defied royal officials. Like them, they hated to pay taxes. It was always easier to collect tithes in Virginia than in Canada. French administrations were alarmed at their spirit of independence. In 1751 the Minister of Marine wrote that Canadians "long only for independence even at the sacrifice of their own security." The governor-general requested more troops to control the people, who manifested *"une indépendance extraordinaire."* As for individualism, that much misused term, no Anglo-Saxon could match the *coureurs de bois.* "We were Caesars," boasted Pierre Radisson, most famous of all Canadian frontiersmen, "[there] being nobody to contradict us."

The only challenge came from the neighboring Anglo-Saxons, who were cultural rivals and territorial competitors. France long ago had abandoned its hopes of wiping out the Atlantic states: they were too strong and stable, solidly occupied, and prosperous, with excellent water communication along the ocean highway. "We must not flatter ourselves that our colonies can compete in wealth with the adjoining English," the governor of Canada, Michel La Galissonière, advised the ministry in 1750. But France expected to control the Mississippi valley by surrounding the Americans and confining them east of the Appalachians. By itself, Canada was not worth much to the French. Emigration there was minimal. Voltaire dismissed the colony as "a few acres of snow." The Count of Vergennes, after the American Revolution, had no desire to recover Canada. "It cannot be denied," wrote La Galissonière, "that Canada has always been a burden to France." As part of a sweeping empire, which stretched in an arc across the heartland of the continent, however, Canada held an enormous attraction. Peter Kalm believed such an empire would be "the foundation to the rise of France," and lamented that his own country (Sweden) had withdrawn from the competition.

The policy that Michel La Galissonière detailed at mid-century might have been followed by France had Montcalm won at Quebec: to link Canada and Louisiana by concentrating on the Illinois lands. "It is a country easy to cultivate and clear," he wrote to the Count de Maurepas, "and greatly coveted by our neighbors. . . . Should a populous Illinois be capable of harassing the English colonies, they possess scarcely less facilities for seizing the Illinois. . . . Of all the countries in our occupation, this is the one they can invade most easily with the smallest force; and could they once succeed in thus intruding themselves between our two colonies, the loss of the Mississippi and the ruin of the internal trade with Canada would be assured."

La Galissonière outlined the steps necessary to populate Illinois. Married soldiers were to be sent there and given land, tools, and livestock at the expiration of their terms of service. Salt smugglers from France as well as "sturdy beggars" "and even some bad women" (*femmes de mauvaise vie*) might be added. Nothing should be spared to strengthen this area. La Galissonière envisioned a Mississippi valley not inhabited by independent *coureurs de bois* and fur traders but by stable agricultural communities that would serve to subjugate the savages and limit the Anglo-Saxons. That the French government agreed can be read in the ministerial minutes of September 2, 1751: "The Beautiful river has always served as a communication between Canada and Louisiana. . . . There is no other course to adopt than to drive from the Beautiful river any foreigners who will happen to be there, so as to make them lose all taste for returning thither."

The Americans, of course, had no taste for the cold marginal lands north of the lakes, but preferred the cheap and fertile frontier lands to the west. It is true that the Continental Congress invited Canada to become a fourteenth state. Also, periodically in the nineteenth century, a few fanatics demanded that Canada be seized by force, and a few deluded romantics assumed that most Canadians wished to join the United States. As late as 1904 a Boston newspaper announced every day, in bold type at the top of the page, that it was the first duty of the United States to annex Canada. Such exotics never represented American opinion. The course of empire was due west, along latitudinal lines, to what George Washington called "a second land of promise." Americans' pride and determination, their impulse toward mobility, and their characteristic belief that distant lands were preferable could not be denied. By the end of the eighteenth century, their expansionist energies began to pulsate, as rivulets of settlers and speculators breached the mountain barriers and poured onto the coveted lands beyond.

Both Canadians and Americans were materialistic enough to profit by trading with one another during the Seven Years War. But that did not lessen their mutual suspicions and deep hatreds. "The most nearly impassable chasm between one group of North Americans and another aside from that between white and negro," the scholar John Brebner has noted, "lay between the French and British colonists." The Canadians regarded Americans as barbarous and overly acquisitive, and spoke derisively of *"les Bostonnais."* Anglo-Saxon Protestants looked upon Catholic Canadians as subhuman, misguided tools of the Pope, on the same level as the perfidious Spaniards. "What we have above everything else to fear," Samuel Adams stated in New England fashion, "is popery." John Jay's reaction to the Quebec Act of 1774 bordered on the paranoid, and was typical. He declared that Catholicism spreads "impiety, bigotry, persecution, murder, and rebellion throughout every part of the world." He prophesied that if the Quebec Act was permitted to stand, the number of Canadian Catholics would multiply, an Inquisition would be imposed, and the Protestant colonies would be reduced to slavery. There were then some 60,000 Americans settled in the Old Northwest. Would they be subjected to the Romish church? If these fears were current while England possessed Canada, one can readily imagine their multiplication had Montcalm won at Quebec.

Thus, for territorial and cultural reasons, the two New World societies would have come to blows. Probably the upper Mississippi valley would have been the area of early skirmishes and then major battles, comparable to the American and Mexican rivalry in the Southwest some 40 years later. From Venango to Pickawillany to Vincennes to Kaskasia, the war would have continued over several seasons. To speculate on its military outcome, however, is to enter the realm of pure conjecture. There are simply too many hypothetical variables to make a balanced judgment. On the one hand, the Americans had a distinct numerical advantage. Even if the French government had encouraged emigration, the weight of numbers still would have favored the Americans. On the other hand, the Canadians could count on a majority of Indian tribes as allies, though some authorities would consider such an alliance of dubious value.* How much help either the Canadians or the Americans would have received from foreign sources is equally problematical. One can well imagine sporadic conflicts between the two, extending well into the nineteenth century, with a cycle of truces negotiated, violated, and reaffirmed.

Had history unfolded as this essay suggests, the national characteristics of Canadians would have been considerably altered. Canada has been a country divided between two identities, the French and the English. Their antagonisms occasionally have erupted in bloodshed and, in the 1960s, threatened to sunder the nation. Moreover, Canada has been without a revolutionary tradition. Neither the American nor the French Revolution made any radical impact, and Canada had none to call its own.† Quite the contrary, American loyalists flocked there; colonial Toryism was given a second chance and quickly came to dominate the economic and political life of Canada. Their goal was to copy the English, and to preserve the old order. As a result, though a democracy and despite its frontier experience, Canada has been more conservative than the United States, the people more reserved, cautious, and restrained. "In Canada," writes the sociologist Kaspar Naegele, "there seems to be a greater acceptance of limitation, of hierarchical patterns. There seems to be less optimism, less

---

*Indians who joined whites on wilderness campaigns frequently refused to follow orders, rejected discipline, and failed to ration food supplies. Nevertheless, anyone familiar with the Indian uprising of 1763 led by the Ottawa chief Pontiac cannot summarily dismiss their fighting qualities. Before peace was restored, George Croghan estimated, the Indians "killed or captivated not less than two thousand of his Majesty's subjects and drove some thousands to beggary and the greatest distress."

†Canada, of course, had serious internal conflicts, as manifested by the Rebellion of 1837.

faith in the future, less willingness to risk capital or reputation." More than one commentator has diagnosed the Canadian character as suffering from a massive inferiority complex.

A wholly French Canada, on the other hand, might well have represented an amalgamation of New World opportunities and the ideology of 1789, forging a race of ambitious and enterprising people. As the Revolution of 1688 helped to provide England with a modern framework for economic and political progress, so the French Revolution would have abetted the impetus for similar developments in Canada.

First of all, religion in Canada was largely rooted in institutional loyalty rather than theological conviction. "Religion here," wrote Peter Kalm, "appears to consist solely in exterior practices." A church official, Monsignor Briand, agreed: "How little faith there is in Canada, although the outer shell remains!" Despite the presence of some ultramontane Catholics, most Canadians were not apt to accept political direction emanating from the local curate or the papal see. Even the pious could be anticlerical and could support fundamental revolutionary changes with no sense of inconsistency. Thus the doctrines of the Rights of Man and the concepts of liberty, equality, and fraternity would have penetrated, for the Canadian character was receptive.

Second, French Canada would have adopted the Napoleonic codes, which not only preserved the fundamental principles of the Revolution, but provided for economic freedom as well. The *Code civil* (1805) and the *Code de commerce* (1807), expressly authorizing loans at interest, were of primary importance for the growth of capitalism in Catholic countries.

French technical knowledge would have been attracted by the enormous challenges of the Mississippi valley. Instead of channeling venture capital into Iberian canals and bridges, Balkan factories and railroads, or Latin American banks and electric companies, French investors undoubtedly would have preferred to develop the Lake Superior copper deposits and Galena lead mines. From being a colony noted for its monopolies, bureaucratic corruptions, and dependence upon the fur trade, Canada would have become a major power in its own right, with a thriving and diversified economy. There would have been countless problems, no doubt: jealousies between old settlers and new, agricultural versus commercial interests, and home rule against imperial regulations. Whether these problems ultimately would have led the Canadians to follow the American example of independence, if such were the case, is difficult to say. Much would have depended upon the wisdom of French administrators, for revolutionaries must work among the discontented or their efforts will be stillborn. A Canada with a substantial economic growth rate in the nineteenth century would not have been particularly receptive to revolution. Undiluted by English stock and threatened by the always encroaching Americans, the Canadians would have possessed a degree of unity, a sense of purpose, and a belief in progress to match those of any Anglo-Saxon.

Contrary, then, to the assumption that the New World worked its magical transformations only upon the English colonists, it is easy to speculate that the Canadians would have developed along similar lines. A trinity of republicanism, Catholicism, and capitalism would have defined the institutional limits within which Canadians operated. In the nineteenth century, there was nothing inherently contradictory among these three. They would have had an American cast, however, that was a blend of the frontier and history. "Here," wrote Alexis de Tocqueville in 1831 after a visit to the French Canadians, "are all the elements of a great people." Then he added with a touch of pride and sadness:

> They have preserved the greater part of the original traits of the national character, and have added more morality and more simplicity. They have broken free from a crowd of prejudices and false points of departure which cause and will cause all the miseries of Europe. In a word, they have in them all that is needed to create a great memory of France in the New World.

One can speculate endlessly on how a looming French-Canadian presence to the north and west might have affected the American character. However, it is safe to say that instead of the United States becoming a haven for all mankind—"a chosen country, with room enough for our descendants to the hundredth and thousandth generation," as Thomas Jefferson said—immigration restrictions would have been demanded and imposed against Catholics. Anti-Catholicism has been an old and familiar prejudice of Protestants, flaring into full-scale bigotry in the decades before the Civil War. Fierce religious riots swept through virtually every major American city, resulting in hundreds of deaths. Nevertheless, the number of Catholics rose from 318,000 in 1830 (3 percent of the population) to 3,100,000 in 1860 (10 percent of the population). In the end, economic necessity proved stronger than religious bigotry. Catholics were needed as laborers in factories, on farms, and on canals, to do the hard, dirty, low-paid jobs others disdained. But with limited opportunities, without an open frontier beckoning all who dreamed of wealth, and with Canadian Catholics challenging Anglo-Saxon Protestants for continental suzerainty, nativism would have become a basic and unshakable tenet of the American faith. Irish Catholics would have been kept out and would have emigrated to Canada or South America instead. The Catholics who remained, remnants of older settlements such as in Maryland, would have lived in separate enclaves under constant vigilance, suspicion, and hostility.

It also seems predictable that the existence of a fortified boundary, in addition to territorial quarrels carrying the potential of armed conflict, would have forced the Americans (and Canadians) to become more militaristic. Instead of deep suspicions of professional armies; instead of emphasizing the primacy of civilian superiority; instead of revering leaders such as George Washington and Dwight Eisenhower for other than soldierly traits, Americans might have created a substantial military elite supported by large defense budgets. In other words, the United States might have followed a European pattern in which the military occupied an important, if not a dominant, social and political position.

"The sense of collective power, demonstrated in the rapidity and extent of westward expansion," the philosopher Ralph Barton Perry has commented, "led Americans to confuse bigger and better, and to identify value with velocity, area, altitude and number." That they were the only hope of mankind became axiomatic, and their mission to save the world became a part of their gospel. These traits might well have been modified in subtle ways had the course of empire not been so open, and had the competitive struggle for possession of the West been played out by two equally formidable contestants. Limited in area, Americans might have been less profligate. Limited in direction, they might have been less provincial. Limited in success, they might have been less optimistic.

All this might have happened, since North America initially was a projection of Europe, with its feuds, divisions, ancient prejudices, and historic rivalries. On the other hand, given time, experience, wisdom, circumstances, and a measure of luck, the two nations might have learned to live in harmony, with respect if not affection, as equals, neither dwarfing the other in size or in strength, but bound by a set of continental interests to cooperate for survival against a hostile world.

SUGGESTED READINGS

John B. Brebner, *North Atlantic Triangle,* 1945

Norman W. Caldwell, *The French in the Mississippi Valley,* 1941; reprinted 1974

Gerald M. Craig, *The United States and Canada,* 1968

Sigmund Diamond, "An Experiment in Feudalism: French Canada in the Seventeenth Century," in *Essays in Colonial History,* ed. Paul Goodman, 1967

W. J. Eccles, *Canada Under Louis XIV,* 1964

William Ellis, "Six Minutes That Changed History," *American West,* May 1974

Lawrence H. Gipson, "The American Revolution as an Aftermath of the Great War for the Empire," *Political Science Quarterly 65,* 1950

Marcus L. Hansen, *The Mingling of the Canadian and American Peoples,* 1940; reissued, 1970

David Hawke, *The Colonial Experience,* 1966

Victor L. Johnson, "Fair Traders and Smugglers in Philadelphia," *Pennsylvania Magazine of History and Biography 83,* 1959

Howard M. Jones, *America and French Culture, 1750–1848,* 1927

Gustave Lanctot, *Canada and the American Revolution,* 1967

A.R.M. Lower, "Two Ways of Life: The Primary Antithesis of Canadian History," *Canadian Historical Association Report,* 1943

Edgar W. McInnis, *The Unguarded Frontier,* 1942; reissued, 1970

Kaspar D. Naegele, "Canadian Society: Some Reflections," in *Canadian Society: Sociological Perspectives,* eds. Bernard Blishen, Frank E. Jones, Kaspar D. Naegele, and John Porter, 1961

Howard H. Peckham, "Speculations on the Colonial Wars," *William and Mary Quarterly 17,* 1960

Ralph B. Perry, *Characteristically American,* 1949

John C. Rule, "The Old Regime in America: A Review of Recent Interpretations of France in America," *William and Mary Quarterly 19,* 1962

C. P. Stacey, *Quebec, 1759,* 1959

Alexis de Tocqueville, *Journey to America,* ed. J. P. Mayer, 1971

Mason Wade, ed., *Canadian Dualism: Studies of French-English Relations,* 1960

What If Slavery Had Been Geographically Confined?

From the colonial period to the present, the deepest, most tenacious, and volatile issue troubling American society has been the relationship between white and black. For more than two hundred years blacks were slaves, and the incipient roots of white racism flourished as the economic value of the slave system increased. Once slavery became well established, there never was a chance to eradicate it by peaceful political means. England did so by a simple act of Parliament in 1833, but the slaves were thousands of miles away in the remaining British colonies, and few members of Parliament had a direct monetary interest in them. In America, on the other hand, the same men who owned slaves fought in the Revolution, sat in the national legislature, and helped devise a federal compact that did not dare interfere with their possession of human property.

Voices against slavery were heard with greater frequency after the middle of the eighteenth century. Before that time, except for some Quaker protests, the colonial conscience had remained dormant. But coincident with arguments against parliamentary despotism, as well as Revolutionary appeals to natural-law rights, the institution of slavery came under attack. "It always appeared a most iniquitous scheme to me," Abigail Adams told her husband, "to fight ourselves for what we are daily robbing and plundering from those who have as good a right to freedom as we have." Critics pointed out that slavery was cruel, un-Christian, and contradictory to the commitment made in the

17

Declaration of Independence. Such arguments were effective in the Northern states where slavery was not crucial to the economy, where blacks made up only 4 percent of the total population, and where even that small number was viewed as a threat by free white labor. A Massachusetts slave, Quork Walker, won his freedom in 1781 by a court order, on the ground that the state constitution declared "all men are born free and equal." New Hampshire also eliminated slavery by judicial decree. Pennsylvania passed a law providing for gradual emancipation in 1780, New York in 1799, and New Jersey in 1804. Slowly, and not without a struggle, and not for many decades, the North became free.

In the South, slavery was morally and philosophically disturbing to many leaders of the Revolutionary generation. Patrick Henry, for example, declared his "abhorrence of slavery." The Marquis de Chastellux, traveling in the Chesapeake region, reported that people "seem grieved at having slaves, and are constantly talking about abolishing slavery, and of seeking other means of exploiting their lands." Between 1782 and 1790 individual owners in Virginia manumitted some 10,000 blacks. Nevertheless, no proposal for emancipation was ever made in the South, because the vast majority of slaveowners were decidedly hostile to it. Even if they were not, the economic costs of compensated emancipation would have been prohibitive. In 1790 the value of slave property was approximately $140 million (700,000 slaves at $200 each), nearly double the entire Revolutionary War debt. Moreover, the freed blacks would have to be resettled elsewhere at an additional cost of several hundred million dollars. "Among the Romans," wrote Thomas Jefferson, who had mulled over the idea, "emancipation required but one effort. The slave, when made free, might mix with, without staining the blood of his master. But with us a second is necessary, unknown to history. When freed he is to be removed beyond the reach of mixture." Thus, abolition would be too expensive; it would wreck the Southern economy as well as its social system; and it would leave behind the problem of large numbers of freed blacks whom whites, in both North and South, would not accept.

Jefferson was no radical idealist but a man of moderation and common sense. He was acutely aware of what could and could not be accomplished in reforming society. His dream was of a white America, without slaves and without blacks, but he knew that abolition in the South was impractical and, indeed, impossible in his lifetime. Yet, if nothing was done, Jefferson foresaw "bloody scenes which our children certainly, and possibly ourselves (south of the Potomac), [will] have to wade through."

However, if slavery could be confined to the original states, if it could be kept out of the Western territories, then the future collision course of American history might be radically altered. Jefferson originated what Abraham Lincoln and the Republican party espoused seventy years later, that slavery be sectional, and freedom national. In March 1784, he proposed a congressional ordinance, one clause of which stated "that after the year 1800 of the Christian era, there shall be neither slavery nor involuntary servitude in any of the said states" to be carved out of the West, whether north or south of the Ohio River.

Of the eleven states present in Congress, seven affirmative votes were necessary to retain the clause.* Six voted yes—New Hampshire, Massachusetts, Rhode Island, Connecticut, New York, and Pennsylvania. Three voted no—Maryland, South Carolina, and Virginia by a split ballot of two to one against. North Carolina divided evenly, nullifying its vote. New Jersey's affirmative vote did not count, since only one member was present instead of the mandatory minimum of two. The absent representative, John Beatty, was ill and confined to his lodgings. "Thus," Jefferson later reflected, "we see the fate of millions unborn hanging on the tongue of one man, and heaven was silent in that awful moment."

What if Jefferson's proposal had succeeded? What would have been the political and economic consequences? Obviously the West would have been the whitest of all sections. Slaveowners could not risk taking valuable property to any territory that did not recognize the legality of slavery. This can be verified by a study of what did happen when part of Jefferson's plan was salvaged in the famous Northwest Ordinance of 1787, which forbade slavery north of the Ohio River. By 1820 only 1 percent of the population in Ohio, Indiana, Illinois, and the Michigan Territory was black. By that date, in Kentucky, 22.9 percent was black; and in Mississippi, 44.1 percent. In effect, the Northwest Ordinance continued the line between free and slave states to the Mississippi River. Had Jefferson's plan succeeded, the Mason-Dixon line would have stopped at the Appalachians.

There would have been considerable agitation to rescind the law and to open the territories to slavery. South Carolina and Georgia delegates to the Philadelphia convention of 1787 would have insisted upon it. Disputes did, in fact, take place in the Northwest after that date. Indiana settlers, led by William Henry Harrison, petitioned Congress to reopen the area to slavery. When Congress refused, the Indiana legislature easily enacted an indentured-servitude law for blacks, which reduced them to virtual slavery. In Illinois, proslavery forces were barely defeated, mainly through the efforts of Edward Coles. A transplanted Virginian, Coles had served as James

---

*One delegate had asked that the clause be struck from the ordinance. The question was: Should Jefferson's words stand as written? A majority of all states, present or not, had to vote in the affirmative. Since there were 13 states, the clause needed seven affirmative votes to be retained.

Madison's secretary, and later migrated to Illinois where he freed his slaves. In 1822 Coles won the governorship of Illinois over his proslavery opponent in a closely contested election. Two years later, proslavery forces supported a referendum which, opposed by Coles, was defeated by the narrow margin of 6,640 to 4,973. What happened in Indiana and Illinois was repeated beyond the Mississippi River as the boundaries of the United States were enlarged. Antislavery and proslavery groups continued their rivalry with increasing bitterness, to the point of turning Kansas into a bloody battlefield. Slavery in the West was a persistently divisive problem in American history, crumbling the cement of nationalism, until the matter was settled by the Civil War.

Whether Jefferson's attempt to keep slavery out of the entire West could have withstood the considerable pressures to expand that institution is questionable. The main body of settlers would have been yeomanry without slaves, and farming would have been based on the family unit. As the profitability of cotton culture multiplied after 1800, many of these farmers, in regions where that crop could be harvested, would have agitated for slave labor. Others would have resisted, however, in part because of moral compunctions, but mainly because of racial prejudice and antiblack fears. Even Owen Lovejoy, an abolitionist congressman from Illinois, whose brother had been killed by a rampaging mob because of his antislavery activities, wrote as follows: "We may concede it as a matter of fact that [the black] is inferior, but does it follow, therefore, that it is right to enslave a man simply because he is inferior?"

The black was judged to be an alien element, certainly not a constituent member of society. Ohio prohibited any black from entering the state unless he or she posted a $500 bond for good behavior. Illinois in 1813 ordered any entering free black to leave the state or suffer a penalty of thirty-nine lashes, to be repeated in 15 days if the black had not left. Indiana kept blacks from testifying in court against whites and from serving in the militia. None of the Northwestern states, including Michigan, Wisconsin, and Iowa, permitted blacks to vote before the Civil War. In 1858 Abraham Lincoln told an Illinois audience: "I am not, nor ever have been, in favor of bringing about in any way the social and political equality of the white and black races." A friend of Lincoln, Lyman Trumbull, announced that "we, the Republican Party, are a white man's party." Westerners were opposed to slavery expansion because they did not want an enormous black population, as in South Carolina, with all the attendant problems it would introduce. White America was not so much antislavery as it was antiblack.

If Jefferson's proposal to keep slavery out of the entire West had been adopted by Congress and been reasonably well enforced, its impact upon the South would have been profound. The policy would have had one of two possible effects. On the one hand, it might have made the plantation system less profitable or even unprofitable, reduced the power of the planter class, increased the harshness of the treatment of slaves, forced the manumission of the nonproductive ones, evoked more numerous and more serious black rebellions, and quickened the demand that all free blacks be removed from the South. On the other hand, Southern prosperity might have been considerably enhanced if the plantation aristocracy had abandoned its historic agrarian bias, invested in factories rather than in land, supported the use of slaves as industrial workers, and thus achieved a healthy economic diversification. In either case, the closing of the West to slavery would have neither spurred any general movement for emancipation nor substantially reduced the degree of white racist hatreds. It would, however, have avoided a Civil War.

The way the South did develop in the nineteenth century precluded any substantial discussion of the merits of slavery. The Virginia convention of 1831–32 wrestled with the issue of abolition in the last significant debates on that subject in the South. Minor abolitionist attempts were made in Tennessee in 1834 and in Kentucky in 1849. Gradually the collective intellectual abilities of the South seemed to be directed toward proving that slavery was a superior and beneficial system. Southern ministers appealed to the Gospel as a theological defense. Southern historians cited the existence of slavery in ancient and contemporary cultures. Southern politicians reproached their Northern brethren for violating what the Constitution protected. Southern planters insisted that blacks were mentally and physically suited to slavery and were better treated than Northern workers. The few who held contrary views had to remain silent or leave. For the overwhelming majority of Southern whites, slavery was a positive good. In the words of James H. Hammond of South Carolina, it was "the greatest of all the great blessings which a kind providence has bestowed."

All arguments in defense of slavery rested fundamentally on its profitability. The South was not, as it has often been pictured, an economically backward and stagnant region. True enough, investments in slaves used capital which might have been employed in achieving greater diversification. But for at least two decades prior to the Civil War, the rate of Southern economic growth rose faster than the national average. Cotton was king, as far as exports were concerned, heading the list of commercial crops that were responsible for Southern prosperity. That crop, as well as tobacco, hemp, sugar, and rice, was produced by slave labor. All other variables being equal—soil fertility and transportation costs, for example—slave labor was cheaper than free labor. Thus, the plantation owners wielded immense economic power and, with it, social control and political domination.

Slave labor was cheap, however, because the cost of rearing slaves was low compared to their market price. To maintain the high market price, there had to be demand, and that demand came largely from the West. Female slaves were prized for their ability to produce children. Children were prized because they helped in the fields and could be sold at handsome profits later on. Indeed, no comparable investment available in the antebellum period was as lucrative or yielded as high a rate of return as raising and selling slaves.

Southerners indignantly denied that they were slave breeders, and in a technical sense they were not. There were no examples of actual business ventures aimed solely at producing slaves. Nevertheless, Thomas Jefferson Randolph of Virginia stated that slaves were "reared for the market like oxen for the shambles." Slave women were more esteemed for their reproductive abilities than for any other quality. With the African slave trade closed, with the original imports inadequate to meet the increasing requirements for plantation labor, and with the market price rising, the incentives were overwhelming. It was common for slaveowners to promote sexual promiscuity among their female chattels and to reward the fecund more than the sterile. Fanny Kemble, a planter's wife, reported with some distaste "the meritorious air [with] which the [slave] women always made haste to inform me of the number of children they had borne, and the frequent occasions on which the older slaves would direct my attention to their children, exclaiming, 'Look missis! little niggers for you and massa; plenty little niggers for you and little missis!'" The net result was a phenomenal rate of natural increase of the slave population.

Had the extension of slavery been stopped by Jefferson's law of 1784, plantation owners would have felt the pinch of declining profits—not immediately, but ultimately. Unable to move their operations to the West, they would have cultivated the remaining vacant land in the South (much of which, presumably, would have been sold or abandoned by slaveless farmers who had left). Year by year the soil would have become depleted as it in fact did. Southerners were not ignorant of methods of crop rotation or the benefits of fertilizer—these were among George Washington's favorite subjects—but planters had formed the habit of exploiting plantations and abandoning old ones for new. Placing a geographic limit on slavery expansion might have curbed this habit, but would not have cured it. Moreover, planting by slave labor in large units was more wasteful than the skilled, intensive care with which yeomen farmers tended their lands. Gradually, then, yields per acre for cotton and tobacco would decline.

Concurrently, the market price of slaves would fall, cutting into the planter's margin of profit. He would have to bear the expense of feeding, housing, and clothing female slaves and their children, whose later monetary value on the auction block would be less than the rearing costs. Stocked with an oversupply of a property declining in value and which drained his wealth, but not daring to emancipate because of racial nightmares, the plantation owner—being a good businessman—would try to cut his costs by getting rid of the nonproductive slaves. His treatment of blacks would have become quite heartless.

There were, of course, countless examples of extreme cruelty in the South. Whipping was the most common practice, used even by enlightened masters, as it was in the army and navy at that time. To maintain discipline, to establish authority, to instill fear, to increase output, and to punish, slaves were beaten, flogged, and put in chains. An element of savagery runs through the well-documented accounts to be found in travel journals, in newspapers, in law cases, and in plantation records. Blacks accused of rape, murder, or conspiracy to revolt were frequently seized and hanged by mobs. "Let every tree in the country bend with negro meat," an aroused Mississippian advised. Nevertheless, in general, most masters were stern rather than sadistic, regarding themselves as paternal rather than oppressive. "My great desire is to have my blacks taken care of," a North Carolina plantation owner noted. "I should consider myself an unjust and unfeeling man if I did not have a proper regard for those who are making me so much money." He might not have been so solicitous if, with the West closed to that property, the slave system had become too expensive a form of labor.

The Brazilian experience might well have been repeated in the United States. In Brazil, the slave trade remained open until 1850, the market price of slaves remained low, and it was better for planters to import new slaves than to breed, raise, and care for the indigenous stock. As a result, *for economic reasons,* the treatment of slaves in Brazil was considerably more severe than in the United States. "It was considered cheaper, in the country [coffee] plantations," a visiting American reported, "to use up a slave in five to seven years, and purchase another, than to take care of him." The death rate of slave children was so high as to amount to a form of infanticide. Four times more male slaves than females were imported, and females were encouraged to work rather than to reproduce. On some plantations, males and females were deliberately kept apart after returning from the fields (though the white master, as in the United States, exploited his female slaves sexually). Pregnant females were an economic liability, as were their black children, and there was no incentive to provide for either. "Simple hygienic measures are almost always neglected by the owners of slaves," a French traveler wrote, "and the mortality of *negrillons* is very considerable." The same was true for the aged, the lame, and the sick, who were often turned out of the plantation to fend for themselves. Only after the slave trade was halted in Brazil and the value of slaves increased did their treatment improve.

In the United States, if the plantation structure had faltered because of soil depletion, rising costs, and surplus slaves, Southern planters would have been equally heartless. Feelings of paternalism would have dissipated, and polite forms of infanticide and euthanasia would have come into practice. Instead of furthering the breeding of slaves, masters would have done all they could to separate the sexes and to forbid intercourse. The mortality rate of black children would have climbed, as slaveowners with heavy expenses cut rations, reduced medical attention, and ignored housing and clothing necessities. The selective manumission of nonproductive slaves, particularly the old and the infirm, would have condemned tens of thousands of indigent black people to beg or to starve. Black suicides would have been numerous, as they were in Brazil. Some females would have prostituted themselves or been hired out as prostitutes by their master-pimps, as was the case in Brazil. Barred from the West, unwanted in the North, uncared for by the state, the more desperate blacks would have robbed, pillaged, or headed rebellions; white retaliation would have been swift.

The black slave was not the docile, contented, loyal servant that romantics like to imagine. Nor was he the rebellious firebrand some authors have portrayed. Statistically, many more slave conspiracies were plotted than the small number of open rebellions that were actually attempted. Both were numerous enough, however, to keep Southern whites in a state of fear sometimes bordering on hysteria. "We regard our Negroes," one Southerner commented, "as the *Jacobins* of the country, against whom we should always be on our guard." When the blacks in Santo Domingo rebelled in 1791, and a brutal slaughter ensued, the United States government responded on racial grounds, sending aid immediately lest the uprising spread. "Lamentable!" George Washington told a friend, "to see such a spirit of revolt among the blacks. Where it will stop, is difficult to say."

Since many more rebellions would have erupted as the plantation economy suffered, and free blacks would have been blamed for inciting them, Southerners would have demanded legislation to rid their section of all blacks who were not slaves. It would probably have become a national issue, attracting the support of a number of politicians from the North and West. Speeches would have been made, calling for the removal of free blacks, like Indians, to special reservations, or for their resettlement in the Caribbean or in Africa. In 1862, in fact, Congress did appropriate $600,000 to pay for the voluntary emigration of blacks from the District of Columbia. There were some Northern freedmen who, convinced that equality was meant for whites only, did not wish to remain in the United States. Scores of them went to Canada, Haiti, or Liberia. But the overwhelming majority would have resisted expatriation. "Here we were born, here we will live, and here we will die," a Pittsburgh black group resolved. James Forten, a wealthy black Philadelphia sail-maker and supporter of William Lloyd Garrison, spoke for his race by calling expatriation "little more merciful than death."

The state governments in the South, however, might well have taken action. In 1849 a petition from Augusta County, Virginia, requested an appropriation of funds from the state legislature for removing all free blacks to Liberia within five years. Such petitions were frequent, and some might have been heeded under deteriorating economic and social conditions. After all, the idea that blacks were unassimilable and should be colonized attracted prominent supporters ranging from Thomas Jefferson to Abraham Lincoln.

There was a possible safety valve for the explosive problem of surplus slaves: their potential use as nonagricultural workers. Employing slaves in industry was, in fact, a functioning part of the economy below the Mason-Dixon line. "In all departments of mechanical labor," a Virginia newspaper reported, "the slaves of the South are profitably employed. . . . They are far more valuable than field-laborers—indeed, intellectual expertness and manual dexterity are much more important elements in the price of a slave than mere physical strength and power of endurance." Slaves could be found working not only as domestic servants or common laborers doing the heavy, dirty work whites rejected, but as skilled craftsmen: as carpenters, cabinet-makers, blacksmiths, river-pilots, painters, firemen, coopers, masons, shoemakers, and tailors. Slaves worked in the gold mines of Georgia, on railroads and canals, in textile and tobacco factories, in ironworks and brickworks, and in forest industries and milling operations. Five percent of the total slave population—some 200,000—were so employed in 1850.

Slave labor in industry was indisputably profitable. "The experience of the entire South is in favor of building [rail]roads with negro Labor, as the *cheapest,* the most reliable . . . the best," wrote one entrepreneur, "and not liable to strikes and riots." Southern railroads were less expensive to construct than those in the North and yielded better profits because of slave labor. The owner of the famous Tredegar Iron Works in Richmond believed that his introduction of slave labor reduced costs enough to give his company a competitive advantage. In the West Florida lumber industry, another Southerner testified that "more money can be made in this business when [slave] labor is used." An unskilled white worker cost, on the average, $335 per year; an industrial slave, less than one-third as much. Moreover, the maintenance of slave women and children was considerably less, and they were used extensively in textile and tobacco factories. A liability on some plantations, they were an asset in industry. "Slaves not sufficiently strong to work in the cotton fields can attend to the looms and spindles in the cotton mills," a visitor to one such factory reported, "and most of the girls in this establishment would not be suited for plantation work." A Southern textile promoter observed that the use of young blacks in mill work "renders many of our slaves who are generally idle in youth profitable at an early age."

If slave labor in industry was a proven success in hundreds of cases, why did the South fail to develop its manufacturing potential more rapidly? Why did it remain an economically colonial area, exporting raw materials and largely depending upon Northern and foreign sources for finished products? Part of the explanation may be the pronounced hostility of planters to industrialization and to what they assumed was its consequence—urbanization. Antiurban sentiment had become an axiom of their political faith. "When we get piled upon one another in large cities, as in Europe," Jefferson once predicted, "we shall become corrupt as in Europe, and go to eating one another as they do there." Cities were regarded as centers of immorality, of slums, of fires, of plagues, and of a propertyless class that had no stake in orderly government and existed like a leech upon the landed part of society. Cities were noisy, bustling centers of change, which disturbed the quiet, traditional routine that agrarian Southerners preferred. In Charleston, an ordinance was passed prohibiting the use of steam power. "Why are our mechanics forbid [sic] to use it in this city?" William Gregg, a champion of industry, asked. "This power is withheld lest the smoke of an engine should disturb the delicate nerves of an agriculturist or the noise of the mechanic's hammer should break in upon the slumber of a real estate holder . . . while he is indulging in fanciful dreams."

Southerners wished to preserve their idyllic, rural lifestyle of country gentlemen, one in which social prominence depended upon possession of land and slaves. The institution of slavery created a leisure class of whites, giving them the time and wealth to build beautiful mansions, to educate their children abroad, to cultivate social graces, and to acquire qualities of command. Even if a Southerner initially was successful as a lawyer, a doctor, a clergyman, or a merchant, his ideal was to invest his professional profits in land and slaves and to retire as a plantation owner. Cities would destroy this perfection. Moreover, slaves could not be as well controlled in cities, where they were more mobile and could gamble and obtain liquor, learn to read, be influenced by free blacks, fraternize with each other, and conspire against whites. "A city slave is almost a free citizen," wrote Frederick Douglass, the black abolitionist. "He enjoys privileges altogether unknown to the whipdriven slave on the plantation." Partly because of this conscious resistance to urbanization, only 10 percent of the Southern population lived in cities in 1860; in the Northeast, the figure was 36 percent.

Emotionally and ideologically, the Southerner was committed to the slave system and to agrarian pursuits. He preferred to invest capital in land and slaves rather than in industry, according to his own arguments, because of paternalistic responsibilities to blacks and the need for social stability. He insisted that it was not profits, but racial necessity, that justified the plantation economy. Alexander H. Stephens, vice-president of the Confederacy, stated in 1861 that the foundation of the Confederate government "rests upon the great truth that the Negro is not equal to the white man, that slavery—subordination to the superior race—is his natural and normal condition." Planting was a more virtuous pursuit than manufacturing, and planting with slaves the best means of preserving Southern civilization. Industrialization and urbanization were twin threats which would upset the separation of the races and the subordination of blacks.

Yet, if Jefferson's attempt to set a geographic limit to slavery expansion had been adopted in 1784 and the ownership of slaves had become an economic burden to planters, they would certainly have shifted to manufacturing. The South possessed the requisites for substantial industrial growth: cheap labor, sufficient capital, raw materials, power sources, and a market—not with the equivalent purchasing potential of Northern consumers, but large and standardized enough to favor mass production. Moreover, the Old South would have become the industrial supplier to the yeomanry of the Southwest. Hundreds of textile plants, shoe factories, ironworks, and other establishments would have sprung up, not necessarily in seaboard cities, but in river valleys and country towns. There the slaves could be kept separate and controlled almost as well as on a plantation. Initially there would have been scattered opposition, on the part of white workers, to the use of slave labor—as indeed there was, especially during periods of economic recession. However, the sheer necessity of finding a profitable outlet for surplus plantation labor would have overcome these objections.

Cheap slave labor in the factory ultimately would have driven out free white labor, except perhaps for foremen (the industrial equivalent of the plantation overseer). Some planters, or their sons, would have abandoned cotton growing for cotton manufacturing, while others would have held firm, denouncing change and lamenting the passing of old values. Conflicts between these two elite groups for social position and courthouse control would have monopolized Southern politics. Planters would have continued to emphasize states' rights and to oppose high tariffs. Manufacturers, though competing with Northern firms for Western markets, would have joined with them to keep out foreign goods.

Yet, in most respects, the South would have remained unchanged. Planters and manufacturers would still have had their peculiar institution in common. Their racism would have continued unabated. Both would have demanded that the North return fugitive slaves. Both would have lived in dread of slave rebellions. Such might have been the consequences if Thomas Jefferson's proposal in 1784 had been adopted and enforced. Without the issue of slavery expansion to divide Americans, there would have been no Civil War. But with no war, and with a strong and energetic South effectively using chattel labor in both agriculture and industry, there is no telling how long slavery would have endured.

SUGGESTED READINGS

Hugh G. Aitken, ed., *Did Slavery Pay?* 1971

Eugene H. Berwanger, *The Frontier Against Slavery: Western Anti-Negro Prejudice and the Slavery Extension Controversy,* 1967

Carl N. Degler, *Neither Black Nor White: Slavery and Race Relations in Brazil and the United States,* 1971

Stanley M. Elkins, *Slavery, A Problem in American Institutional and Intellectual Life,* 1968

Robert W. Fogel and Stanley L. Engerman, *Time on the Cross,* 1974

William W. Freehling, "The Founding Fathers and Slavery,"*The American Historical Review,* February 1972

Winthrop D. Jordan, *White Over Black: American Attitudes Towards the Negro, 1550–1812,* 1968

Staughton Lynd, *Class Conflict, Slavery, and the United States Constitution,* 1968

Robert McColley, *Slavery and Jeffersonian Virginia,* 1964

Merrill D. Peterson, *Thomas Jefferson and the New Nation,* 1970

Donald L. Robinson, *Slavery in the Structure of American Politics, 1765–1820,* 1971

Kenneth M. Stampp, *The Peculiar Institution: Slavery in the Ante-Bellum South,* 1956

Robert S. Starobin, *Industrial Slavery in the Old South,* 1970

Richard C. Wade, *Slavery in the Cities: The South, 1820–1860,* 1964

Allen Weinstein and Frank O. Gatell, eds., *American Negro Slavery: A Modern Reader,* 1973

Arthur Zilversmit,*The First Emancipation: The Abolition of Slavery in the North,* 1967

Could the Articles of
Confederation Have Worked?

Quite a bit of prejudiced history has been written about the defects of the Articles of Confederation and the merits of the Constitution. The one-sided assessment began rather early when nationalists—who called themselves Federalists—portrayed the United States as being feeble, divided, and anarchical, tottering on the verge of economic ruin and civil dissension unless the Constitution was ratified. The Constitution, one Federalist declared, was formulated "under the guidance of Divine Revelation" to save America from catastrophe. Such claims were ridiculous, of course, since the Founding Fathers were practical politicians rather than divine instruments and many, in fact, harbored serious reservations about the Constitution. In time, however, as the United States grew and prospered, these reservations were forgotten, and the Federalist account of chaotic post-Revolutionary conditions due to the inherently defective Articles of Confederation became the basic story line of American history. The Confederation had failed. The Constitution had succeeded. Thus, by the one infallible test that Americans favored—success or failure—the Constitution became sacrosanct.

Of course, the Constitution is no longer sacrosanct. Many question its usefulness in the twentieth century. Both scholars and politicians have made proposals either to alter the political structure within the Constitution or to fashion a completely new one. Barbara Tuchman, for example, believes that the presidential office "has become too complex and its reach too extended." She suggests that it be replaced with a six-person directorate with a rotating chairman. Max Lerner prefers a Council of State, with half its members drawn from Congress. Walter Coombs wants to restore the electoral college as a meaningful screening device, since he believes political parties are excessively partisan and promote the election of mediocrities. A substantial number of citizens are receptive to the idea of making fundamental alterations in the Constitution. Some want to streamline the national government, permitting it to deal more efficiently with modern problems. Some want a selective but substantial decentralization of power, believing the individual states to be a safer repository and more democratic agency of government. It is an old dichotomy in the American mind: the locus and division of authority in a federal system. In a sense, the conflicting arguments mirror those of 1787, except that the positions of liberals and conservatives are somewhat reversed.

Those who opposed the Constitution objected to the circumstances surrounding its birth, to its contents, and to the method of ratification. Delegates to the Philadelphia convention in 1787 had been instructed by the states to suggest amendments to the Confederation, nothing more. They chose, however, to violate these instructions. Moreover, they met in secret, purposely excluding any observers or reporters. Then they submitted their work, not to state legislatures, but to special conventions of the people, which could either accept or reject the Constitution without prior conditions or qualifications. Anti-Federalists saw no reason for, and many dangers in, a document that had been conceived secretly and extralegally, that radically altered the conditions of union, and that permitted only yes or no ratification alternatives cleverly imposed by the Founding Fathers.

First of all, the Anti-Federalists did not believe any emergency existed that called for a hasty decision. The country was in no danger from foreign or domestic foes. No wars or insurrections threatened. Shays's Rebellion in western Massachusetts had been quickly and easily suppressed. The laws were well executed. "We are now told . . . that every calamity is to attend us, and that we shall be ruined and disunited forever," a Virginia Anti-Federalist argued, "unless we adopt this Constitution." These specious claims of impending calamity, a Pennsylvania writer suggested, arose "from the artful suggestions of designing men." The Confederation could scarcely be blamed for normal postwar economic dislocations, which all admitted. True enough, Revolutionary War debts were a vexatious problem, but some states were repaying those debts. Time alone, the Anti-Federalists argued, would cure many of the young nation's economic headaches.

Second, the Confederation was the true fruit of the Revolutionary tree. Its philosophy rested on the same natural-law foundation as the Declaration of Independence. It functioned by means of state cooperation rather than national coercion. It emphasized liberty rather than property. Had America fought to free itself from British despotism, Anti-Federalists asked, merely to create a similar despotism in the United States? Anti-Federalists predicted that ratification of the Constitution would lead to the imposition of heavy taxes, to large standing armies, to presidential dictators, to aristocratic senators, and to a federal city populated by self-serving politicians; in short, it would doom America to repeating the sad history and unhappy fate of European nations. Ratification of the Constitution would mean that the Revolution had been fought in vain.

Third, the Anti-Federalist position was based on the premise that government was, at best, a necessary evil, and preferable when controlled at the local level. The Confederation called itself a "perpetual union" of sovereign states. Under its terms, there would be unity in dealing with Indians, with foreign countries, and with Western lands. Congress could fix standards of weights and measures, regulate the value of money, establish a postal service, appoint and receive ambassadors, enter treaties, and determine questions of peace or war, all under the express powers specifically delegated by the states. Ultimate authority, however, was reserved for the states. The Constitution, on the other hand, created a consolidated national government masquerading in federal form.

Finally, the Anti-Federalists envisioned an America that was peaceful, rural, agrarian, and virtuous, independent of foreign entanglements and innocent of burdensome bureaucracies. Under the Confederation, they hoped that America could fulfill that vision. Certainly it could not under the Constitution. "That a *national* government will add to the dignity and increase the splendor of the United States abroad," wrote an opponent of the Constitution, "can admit of no doubt. . . . We wish to make a noise in the world. We are desirous of cutting a figure in history. Should we not reflect that quiet is happiness? That content and pomp are incompatible? I have either read or heard this truth, which the Americans should never forget: *That the silence of historians is the surest record of the happiness of a people.* The Swiss have been four hundred years the envy of mankind, and there is yet scarcely an history of their nation."

Despite the endorsement of George Washington, Benjamin Franklin, James Madison, Alexander Hamilton, and other elite leaders, ratification was not easily achieved. "Throughout the course of the whole transaction," one contemporary remarked, the Constitution appeared "to have been on the brink of failure." Massachusetts became the sixth state to approve, 187 to 168, and New Hampshire the ninth, 57 to 46. The Virginia ratifying convention witnessed a brilliant exposition of the Constitution by both sides. When all the arguments were exhausted and political lines had firmed, the Constitution narrowly carried, 89 to 79. News was relayed to Poughkeepsie—site of the New York ratifying convention—as soon as possible, for the Federalists there needed help. George Clinton, governor of the state, was firmly opposed to the Constitution, and a substantial majority of the convention seemed to agree with him. Alexander Hamilton's speeches had little effect. If any one factor should be singled out to explain the switch, it was that ten states had ratified, and New York would be excluded from the Union when it was in her interest to participate. Still, 27 irreconcilables continued to vote negatively on the final ballot, which was taken on July 26, 1788. Thirty delegates, including those moderate Anti-Federalists who decided to swallow their misgivings and risk the Constitution, cast affirmative ballots. Thus, less than a handful of votes decided the outcome.*

What if one of the key states had aborted the birth of the Constitution? What would have been the short-term results? And the long-run consequences? We can speculate with assurance that there would have been no invasions, no revolutions, and no wars between the states—for none of these threatened. Nor would there have been an economic breakdown, social chaos, or mob rule—for the state governments were functioning effectively. "Does not every man sit under his own vine and under his own fig-tree, having none to make him afraid?" an Anti-Federalist asked. "Does not everyone follow his own calling without impediments and receive the reward of his well-earned industry?" For the average farmer or worker, the acceptance or rejection of the Constitution was not an important issue. That whole debate was carried on by a small ruling class who were divided according to their local and personal circumstances. Many defended the Confederation for its positive accomplishments. The war debts were in the process of reduction, and the Western territories were being settled under the Northwest Ordinance. Patrick Henry praised the government as being "strong and vigorous," and said it deserved "the highest encomium." An anonymous Anti-Federalist complimented Rhode Island for rejecting the Constitution and abiding "by the old articles of confederation, which, if re-examined with attention, we shall find worthy of great regard."

Nevertheless, had the Constitution been rejected, there would have been a Second Constitutional Convention in 1788 or 1789 to do what the first had not done: to suggest necessary changes in the Confederation. Anti-Federalists realized that the Confederation contained defects which, they believed, could be corrected by minor surgery. It could be accomplished without haste, without secrecy, without turmoil, but not without considerable effort.

National control of commerce was an immediate need. British-manufactured goods of high quality and low price were flooding the American market, which delighted the consumer but disturbed the merchant and businessman. Moreover, American vessels were barred from the British

---

*Sixteen months later, North Carolina entered the Union, followed by Rhode Island in May 1790.

West Indies. A national tariff, perhaps, could limit imports and force commercial concessions from the British. As early as 1781, Congress sought authority to impose a duty on foreign goods, and 11 states agreed. However, unanimous consent was necessary to amend the Confederation. Again, in 1786, congressional power to enact tariffs was blocked by a single state (New York). Had a Second Constitutional Convention recommended such an amendment, there is every reason to assume its acceptance, for the indications were positive that the American people recognized its practical necessity. Had the Confederation been strengthened by such an amendment, there is every reason to speculate that it would have met the immediate needs of federal union. "A transfer to Congress of the power of imposing imposts on commerce, the unlimited regulation of trade," stated one Anti-Federalist who spoke for most, "I believe is all that is wanting to render America as prosperous as it is in the power of any form of government to render her."

A uniform tariff would provide supplementary funds to meet federal expenses, and commercial regulations would foster the return of favorable economic indicators, permitting the states to meet their tax allocations. With funds derived from the tariff, from the states, and from the sale of Western lands, the Confederation could begin systematically to reduce Revolutionary War debts.

With prosperity the Confederation could borrow time, and with time would come loyalty. In the 1780s people grumbled about the inadequacies of the Confederation; in the 1790s they would have cheered its success. The symbol of continental union was already present in the Great Seal of the United States, adopted in 1782, displaying a proud eagle carrying in its beak a ribbon on which is inscribed *E Pluribus Unum.* The frame of continental union was present in their common history, their common Revolutionary tradition, their common frontier, their common problems, and their common desire to prove to the world that Americans could live harmoniously in a federal republic of independent sovereignties. To be sure, there were sectional jealousies and local interests to surmount, but these need not have resulted in hostile rivalry; planter and farmer, merchant and manufacturer could exchange goods and services in a friendly commercial intercourse that would be complementary rather than competitive. Slowly the tissue of friendship would form, binding Americans to revere the Confederation as a wise instrument of government to be preserved for future generations, to endure through a cycle of centuries. Thomas Jefferson called the Confederation "the good, old venerable fabric." So would others had it been given time.

As the experience of Revolution faded into memory, and as the Confederation acquired respect, the authority of Congress to lead the states in a unified, comprehensive, well-balanced government would have emerged.

Congress was endowed with the power to make war and peace, to regulate Indian tribes, to coin money, to establish a post office, and to create courts to deal with interstate disputes. Under the Confederation, moreover, there were "interstate comity" provisions to ensure the extradition of criminals. One state could not deny citizens of another state the "privileges and immunities" it accorded to its own. The Confederation "was not without merits," Carl Friedrich and Robert McCloskey have noted, "both present and potential. . . . The single-house legislature could quite possibly have evolved into a more efficient body than the modern American Congress."

One should also bear in mind that the Confederation, like the Constitution, was subject to interpretation. Both were capable of broad and strict constructions. Both had the potential of elasticity. As early as 1781, Congress debated an act chartering a bank, though there was no clause in the Confederation authorizing Congress to create corporations. In fact, the second article of the Confederation stipulated that each state retains "every power, jurisdiction, and right which is not by the Confederation expressly delegated to the United States in Congress assembled." Many doubted its constitutionality, as they did in comparable circumstances ten years later when Alexander Hamilton proposed a national bank under the Constitution. But Congress, James Wilson argued, could enact such a law:

> To many purposes the United States are to be considered as one undivided nation; and as possessed of all the rights and powers and properties by the law of nations incident to such. Whenever an object occurs in the direction of which no particular state is competent, the management of it must of necessity belong to the United States in Congress assembled.

The law passed, providing a precedent which would have supported an entire range of legislation that the originators of the Confederation never suspected. In 1783 Hamilton reasoned that since Congress had the discretion of assigning financial quotas to each state for the support of the general government, it also in effect possessed "the constitutional power of general taxation." Such an argument was rejected then, but it was only a matter of time before the nationalistic impulse successfully promoted this canon of construction. Through the doctrine of inherent or implied powers, the federal government under the Confederation—as under the Constitution—would have broadened its scope to include issues of national concern. Moreover, the various executive departments created by Congress, such as foreign affairs, finance, war, admiralty, and post office, would have grown to exercise a crucial role in national affairs.

Had the United States survived under the Confederation, the heroes whom Americans revered would not have been too different from those under the Constitution. The process of myth-making, whereby fallible humans are converted to infallible saints, is common to all nations and all governments. Washington, Franklin, Jefferson, and Adams were assured a place in history as prime movers of the Revolution. Instead of James Madison, perhaps, Americans would have enshrined John Dickinson as the father of the Confederation. Instead of Alexander Hamilton, the economic wizardry of Secretary of the Treasury Robert Morris would have been honored. After all, it was Morris who performed the financial miracle of the Revolution by putting the nation on a hard-money basis before the war ended.

Even the name of Samuel Huntington, president of Congress under the Confederation, would have been singled out for special notice if only because he was first to occupy that position. Mason Weems could have concocted a set of spurious stories and called it *The Life of Samuel Huntington; with Curious Anecdotes, Equally Honorable to Himself and Exemplary to His Young Countrymen;* or Morrison Heady could have written a book of grander invention, *The Farmer Boy, and How He Became America's First President.* Of course, that office was originally nominal, carrying no special privileges. Those who believed in the Confederation were hypersensitive to the dangers of magisterial despotism, and they deemed a separate executive office neither wise nor necessary. They wanted no Caesar. They trusted no single man. In fact, they opposed the Constitution because the presidential office as defined therein was too powerful and the risks too great that ambition would tempt its holder to absolutism. "To be the fountain of all honors in the United States," wrote an opponent, "is in reality to be a king, as much a king as the king of Great Britain, and a king too of the worst kind: an elective king."

What happened to the presidency under the Constitution was essentially as the Anti-Federalists had feared. Some of America's so-called "greatest" Presidents have shown little regard for democratic means and constitutional scruples. They have assumed powers, abused them, and none have been impeached and found guilty. Foreign affairs have been the opening wedge by which successive Presidents have seized power. For example, the Constitution is silent on the question of neutrality; George Washington, without using the word, issued a proclamation to that effect. Again, the Constitution does not mention executive agreements; James Monroe first employed that subterfuge in 1817. Also, the Constitution contains not a word about executive control of information; starting with Washington, Presidents on occasion have refused to release diplomatic papers to Congress, and have since enlarged this refusal to include nondiplomatic material.

Even the separation of powers, on questions of peace and war, so precisely drawn in the Constitution, has blurred. As commander-in-chief, James K. Polk in 1846 dispatched American troops into disputed territory between Texas and Mexico, thereby inciting an attack and beginning a war. Congress was presented with a *fait accompli.* In effect, Polk's unilateral action compelled Congress to declare war against a foreign state. By the

1970s an American President, Richard M. Nixon, was forced to resign. But it is noteworthy that a committee of Congress refused to consider Nixon's order for the secret bombing of a neutral country to be an impeachable offense.

Such an extreme development would have been unlikely under the Confederation. The prestige and authority of the president of Congress would have grown, especially as men of major stature and national reputation began to occupy that position. An energetic, articulate, and charismatic personality, backed by public opinion, could have bedazzled Congress, which in turn might well have delegated authority to him. In moments of crisis, the tendency to endow a leader with emergency power is irresistible. But where would that crisis originate in the first century of American growth? Neither Canada nor Mexico was apt to invade. Indian tribes were too divided to constitute any major peril. The Atlantic was a barrier to any sudden aggression by hostile European countries. Before the jet or missile, before the plane or submarine or steamship, America's secure geographic location simply did not require instantaneous military decisions by one man.

The Confederation, moreover, contained various checks against a president becoming too powerful. The national government consisted of a single-chamber legislature composed of equals and enacting laws that the states enforced. Delegates were annually elected by the states, were paid by them, and were subject to recall at any time. No delegate could serve more than three years in six; and no delegate appointed to the presidency could serve more than one year in three. Finally, while each state had the option of sending two to seven delegates, they voted as a state unit. Thus, the man chosen to be president of Congress was checked by his short tenure in office, by the threat of instant recall, and by the limited weight of his individual vote.

Surely some outstanding individuals would have put their stamp upon an age, but in general Americans would have come to view their political history by congressional rather than by presidential terms. Leadership within Congress would probably have concentrated, not in one man, but in committees. During the long recess of Congress—up to six months, the Articles of Confederation specified—a "Committee of the States" was to be appointed, composed of one delegate from each state. A majority of nine members of this committee had the authority to execute all powers granted by the Confederation. Other special committees of Congress "as may be necessary" were to manage "the general affairs of the United States."* One can

---

*Of course, it is distinctly possible that these committees would have evolved into departments; that committee heads in time would have formed into a cabinet; that one member would have emerged as a prime minister; that the United States eventually would have had a parliamentary system of government. If so, because of the confederated system and the limited tenure, the American prime minister would not have possessed the power of his British equivalent.

assume that the same kind of problems would have prevailed under the Confederation as under the Constitution, and that there would have been committees on Western lands, on neutral rights, on runaway slaves, and on internal improvements. Without a doubt, political parties would have emerged, sectional quarrels would have been widespread, and the country would have passed through the ordeal of transformation from a deferential to a more equalitarian society. There is reason to speculate, however, that the Confederation could have resolved these problems as well as, if not better than, the Constitution could.

First, the Constitution contained provisions, such as the three-fifths rule, that left a legacy of distrust and dissatisfaction. The Confederation was wisely mute on the subject of slavery. Second, the Constitution is an ambiguous document that evoked partisan wrangling from its inception. Virtually every generation of Americans has been subjected to the unhappy fate of rearguing its meaning. The Confederation, while capable of broad interpretation, was not riddled with uncertainties on the fundamental issues of federalism. Third, the Constitution counted on a President to unite all Americans, a President who, as Alexander Hamilton predicted, would be "preeminent for ability and virtue." Few Presidents have possessed the high stature that Hamilton envisioned. When one did—Abraham Lincoln— his election in 1860 was due to an overwhelming sectional vote. The South, feeling that Lincoln was being imposed upon them by a hostile Northern majority, seceded. The Confederation, on the other hand, avoided any pyramid of power with one man at its apex. Secessions or threatened secessions of individual states undoubtedly would have taken place. Indeed, it would have been easier, since a state could refuse to raise money, to elect delegates, to pay them, or to obey federal laws.

Under the Constitution, secession led inevitably to war, since the national government enforced the law upon every citizen. Under the Confederation, economic and social pressures upon the state, but not military coercion, were the only devices the government could use to force the secessionists to rejoin the Union.

This much is certain: some foreign wars would have been avoided if the Confederation had been kept—especially the War of 1812, next to Vietnam perhaps the least wise and least necessary in American history. Statistics tell the story. Seventy-nine members of the lower House heeded James Madison's message and voted affirmatively for war on June 4, 1812, against Great Britain, while 49 voted negatively. There was a similar division in the Senate. If the balloting had been by states rather than by individuals, and a three-quarter majority required for passage as the Confederation stipulated, the result would have been otherwise. Counting by states, there would have been ten affirmative (New Hampshire, Vermont, Pennsylvania, Maryland, Kentucky, Tennessee, Virginia, North Carolina, South Carolina, and Georgia), six negative (Connecticut, Rhode Island, Massachusetts,

New York, New Jersey, and Delaware), and one split (Ohio)—two short of the required number. The Confederation is often criticized for being too idealistic and too rigid—difficult to amend, difficult to apply, and difficult to enforce. To some extent, the criticism is correct. It is obviously harder to obtain a three-quarter than an ordinary majority vote in Congress. By the same token, the Constitution can be criticized for being too pragmatic, for allowing Presidents the opportunity of leading the nation into costly military adventures, and for permitting a simple numerical majority of Congress the right to decide on such a drastic measure as war.

It has been alleged that the Constitution represents a superior form of government because it provides for an independent judiciary, while the Confederation did not. One nineteenth-century writer assumed that this superiority "is too universally conceded to require any argument." But those who supported the Confederation foresaw and warned of the pitfalls of a judicial oligarchy that could evolve—and that has evolved—under the Constitution. More than two centuries ago, Bishop Hoadly stated what is still true today: "Whoever hath an *absolute authority* to interpret any written or spoken laws, it is He who is truly *Law Giver* to all intents and purposes, and not the person who first wrote or spoke them." In the United States, the Supreme Court justices are neither elected by, nor directly responsible to, the people. Yet they have the power to review and to strike down laws passed by elected representatives of the people. The institution represents a deep distrust of democracy on the part of the Founding Fathers.

Moreover, the Supreme Court has a miserable record of constitutional interpretation, time and again having to reverse itself after years of the grossest social inequities that received its judicial sanction. In *Hammer* v. *Dagenhart,* the Court declared a child-labor law unconstitutional. In *Adair* v. *United States,* the Court voided a law that banned yellow-dog contracts. In *Matter of Heff,* the Court ruled that the illegal sale of liquor to Indians could not be punished. All these decisions have been reversed. The income tax law of 1894 was struck down in *Pollock* v. *Farmers' Loan and Trust Co.* The effect was to delay for two decades, until the Sixteenth Amendment, the effective imposition of a federal income tax. The record is certainly not all black, of course, and the Court has accomplished useful social changes at times when Congress could not or would not act. But in a democratic state, in one which operates on the basis of majority rule and minority rights, the legislature generally is less apt to violate the fundamental law. One need only scan the history of Great Britain for proof.

There is no particular technical merit in having a federal government consisting of a separate executive, a bicameral legislature, and an independent judiciary. People learn to admire the forms of government they become used to, and then argue that the forms are infinitely wise since they fit the national character. Within the federal trinity, Americans have long considered the Supreme Court the most holy. In fact, Americans distrust their congressmen—politician is a dirty word—and count upon the Court to check the actions of their elected officials. Had the Confederation been kept, American perspectives on government would have been considerably altered. Congress would have been revered as the central fountain of power in a league of republican sovereignties, and courts would not have become the super-legislatures on which Americans depend.

Contrary to legend, the beginning of the federal judicial system prior to the ratification of the Constitution was rather auspicious. During the Revolution, each colony or new state established admiralty courts to adjudicate disputes arising from prize cases (enemy vessels seized by Americans). As early as November 1775—before the Declaration of Independence—the Continental Congress resolved that it would entertain appeals from colonial courts involving prize cases. Committees of Congress were selected to sit in a judiciary capacity. Then, in 1780, a national law established a Court of Appeals for that purpose, which was composed of three judges appointed and commissioned by Congress.

Much had been made of one particular prize case to illustrate the essential weakness of the Confederation. A Pennsylvania admiralty judge, George Ross, defied an appellate decision that had reversed his finding. What could Congress do? It had no direct coercive authority. It depended solely upon state officers to enforce its judgments. It even refused to pass a resolution of contempt against Ross, "lest consequences might ensue at this juncture dangerous to the public peace of the United States." This case, however, should be balanced by other evidence. Over a hundred appeals in prize cases were submitted to federal courts between 1776 and 1787. Over forty decisions of state courts were reversed. It was rare, indeed, for a state judge to refuse to obey the mandate of the federal courts. (Have state officials always obeyed federal court rulings under the Constitution? The state of Georgia continued to strip the Cherokees of their land despite the findings of the Supreme Court in *Worcester* v. *Georgia* in 1832. "John Marshall has made his decision," President Andrew Jackson is alleged to have said. "Now let him enforce it." And can anyone claim that the 1954 decision in *Brown et al.* v. *Board of Education,* ending racial segregation in the public schools, has been fulfilled?) The fact is that the Confederation at one time represented the political will of the American people. Its power rested ultimately upon the respect for law which forms the fundamental element of American political consciousness.

Article 9 of the Confederation made the United States, in Congress assembled, "the last resort on appeal in all disputes and differences now subsisting, or that hereafter may arise between two or more States concerning boundary, jurisdiction, or any other cause whatever." The remainder of the article outlined an elaborate method for choosing special courts to settle these disputes between states. Would it have worked? Would the federal government have been able to act as judicial arbitrator? Would not state jealousies have erupted against unpopular decisions?

Six such disputes came before Congress before 1789. Five of them, however, were settled between the contending parties. A scholar of the subject has remarked that "one is struck with the very remarkable success of the method under the Articles, cumbersome though it was, in bringing the parties together, and with the willingness of these infant States to yield something of their supposed rights in the interests of national harmony." The remaining case, involving a land dispute between Connecticut and Pennsylvania, was fully adjudicated according to the provisions of the Confederation. A federal court of seven judges sat at Trenton, New Jersey, and decided unanimously that "Connecticut has no right to the land in question." Settlers upon the lands in dispute were not a party to the proceedings, and continued to fight in what amounted to a virtual civil war. A leader of those who held title under Connecticut law, John Franklin, was arrested and brought to Philadelphia to be put on trial for high treason. In retaliation, Timothy Pickering, then quartermaster-general of the Revolutionary army, was kidnapped, carried into captivity, and held as a hostage. Yet the important fact is that both states abided by the decision of the court. A contemporary, Robert R. Livingston, cited the case as an important precedent: "There are few instances of independent States submitting their cause to a court of justice. The day will come when all disputes in the great republic of Europe will be tried in the same way, and America will be quoted to exemplify the wisdom of the measure."

The Confederation was as bold an experiment in its own way as the celebrated Constitution. Rarely, perhaps never, had a number of powerful and independent states joined together as equals in successful federation. Alexander Hamilton and James Madison, in *The Federalist,* offered illustrations of numerous failures. The Amphictyonic council was marked by "weakness . . . disorders, and final destruction." The Achaean league "was seduced . . . [and] the union was dissolved." The Germanic confederacy consisted "of the licentiousness of the strong, and the oppression of the weak . . . of general imbecility, confusion, and misery." Even the vaunted Helvetian league of Swiss cantons, which "scarcely amounted to a confederation," broke down whenever "a cause of difference sprang up." Would this have been the fate of the Articles of Confederation? Hamilton and Madison thought so, since the history of mankind seemed to have proved the case.

But the Confederation need not have ended as they predicted. It could have worked. It would have set an example to the world of government based upon cooperation. The lesson would have been invaluable to twentieth-century African and Asian nations struggling to achieve the political unity of groups separated by linguistic and cultural differences. Within the United States, the Confederation would have fulfilled an idea Americans really have never abandoned: that government is safest and best administered on the local level. Under the Constitution, the states are junior partners at best, and some would argue that they are really anachronistic leftovers. Many, of course, are poorly administered, corrupt, and slow (or unable) to respond to social needs. On the other hand, the effects of state reforms frequently are weakened and even reversed by national legislation. Under the Confederation, the states would have become true testing areas for new political and social experiments. Failures—for example, Prohibition—would have been limited to a few states. Successes—for example, woman suffrage—gradually would have extended to most states. The Articles of Confederation would have derived its unity from tradition and necessity, and its strength from the healthy multiplicity of its sovereign membership.

SUGGESTED READINGS

Morton Borden, ed., *The Antifederalist Papers,* 1965

R. G. Caldwell, "The Settlement of Inter-State Disputes," *American Journal of International Law 14,* 1920

Henry S. Commager, *Majority Rule and Minority Rights,* 1943

E. S. Corwin, "The Progress of Constitutional Theory Between the Declaration of Independence and the Meeting of the Philadelphia Convention," *American Historical Review 30,* 1925

William W. Crosskey, *Politics and the Constitution,* 2 vols., 1953

J. C. B. Davis, "Federal Courts Prior to the Adoption of the Constitution," *Appendix to the United States Supreme Court Reports 131*

Martin Diamond, "Democracy and the Federalist: A Reconsideration of the Framers' Intent," *American Political Science Review 53,* 1959

Merrill Jensen, *The Articles of Confederation,* 1940

Merrill Jensen, *The New Nation,* 1950

Leonard W. Levy, ed., *Essays on the Making of the Constitution,* 1969

Richard B. Morris, "The Confederation Period and the American Historian," *William and Mary Quarterly 13,* 1956

William P. Murphy, *The Triumph of Nationalism,* 1967

Robert A. Rutland, *The Ordeal of the Constitution,* 1966

Arthur M. Schlesinger, Jr., *The Imperial Presidency,* 1973

Charles Warren, *The Making of the Constitution,* 1928

Benjamin F. Wright, *Consensus and Continuity,* 1958

Would Aaron Burr Have Been a Great President?

In 1800 it was well understood that Thomas Jefferson was the recognized leader and presidential candidate of the Republican party. No convention or congressional caucus met to go through any unnecessary formality. He had no challengers. The Republicans, however, decided to wait until the all-important New York City election for the state legislature was completed before they decided on a vice-presidential candidate. Astute observers believed that the entire national election depended upon its outcome. "If the city election of N[ew] York is in favor of the republican ticket, the issue will be republican," Jefferson told James Madison, and "if the federal ticket for the city . . . prevails, the probabilities will be in favor of a federal issue."

Aaron Burr, an early version of what would later be termed a "city boss," guided his smoothly oiled ward machine to victory in that election. At midnight on May 1, 1800, Matthew Davis, the young and loyal aide to Burr, joyously scribbled a note to Albert Gallatin: "REPUBLICANS TRIUMPHANT," and then added, "To Colonel Burr we are indebted for everything." John Dawson wrote James Monroe: "To his [Burr's] exertions we owe much—he attended the place of voting within the city for 24 hours, without sleeping or eating." Twelve days later he received his reward. A large meeting of Republican congressmen formally and unanimously endorsed Aaron Burr for Vice-President.

Election dates varied from state to state over the next six months, and Jefferson's friends scanned each return with a mounting sense of impending trouble. The first problem was to defeat the Federalist candidates, John Adams and Charles C. Pinckney, which would not be easy. Ever since John Adams sent a new mission to France, and despite the split in Federalist ranks, his popularity had increased. But the second problem was to be sure that Burr did not receive an equal number, or a majority, of votes over Jefferson. Prior to the Twelfth Amendment (which resulted from the election of 1800), there was no distinction made in electoral college balloting for President and Vice-President. Each elector voted for two persons. The one having the greatest number of votes, "if such number be a majority of the whole number of electors," became President. However, if there should be more than one person with such a majority—that is, two with an equal number—then the decision between them rested with the House of Representatives.

The problem was, indeed, complex. If Republicans withheld a vote or two from Burr in some Southern states, he might accuse them of bad faith. In fact, intimations that this had occurred in 1796 were broadcast by Burr's agents. Besides, the election would be close. Burr might lose the vice-presidency if Republicans did not give him every vote. "You know," a Virginian warned, "it has sometimes happened that a proposed secondary has become chief." Haphazard plans, informal and sudden, were made to detract one vote from Burr. Peter Freneau wrote from South Carolina: "The vote tomorrow I understand will be Jefferson 8, Burr 7, Geo. Clinton 1. *You will easily discover why one vote was varied.*" Stevens T. Mason reported that in Kentucky and Tennessee "in each . . . a vote will be diverted from Mr. Burr." But none of these plans were carried out. By late December 1800, it was apparent that Jefferson and Burr would have an equality of electoral votes.

Without hesitation, the Federalists in the lower House decided to support Burr. Alexander Hamilton wrote from New York, pleading with Federalist leaders to vote for Jefferson as the lesser of two evils. "I admit," Hamilton said of Jefferson, "that his politics are tinctured with fanaticism; that he is too much in earnest in his democracy; that he has been a mischievous enemy to the principal measures of our past administration; that he is crafty and persevering in his objects; that he is not scrupulous about the means of success, nor very mindful of truth, and that he is a contemptible hypocrite." If Jefferson was all this, Burr was worse. The adjectives Hamilton used to describe Burr included: extreme, irregular, selfish, profligate, and artful. He was, in short, "a complete Catiline." Hamilton's influence had declined, however, and his advice went unheeded. The Federalists in Congress were determined, Jefferson noted, to "reverse" the obvious "wishes of the people as to their President and Vice President, wishes which the Constitution did not permit them specifically to designate."

The vote in the lower House was taken by states, as the Constitution prescribed, and the first ballot—on February 11, 1801—resulted in a deadlock: neither Burr nor Jefferson obtained a majority. Jefferson had eight states, Burr six, and two were tied. Almost immediately, the rumors began to fly of proposed political deals to attract wavering delegates. Republicans approached Federalists who might swing over, and Federalists scanned Republican ranks for the same purpose. New Jersey, for example, was three–two for Jefferson. James Linn of that state was offered the governorship if he switched to Burr. Vermont's vote was tied. Matthew Lyon of that state later testified that he was approached with these words: "What is it you want Col. Lyon, is it office, is it money? Only say what you want and you shall have it." Maryland's vote was also tied. Thomas Jefferson noted in his diary that a Federalist "applied . . . to General Samuel Smith [of Maryland] and represented to him the expediency of his coming over to the states who vote for Burr, that there was nothing in the way of appointment which he might not command, and particularly mentioned the Secretaryship of the Navy."

These offers did not originate with Aaron Burr, which is part of the reason none of them succeeded. Burr was cognizant of Federalist efforts to elevate him to the first office, which he certainly wanted, but he was reluctant to offend the Jeffersonians. Uriah Tracy credited Burr with being a "cunning man. If he cannot outwit all the Jeffersonians I do not know the man." In this case, however, Burr's strategy misfired. He played a game of wait and watch, of not making any commitments, of leaving his political alternatives open to move in any direction circumstances dictated. Burr had received a letter from a Federalist, Robert Goodloe Harper, who told him "to take no step whatever, by which the choice of the House of Representatives can be impeded or embarrassed. Keep the game perfectly in your own hands, but do not answer this letter, or any other that may be written to you by a Federal man, nor write to any of that party."

The advice was bad, since Aaron Burr's behavior antagonized both parties. The Jeffersonians tried to extract a positive declination from Burr, a statement that he had no aspirations towards the presidency, and that he would not serve if elected. Burr refused to issue one. Instead, he told the Republican representative, Gabriel Christie of Maryland, that "the House could and ought to make a decision, meaning if they could not get Mr. Jefferson, they could take him." He repeated the same message in a conversation with Benjamin Hichborn of Philadelphia: "We cannot be without a president, our friends must join the federal vote." Hichborn responded: "But we shall then be without a vice president. Who is to be our vice president?" Colonel Burr answered: "Mr. Jefferson."

On the other hand, Burr declined to participate in any political deals with the Federalists. He sent no agents to Washington. He made no promises. He remained discreetly silent. In late January 1801, James A. Bayard of

Delaware calculated the votes and concluded: "It is . . . certainly within the compass of possibility that Burr may ultimately obtain nine states." Nine states meant the presidency. By mid-February, however, Bayard affirmed that though "the election was in his power," Burr "had refused the offers of the Federalists."

The lower House had decided to ballot to a conclusion, without adjournment. One Republican member from Maryland, sick with a high fever, brought his bed into Congress in order to be present and to maintain the tied vote of his state. Ballot after ballot was taken, with the same results: stalemate. Tension mounted. Some predicted that the young nation was at the point of collapse, since there would be no constitutionally elected President by inauguration day. A chilly snow drifted down on the House chamber, since the roof was not yet completed. A few congressmen went off to committee rooms to snatch some rest, returning with "night caps on" whenever a vote was taken. By Thursday morning, February 12, the members "looked banged badly," a contemporary wrote, "as the night was cold, and they had the most of them not slept a wink; and those who had were none the better for it." After thirty-six successive roll calls, the Federalist ranks cracked. On Tuesday, February 17, some remained absent, others cast blank ballots, and Jefferson was chosen President. "Thus has ended," Albert Gallatin remarked, "the most wicked attempt ever tried by the Federalists." The combination of Republican determination and Burr's refusal to cooperate brought an end to the struggle. But the result could easily have been different. "Had Burr done anything for himself," William Cooper, a New York Federalist, said in disgust, "he would long ere this have been president."

What if Aaron Burr had cooperated, the Federalists had remained firm, a few Republicans had been won over, and he had been chosen America's third President? The probabilities are that Jefferson's supporters would have been incensed, but not to the point of provoking civil war. Threats to that effect had been common in the early months of 1801. Republican militants in Pennsylvania and Virginia announced their determination to march on Washington if the choice was other than Jefferson. "Nothing but an appeal to arms will do," General Meade of Virginia thundered. "I will go wherever there is a call for men. . . . I wish for the opportunity of sacrificing the Devils and sending them to Moloch, their King."

The Federalists were not intimidated. "Our General [Burr]," the Boston *Centinel* declared, ". . . has seen Southern regiments in former times and knows what they are composed of." Another paper that supported Burr, the *Washington Federalist,* squarely met the challenge: "With the militia of Massachusetts consisting of 70,000 in arms—with those of New Hampshire and Connecticut united almost to a man, with half the number at least of the citizens of eleven other States ranged under the Federal banner in support of the Constitution, what could Pennsylvania, aided by Virginia—the militia of the latter untrained and farcically performing the manual exercise with *corn-stalks* instead of muskets—what would be the issue of the struggle?" It is doubtful, however, whether the choice of Burr would have precipitated a war. Jefferson's commitment was to the pen and the ballot, to legal action, to reason rather than arms, and to effecting democratic changes through the Constitution rather than radical upheavals through revolution. He, and James Madison as well, would have cautioned Republican followers to abide by the decision of Congress. As the frustrated partisans of Andrew Jackson did in 1824, when the lower House gave the presidency to John Quincy Adams, so would the Jeffersonians in 1801: wait four years, with sustained malice, seeking in every way to stymie, badger, and embarrass the Burr administration.

Ironically, despite Alexander Hamilton's frantic efforts against Burr, the latter would have been a President more to his liking. In fact, the two men had much in common, perhaps too much in common for friendship. Burr's blood lines were indisputably aristocratic. He was the son of one president of Princeton, grandson of another, and his distinguished ancestry could be traced to the first Puritans. Hamilton was the illegitimate son of a West Indian woman, and did not leave the islands for the continent until 1772. But in other respects, they seemed cast from the same mold. Alike in age, in size (short), in dress (elegant), and in occupation (law), both were proud, ambitious, and arrogant, and both were happiest in military uniform. Both were family men, with adoring wives and loving children, though each—with good reason—was reputed to be notoriously promiscuous. Burr gets the nod, however, for straying the more frequently. Both sought power. Both were manipulators. Both were ready to sacrifice democratic means for political goals.* Both were fundamentally contemptuous of the public, and the public reciprocated by distrusting their motives.

Later scholars have found it difficult to plumb those motives, to separate appearance from reality, and have alternately praised or condemned Burr and Hamilton as selfless or self-seeking, as patriots or intriguers, as visionary statesmen or meretricious demagogues. Hamilton could always justify his own actions as being principled, grounded in necessity, and taken solely in the national interest.† He regarded Burr, on the other hand, as a corrupt

---

*Hamilton frequently extolled the "great source of free government, popular election, which should be perfectly pure"; yet, in 1800, he attempted to void the popular vote in New York City which resulted in a Republican majority.

†In *The Federalist,* Hamilton expressed his hope of erecting "one great American system, superior to the control of all transAtlantic force or influence"; yet his pro-British sympathies were so deep that he was known to British agents, and the information he provided about cabinet meetings was forwarded to England under the cipher key of "No. 7."

and unprincipled individual whose actions were grounded in expediency, whose interests were solely personal.*

In 1801 Hamilton's hatred of Burr bordered on the pathological. For years, friends of both men had tried to bring them together. Despite his Republican affiliations, Burr always enjoyed substantial Federalist support in New York. As early as 1792, a prominent merchant of that state, James Watson, suggested to Hamilton that Burr could be won over from the opposition. Another Federalist, Isaac Ledyard, reported to Hamilton that Burr had expressed "an entire confidence in the wisdom and integrity of your designs and a real personal friendship." A few years later, the conservative Peter Van Gaasbeck noted that Burr was "as good a friend to the Constitution and good government as you or I." Hamilton then remained unconvinced; yet after 1801, had Burr become President, they might well have allied. In political marriages, neither trust nor respect is vital, but common interests are, and circumstances would have dictated that these inveterate enemies unite in the face of their Republican foe.

Scorned by those who were loyal to Jefferson and supported by Federalist votes, Burr would have inherited the leadership of that party. There were no others of national stature to whom the rank and file could turn. George Washington had died in 1799. John Marshall had been elevated to the Supreme Court. John Adams had left office in a sulk. Alexander Hamilton's influence had waned considerably. The Federalists, divided among themselves, felt rejected, unappreciated, impotent, and swamped by the Republican tide. What they needed most of all was superior political management. "I cannot describe to you how broken and scattered your federal friends are!" Robert Troup told Rufus King in 1800. "At present we have no rallying point; and no mortal can divine where or when we shall again collect our strength." Burr would have been the instrument of Federalist resurrection. In fact, while Troup was Hamilton's political lieutenant in New York City, he was also a longstanding personal friend of Burr. From close experience, he could testify to Burr's genius at political organization. What Burr had accomplished for the Republicans locally he could duplicate for the Federalists nationally.

Older Federalists repudiated the electioneering techniques which the Republicans developed so successfully. "You know," one of them wrote, "they use some weapons which we cannot condescend to." Appeals to voters did not sit well with these aristocrats, whose studied aloofness from the masses was considered a virtue. Solicitation was degrading, and they sneered at the expensive political barbecues, the stump speeches, and intensive canvassings and fund-raisings of Republicans.

---

*It is interesting to note that John Adams described Hamilton as "the most restless, impatient, artful, indefatigable and unprincipled intriguer in the United States."

But younger Federalists were ready to abandon philosophical purity for votes. Even Alexander Hamilton suggested the formation of a Christian Constitutional Society as a front organization which would distribute propaganda, form correspondence clubs, sponsor charitable works, court public opinion, and "use . . . all lawful means in *concert* to promote the election of *fit* men." The Federalists, Hamilton wrote, previously "erred in relying so much on the rectitude and utility of their measures as to have neglected the cultivation of popular favor." By establishing this society as a "principle engine" to restore the Federalists to power, Hamilton concluded, "I do not mean to countenance the initiation of things intrinsically unworthy, but only of such as may be denominated irregular." Hamilton's advice was ignored, though other Federalists did begin to imitate Republican methods. After 1800, step by step, they founded Washington Benevolent Societies, financed a vigorous party press and created impressive statewide tables of organization. Several times, without success, they attempted to unite these fragmented groups into a national party. No interstate conference was ever convened, and their quadrennial presidential conventions accomplished little.

The Federalists were ripe for a change of direction, but no leader of charismatic qualities appeared to rally them, instruct them, unite them, and point out their course of political survival. Jefferson did this for the Republicans, who cooperated in a rare display of party solidarity under his direction. Had Burr become President, he would have done as much for the Federalists. Certainly with his position of authority and control of patronage, with his chameleon character and his acknowledged intelligence, Burr possessed all the requisites for charting the Federalist future.

One might even speculate that Burr's actions as President would have attracted the support of many Republicans. The first significant issue of his term in office undoubtedly would have been—as, in fact, it was while Jefferson was President—the judiciary act of 1801, passed in the closing days of the Adams administration. Sixteen new circuit courts were established by this act, to which Adams had appointed members of his own party as judges. Federalists argued that the act could not be repealed without violating the clear mandate of the Constitution. The basic law of the land guaranteed the tenure of federal judges. So long as they exercised "good behavior," their salaries could not be diminished nor could they be removed except by the process of impeachment. Jefferson complained that the Federalists had retreated "into the judiciary as a stronghold. . . . By a fraudulent use of the Constitution, which has made judges irremovable, they have multiplied useless judges merely to strengthen their phalanx." Taking their cue from Jefferson, Republicans responded that Congress had authority, by constitutional provision, over all inferior federal courts. They were the creations of Congress and by logic they could be abolished by Congress.

Federalists, to a man, lamented the threatened repeal, claiming that the independence of the judiciary would be impaired, if not destroyed. Many Republicans, on practical grounds, agreed that the act should be retained. Supreme Court judges were tired of traveling on circuit, and the new system afforded relief. Thirty-six Philadelphia lawyers, including prominent Republicans such as Alexander J. Dallas, Peter S. Deponceau, and Thomas McKean, Jr., signed a petition requesting retention of the act. In New York, leading Republicans, such as Chancellor John Lansing and Chief Justice Morgan Lewis, were critical of repeal. Yet the repeal passed by an overwhelming party vote, and was signed by Jefferson.

Had Burr been President, there is reason to believe that the result might have been different. We know, for example, that Burr, as Vice-President, kept his friends—including Charles Biddle of Pennsylvania—informed of the progress of the repealing measure, one that he reprobated. We know that Burr privately consulted with the influential Federalist, Gouverneur Morris. He even attended a Washington birthday dinner tendered by congressional Federalists, at which he offered the cryptic toast: *"The union of all honest men!"* As Vice-President, Burr broke a tied vote in the Senate by electing to send the repealing bill to a committee for further consideration. The gesture was symbolic only, for with the return of absentee Republicans the majority resumed control. But Abigail Adams was impressed with Burr's willingness to support the Federalists. "Burr has shown us," she noted, "what he will do when the fate of the Country hangs suspended upon his veto in the National Government."

Abigail Adams was not alone in her admiration. Many observers commented on their preference for Burr rather than Jefferson. "The Vice President was formed by nature to command," William Plumer of New Hampshire declared. He lamented that but for the turn of a few votes in 1800, "we should not live under the feeble, nerveless administration of a dry dock and indissoluble salt mountain philosopher." Thomas Truxtun, the naval commander, felt the same way. He wrote to Burr: "I most sincerely anticipate the pleasure of seeing you in the possession of the first office under our blessed Constitution after the 3d of March, 1805, and I pray that events may turn up to put you there before."

Burr's strategy was to unite Federalists and dissident Republicans, to create a new third force in American politics which would pit these friends of the Constitution against the Virginia party of Jefferson and Madison. Of course, he failed. "Never in the history of the United States," one scholar has concluded, "did so powerful a combination of rival politicians unite to break down a single man as that which arrayed itself against Burr." Had Burr been elected President, however, his opposition to the repeal of the judiciary act, and his veto of that repeal if necessary, would have gained the esteem of virtually every Federalist in the country. It would also have received the endorsement of moderate Republicans who agreed that the judiciary act should be kept. Burr would have capitalized upon the considerable anti-Virginia sentiment in the country to weave a strong network of support for his administration.

As Vice-President, Burr saw his political ambitions frustrated by Jefferson's augmented popularity and Hamilton's sustained enmity. The purchase of Louisiana, in particular, capped a long list of Jefferson's achievements which, one eulogizer predicted, "the historian will not fail to seize, to expand, and to teach posterity to dwell upon with delight." Federalists, however, opposed the purchase, since it seemed to assure the continued Southern domination of the national government. Some extremists, such as Timothy Pickering, were so embittered that they inclined toward a separation of the Union. Pickering declared that he would rather have a "new confederation" than "to live under the corrupting influence and oppression of aristocratic democrats of the South." The three-fifths clause of the Constitution permitted slaves to be counted for purposes of representation. The Louisiana Purchase permitted the South to extend its rule westward. "Without a separation," William Plumer insisted, the Northern states could never "rid themselves of negro Presidents and negro Congresses, and regain their just weight in the political balance." Disunion was the wisest choice.

The secessionist plan was carefully conceived and contained four logically consecutive steps. The conspirators would win the state elections in New England and thus gain control of these governments; electoral laws for national congressmen would be repealed, and senators recalled; each state would sever relations with the central government and establish its own collection of customs; ultimately they would combine into an independent Northern Confederation.

The plotters even made military preparations to defend the new confederation in case the American government should decide to challenge its legitimacy. They also debated the possibility—some thought it was a necessity—of including New York and other middle-Atlantic states. Oliver Wolcott asked whether New York, controlled by Aaron Burr, could be freed "from the abhorred domination of the perfidious Virginians." Only Burr, Pickering wrote, "can break the democratic phalanx." If New York were "detached (as under his administration it would be) from the Virginia influence," Pickering reasoned, "the whole Union would be benefited." The idea was first broached to Burr at a meeting in his Washington home, attended by Pickering, Plumer, and James Hillhouse. The secessionists hoped that Burr, supported by Hamilton, would win the New York gubernatorial race and join with them in confederation. He might even emerge as its first president. Burr's reply to the overture was masterfully enigmatic. Hillhouse came away with the impression that Burr was favorably disposed. Plumer was baffled by the vagueness of his response.

Though well conceived, the entire conspiracy was in fact absurd. Hamilton proved hostile to the idea of secession, and had no intention of working in double harness with Burr. The British minister, Anthony Merry, who had been approached for financial aid, also rejected the scheme. So did various politicians in New Jersey, Pennsylvania, and Delaware. Burr failed to win the New York gubernatorial election. "Few intrigues have ever fizzled out so ingloriously as the secessionist plot of 1804," declares a scholar of that period, "but few plotters have ever built upon so flimsy a foundation. It requires some discontent to arouse a people against their government, and the only dissatisfaction with Jefferson's regime in 1804 existed in the imaginations of the Federalist leaders." The historical fallout which proceeded from the aborted conspiracy resulted in the tragic duel at Weehawken. Hamilton was one of the few Federalists who refused to repudiate the Louisiana Purchase. In 1804, as in 1800, moreover, he successfully labored to defeat Burr's candidacy. "He threw himself against Burr's ambition," Broadus Mitchell, Hamilton's biographer states, "and died to satisfy his rival's revenge." With Burr's avenues to power blocked in New York and in Washington, the Vice-President sought glory elsewhere. He would shortly take the westward road to his doom.

How different it might have been had Burr become America's third President! Louisiana, the very issue that triggered New England extremists to plot secession, and that led to the duel at Weehawken, might have served to precipitate the political cooperation of Burr and Hamilton. Both men were expansionists. Both thought in continental terms. Both recognized the vast potential of Louisiana.

Burr was regarded as a person of considerable knowledge about the West. The Earl of Selkirk made it a point to consult Burr in 1803 about settlements for displaced Scottish peasants. The Mohawk chief Joseph Brant was a close friend. Burr tended to romanticize the wilderness. But his infatuation with the West did not cancel his realistic appraisal of its economic value. Burr was one of the first to envision the use of Niagara Falls as a source of hydraulic power. He was concerned that foreign influence, especially that of France, might interfere with personal investments and national growth. The two went together. Hamilton, like Burr, had long championed the preservation and extension of American territorial interests. "There are rights of great moment to the trade of America which are rights of the Union," Hamilton wrote in *The Federalist*. "I allude to the fisheries, to the navigation of the Western lakes, and to that of the Mississippi." Hamilton wanted all obstacles to commerce on the Mississippi removed. He knew that access to the Gulf of Mexico was economically vital to the United States, and he feared the machinations of European nations, which sought to obstruct American growth and which fostered Western disaffection. Burr was of the same mind. "It has for months past been asserted that Spain ceded Louisiana and the Floridas to France," Burr wrote to his son-in-law in 1802, "and it may, I believe, be assumed as a fact. . . . To me the arrangement appears to be pregnant with evil to the United States."

Had Burr been President, Louisiana would have been acquired, but probably by war rather than by purchase, and with Hamilton's full endorsement. Hamilton's past history indicated a willingness to embark on Western military adventures. As the Spanish empire crumbled, Hamilton hoped, the United States would move into Florida, Louisiana, and even Central and South America. If this were not done, France or England would gain control; even worse, independent confederacies might form beyond the Appalachians, a source of friction that threatened "the permanency of the union." Hamilton was prepared to hasten the demise of the Spanish empire. In 1798 he discussed with Francisco Miranda, a Venezuelan soldier of fortune, plans to liberate Latin America. The American people, Hamilton reported, were not yet prepared for the idea of war, but "we ripen fast and it may, I think, be rapidly brought to maturity." To Senator James Gunn of Georgia, he wrote: "If we engage in war, our game will be to attack where we can. France is not to be considered as separated from her ally [Spain]. Tempting objects will be within our grasp." To Representative Harrison G. Otis of Massachusetts, Hamilton stressed the value of war "for preventing and frustrating hostile designs of France, either directly or indirectly through any of her allies." The United States should immediately seize Louisiana and the Floridas "to obviate the mischief of their falling into the hands of an active foreign power."

All of Hamilton's efforts were to no avail. John Adams' unexpected dispatch of a new diplomatic mission to France and the subsequent peace treaty that ended the quasi-war shattered Hamilton's imperial visions. So proud was Adams that he desired the following inscription on his gravestone: "Here lies John Adams, who took upon himself the responsibility for peace with France in the year 1800."

As Adams paved the way for the Jeffersonian administration, so Burr as President would have followed fundamentally a Hamiltonian program. Even as Vice-President, Burr was known as a man of arms and action. Hamilton once labeled him, with some distaste, an "enterprising and adventurous character." Were those qualities utilized in an imperialistic war for Western lands or for the national benefit, Hamilton might have found them admirable. When the port of New Orleans was closed to American traffic in 1802, James Biddle wrote with some belligerence to Burr: "In my opinion, and it is the opinion of many others, we should immediately take possession, and then treat about it. . . . For my own part, I do not fear a war with France and Spain." Westerners clamored for war, and Jefferson was faced with excruciating alternatives. Either he had to declare war on France to satisfy the martial spirit or, by continuing a pacific policy, he had to risk unpopularity and a possible Federalist renaissance. "If he acts feebly," the French minister, M. Pichon, advised his government, "he is lost among the partisans; it will be then time for Mr. Burr to show himself to advantage."

Jefferson chose peace, and purely by good fortune; since Napoleon had abandoned his idea of a French empire in America, Louisiana was offered for sale. But Burr had neither the patience nor the pacific inclinations of Jefferson. As President, he would have asked Congress for authority, received it, and ordered an attack upon New Orleans. The move would have been politically astute. Federalists, urged on by Hamilton, would have supported an anti-French policy. Republicans would have split, many seeing in Burr an American version of Napoleon. Westerners, however, mainly Republicans, would have responded enthusiastically. One can easily imagine voluntary militia companies forming in Cincinnati, Lexington, and Frankfort, joining regular troops mobilized for an attack. Andrew Jackson, a favorite of Burr's, would have responded to the call. The seizure of Louisiana would have engrossed the entire public mind. Moreover, the United States would have gained an easy victory, since the Spanish garrison at New Orleans was small, and the French were in no position to send substantial aid.

Aaron Burr, instead of Thomas Jefferson, would have been rated as one of America's greatest Presidents. After all, scholars compliment Jefferson's political expertise. They frequently cite his Inaugural Address, which includes the words, "We are all republicans—we are all federalists," as an example of the principles he intended to pursue. Until foreign affairs bedeviled his administration, Jefferson controlled Congress, maintained party cohesiveness, kept sectional pressures submerged, and commanded popular allegiance. But Burr might have done the same. By cooperating with congressional Federalists, by drawing off dissident Republicans, by taking no rash action to upset prosperous conditions, by choosing a path of political conciliation, yet at the same time, by using his office to build a national political machine, Burr could have merited the applause of contemporaries and the praise of posterity. The Federalist party would have remained in power long into the nineteenth century. Their solid New England and strong middle-Atlantic base would have been supplemented by Western support loyal to the party that brought Louisiana into the Union.

Jefferson is credited with obtaining Louisiana, in the words of William Wirt, "without the guilt or calamities of conquest." Had Louisiana been taken by military force, there would have been few calamities and little guilt. Indeed, the war would have been immensely popular, and historians would have found proper justification for it. Some decades later, Polk brought on the war with Mexico for territorial reasons, yet he is listed as a great President. Greatness is not accorded on the basis of creativity, brilliance, courage, or adherence to democratic means, but merely on the successful accomplishment of a goal which the majority of white Americans approve. It would not have mattered how the United States acquired Louisiana.

Jefferson is celebrated as America's premier intellectual statesman, the philosopher-king of democracy. He has left his country a legacy of democratic principles which Burr never could have approached. By comparison, Burr's range of interests was narrower, his commitment to republicanism shallower. But two things should be noted. First, that as President, Jefferson on several occasions had to sacrifice theoretical purity for pragmatic solutions that were less than democratic. The embargo, for example, has been called the most "arbitrary, inquisitorial, and confiscatory measure formulated in American legislation up to the period of the Civil War." In practice, Burr's administration might have been no more or less authoritarian than that of Jefferson. Second, intellectually superior individuals are not necessarily abler Presidents. The ability to command, and especially to command others of greater learning, has been a distinguishing characteristic of many famous rulers. It might well have been Burr's.

Finally, Burr was formidable in his own right. Instead of the tragic conclusion to his life, and that of Hamilton as well, the two men might have lived on—as did Adams and Jefferson—to become venerated elders, the argonauts of the American experiment, to whom others turned for advice. This much seems obvious. Had Burr become President, the growth of democracy would not have been hampered, for that growth emanated not so much from the government in Washington as it did from the fluid society, the mobility of an enterprising people, the equalitarian impulse, and the economic opportunities of a vast land.

SUGGESTED READINGS

Morton Borden, *Parties and Politics in the Early Republic,* 1967
Jonathan Daniels, *Ordeal of Ambition,* 1970
Matthew L. Davis, *Memoirs of Aaron Burr,* 1837
Richard Ellis, *The Jeffersonian Crisis,* 1971
David H. Fischer, *The Revolution of American Conservatism,* 1965
Cecilia Kenyon, "Alexander Hamilton: Rousseau of the Right," *Political Science Quarterly 73,* 1958
Linda Kerber, *Federalists in Dissent,* 1970
Broadus Mitchell, *Alexander Hamilton,* 1962
Herbert Parmet and Marie Hecht, *Aaron Burr,* 1967
Nathan Schachner, *Aaron Burr,* 1937
Lynn W. Turner, *William Plumer of New Hampshire,* 1962
Frank Van der Linden, *The Turning Point,* 1962
Samuel Wandell and Meade Minnigerode, *Aaron Burr,* 1925

CHAPTER
5

What If the Second Bank
Had Been Rechartered?

Every student of American history knows that Andrew Jackson waged and won a mighty battle against the Bank of the United States. It is sometimes presented as a medieval duel, with Jackson as the pure White Knight fighting the financial Monster that fed upon the honest labor of American workingmen. The Monster was controlled by a charming but greedy wizard named Nicholas Biddle. If that analogy seems ludicrous, it is not far from Jackson's own view of the struggle. He saw himself as the man of republican simplicity and biblical virtue, the citizen-soldier who accepted the presidency to restore government to the people. Quite a few admirers saw it that way too. "If elected, which I trust in God you will be," John Branch wrote in 1828, "you will owe your election to the people, Yes Sir, to the unbiased, unbought suffrages of the independent, grateful yeomanry of this country. You will come into the Executive chair untrammeled, free to pursue the dictates of your own judgment."

But no one really knew what Jackson's judgments were, or how strong they might be, when he first assumed the presidency. In the campaign, he had displayed a positive mastery at political double-talk. On the one hand, he swore to uphold states' rights; on the other, he insisted that the states must acknowledge their membership in an indestructible Union. On the one hand, he assured voters of his Jeffersonian beliefs; on the other, he claimed no hostility to "domestic manufactures or internal works." Was he entitled to wear the Jefferso-

57

nian mantle? In 1824 Jefferson told Thomas Gilmer that "one might as well make a sailor of a cock, or a soldier of a goose, as a President of Andrew Jackson." Soon after Jefferson's death, it was claimed that he had changed his mind—the evidence is murky and contradictory—and the matter was debated with some heat. To this day, scholars argue over whether Jackson deserved or violated the Jeffersonian imprimatur. All one might say with certainty is that his intellectual commitments in 1829 were vague, amorphous, dimly perceived, and intuitive rather than reasoned. As for the Bank, Jackson voiced reservations and criticisms designed to reform that institution, but no one anticipated that he would seek to destroy it.

Biddle did what he could to appease Jackson. He investigated charges that some branch managers had contributed funds to anti-Jackson politicians—a policy Biddle deplored. (It was one thing to bribe influential congressmen with "loans," a common enough practice of the Bank; but it was quite unacceptable for the Bank to become frankly partisan.) He cultivated members of Jackson's cabinet, appointed some of Jackson's closest friends to Bank posts, and called upon Jackson personally to assure him of the Bank's goodwill, its value to the country, and its future goals. One of the latter was an offer to pay off the national debt in short order, and to schedule it for the anniversary of the Battle of New Orleans. Both the object and the timing were pleasing to Jackson, but nothing could really alter his distrust of the Bank. At times he masked it, would drop a friendly word, counter that with a threat, and seemed to delight in Biddle's discomfiture. The more erratic Jackson appeared, the more edgy Biddle became.

What Jackson sought was an alternative to the Bank, or some fundamental changes that would strip it of power. Constitutionally, Jackson thought the Bank had no right to establish branches, despite the *McCulloch* v. *Maryland* court decision of 1819; economically, he thought its financial position amounted to a monopoly that must be curbed, despite its numerous services to the government. By the close of 1831, however, Jackson was ready to concede. Instead of insisting upon fundamental changes, he seemed prepared to accept nominal ones. Publicly, his annual message to Congress in December referred to the Bank in noncommittal terms. Privately, he agreed to the Bank's recharter, so long as that issue was postponed until after the election of 1832. Politics came before economics, and Jackson wanted to avoid a showdown.

At this point Biddle erred. Instead of accepting Jackson's face-saving retreat, Biddle took the risk of requesting that Congress recharter the Bank in 1832—four years earlier than necessary. Perhaps he did not trust what Jackson might do after the election; perhaps he trusted too much in the advice of Henry Clay and Daniel Webster. The calculated assumption was that Jackson had to either sign the recharter bill or veto the measure and have that veto overridden by a new Congress pledged to the Bank. Whatever Biddle's reasoning, Jackson regarded it as a challenge and a provocation. Instead of conciliation, he girded for political battle. Senator Willie Mangum of North Carolina recognized Biddle's strategic mistake immediately: "I have no doubt with but slight modification (to save appearances) it [the Bank] would have met with Executive favor—it is *now* more than doubtful whether it will—And the whole may ultimately take the appearance of a trial of strength between General Jackson and the Bank—In that case the Bank will go down."

That is precisely what happened. The recharter bill passed the Senate 28 to 20, and sailed through the lower House, 107 to 85. Four of Jackson's advisors—Roger Taney, Amos Kendall, Andrew Donelson, and Levi Woodbury—helped the President to compose a veto message that amounted to a campaign manifesto. It struck at the "rich and the powerful," who "bend the acts of government to their selfish purposes." It opposed "exclusive privileges" that make "the potent more powerful," and sympathized with the common men "who have neither the time nor the means of securing like favors to themselves." In other words, it was a classic political document designed for votes, and it had the desired effect. Jackson swept to victory in 17 states and rolled up an electoral majority of 219 to Clay's 49. His victory was so commanding and his control of the large Democratic majority in Congress so firm that all hopes for the Bank were dead.

Of course the struggle was not quite over, and in 1833 both Jackson and Biddle pulled whatever economic levers were at their disposal. Old Hickory was determined to remove government deposits from Biddle's Bank and relocate them in state banks. He so instructed the secretary of the treasury, Louis McLane, who refused and was shifted to the State Department. The next secretary of the treasury, William J. Duane, also refused and was dismissed. The next, Roger Taney, later to be rewarded with the post of chief justice of the Supreme Court, accomplished Jackson's purpose. Taney made all government deposits in state banks, known as "pets," and for expenditures drew upon the reserves in the Bank of the United States. Biddle was forced by the dwindling reserves to curtail the Bank's operation. However, the credit contraction he ordered—a drastic reduction of loans to businessmen, and pressures upon state banks to redeem their notes and checks in specie—was undoubtedly exaggerated. Biddle expected the economic distress to force Jackson to restore the government deposits. Hundreds of businessmen petitioned the President for relief, and some called upon him. "Go to the monster, go to Nicholas Biddle," Jackson stormed. "I will never restore the deposits." By 1834 Biddle relented, reversed his policy, and ended the artificial shortage of credit. The value of Bank stock continued to fall, and in 1836 the Bank ceased to function as a nationally chartered institution.

Contemporaries argued over the wisdom—or lack thereof—of Jackson's destruction of the Bank, and so have scholars, who more or less reflect the same disagreements. To his supporters, Jackson's accomplishment was democratic and monumental, "a crowning glory," in the words of Nicholas Trist, "and the most important service he has ever rendered his country." The editor of the *Boston Post* exulted that the Bank was "BIDDLED, DIDDLED, and UNDONE." Theodore Sedgwick, Jr., boasted that "we have as yet scarcely begun to see the advantageous results . . . which are yet to ensue." One contemporary likened the result to Christ's expulsion of the money-changers from the temple. Even a hostile nineteenth-century biographer, James Parton, conceded that "every one is glad the bank was destroyed."

A more recent and sympathetic scholar, Claude Bowers, concluded that Jackson's "war on a moneyed monopoly . . . put democracy on an even keel. It served notice that ours is a government by men and not by money. It asserted and maintained the preeminence of the people's government in the affairs of the country. It made good the Jeffersonian formula of equal rights with special privileges for none. And the arrogant plutocracy that had dared challenge the national government of all the people was buried in the grave of the national bank." Finally, Arthur Schlesinger's *The Age of Jackson* turned the hero of New Orleans into a latter-day Franklin D. Roosevelt, battling the economic royalists, contending for reforms, and ushering in a new age of democratic participation. It was the final stage in the gradual apotheosis of a Tennessee squire and plantation aristocrat into a champion of the masses. In that respect, the comparison to Roosevelt is most apt.

To his opponents, of course, Jackson was an economic illiterate, a hard-money man with no appreciation of the role of credit in a capitalist society. His destruction of the Bank was a disaster that furthered the very frenzy of paper speculation which he deplored. Before the removal of the deposits, pro-Bank people boasted that the United States had the best monetary system in the world. Within three years, with the brakes removed, note issue of state banks increased by 50 percent in the East, 100 percent in the West, and 130 percent in the South. Thomas Hart Benton, in an angry speech to the Senate, declared: "I did not join in putting down the Bank of the United States, to put up a wilderness of local banks. I did not join in putting down the paper currency of a national bank, to put up a national paper currency of a thousand local banks. I did not strike Caesar to make Anthony master of Rome."

But that was precisely the effect of the Jacksonian program, according to those who lived through the rapid inflation followed by the Panic of 1837. It was not that Jackson was evil; he was merely stupid and easily manipulated by Martin Van Buren, who sought to further the interests of the Albany Regency, a political-financial oligarchy in New York State. Such is the conclusion of Bray Hammond, who writes in *Banks and Politics in America* "that Andrew Jackson himself did not understand what was happening." An acquisitive class of entrepreneurs, precursors of the robber barons of the late nineteenth century, using the rhetoric of agrarianism to achieve a freedom from governmental restraints, benefitted from the demise of the Bank. Certainly the public interest was not served by the absence of a national banking system, Bray Hammond argues.

But would it have made much difference? Was the Bank that important to the economy? What would have been the consequences had Biddle not forced the issue in 1832, and a grateful Jackson had signed a 20-year recharter bill in 1833? What alterations would the presence of a national Bank have made upon the total economy of the United States? Would it have fostered interregional investments? Would it have provided a source of domestic capital for agriculture, industry, or transportation not readily available elsewhere? Would it have significantly affected the business cycle? This speculation holds that the Bank was a valuable institution but not indispensable, powerful but not crucial. Its major role in political history has caused scholars to overrate its economic impact. The presence or absence of a central Bank would not have mattered very much until the time of the Civil War.

It is true that many state banks in the 1830s, without the moderate controls exercised by the Bank, failed to maintain adequate specie reserves in proportion to their loans; that a degree of heavy speculation ensued; and that the inflationary bubble burst with the Panic of 1837. This was followed by a brief period of economic recovery, and then by a severe deflation that lasted for five years. A cause-and-effect presumption—that the destruction of the Bank led to the monetary disturbances of the 1830s and 1840s—is widely accepted by scholars who have failed to consider all the variables that affected the American economy. The overextension of bank credit was, in fact, an aggravating factor of the 1837 panic. But its basic causes were due to external circumstances which a central Bank, had one been in existence, could not have altered: cotton production and prices on the international market, the agricultural needs of England and Europe, the withdrawal of British investment capital, and so on.

Students should beware of the simplistic explanations sometimes offered for the periodic economic depressions in American history. At least for the period before 1860, the most important elements controlling the American business cycle—up or down—were the demand for American products abroad and the volume of investment, which was critically dependent upon English capital. Even if the Bank had been rechartered, it would not have had the resources, nor would it have been expected, to alleviate the distress of banks temporarily caught in periods of monetary stringency. The Bank of the United States was not a precursor of the Federal Reserve System. It was a powerful competitor, not an ally of other banks. It might act as a puritanical guardian but not as a kindly rich uncle. In other words, the Bank did not conceive its purpose to be one of rescuing distressed banks with loans, nor did it possess the reserves for such a mission.

Bray Hammond, no less than Arthur Schlesinger, Jr., has interpreted antebellum economic history in twentieth-century terms. He laments the Bank's destruction as an interruption of the orderly progression of central banking in the United States. He sees the country adrift in the 1840s and 1850s without a central Bank. "Being without any leadership and without any lender of last resort," writes Hammond, "such as the Bank of England was to British banks, and such as the Bank of the United States might have become to American ones," this country had no institution to moderate the financial panics that occurred periodically. Such a conclusion assumes too much, given the primitive understanding of the functions of central banking in the Jacksonian period. It assumes that the directors of a quasi-public Bank would put the national interest ahead of protection of Bank assets. It assumes that they would be sophisticated and powerful enough to equalize business fluctuations by a prudent use of Bank reserves and loan policy. And it assumes that there was no alternative. As a matter of fact, the United States Treasury had accepted such responsibility at a very early date. By taking 30-day paper (Secretary Alexander Hamilton in 1792), by increasing government deposits (Secretary Samuel Dexter in 1801), by prepaying the public debt (Secretary William Crawford in 1824), or by issuing notes and bonds (Secretary Levi Woodbury in 1837), the federal government utilized its reserve power to aid banks during times of necessity.

The significance of the Treasury's role as the "lender of last resort" became more apparent after the demise of the Bank. In 1837 William Gouge, an influential pamphleteer, argued for the separation of the fiscal operations of government from banks. In effect, he espoused what later became the Independent Treasury System. But that system never intended the separation to be absolute. On the contrary, Gouge argued that if government funds are kept "in public depositories" rather than banks, "more or less of it will come to their aid in times of emergency." Warning signals of an impending depression again flashed in the early 1850s when a number of banks, because of heavy investments in railroads, faced a liquidity crisis. Secretary James Gouge in 1853 pumped money into the market, temporarily averting a panic. Three years later, Secretary Howell Cobb did the same,* to such an extent in fact that the Treasury exhausted its funds and had to borrow $20 million. If the Treasury, with all its reserves, could not prevent a depression, surely a national Bank would have been powerless to

---

*Cobb had a deep appreciation of the Treasury role as a stabilizing force. He went so far as to suggest that unemployment caused by depressions should be relieved by government expenditures on public works—a twentieth-century concept.

reverse the cycle. Indeed, since the Bank was a commercial competitor with extensive investments of its own, one must conclude that its existence in the 1850s would have exacerbated, not alleviated, the effects of the panic.

Friends and enemies of the Bank of the United States had exaggerated notions of its influence over prices and business. Walter B. Smith reasons as follows:

> . . . price fluctuations would have occurred, Bank or no Bank. Years of prosperity would have been followed by years of dull business, Bank or no Bank. American business operated in the context of a world market, and the Bank certainly did not govern the latter. Prosperity and depression in the United States were much influenced by variations in the amount of foreign capital coming this way. The Bank of the United States had something to do with this, but so did the Bank of England and so did the whole complex of influences which operated in the foreign capital markets. The fiscal policies of both the federal and state governments were potent factors in the uneven economic developments of this period. But fiscal policy influenced the Bank more than the Bank influenced fiscal policy.

When the Bank issue was debated in Congress, numerous supporting memorials forecast devaluation, industrial paralysis, and massive unemployment if the recharter failed. Even a hostile minority report of the Committee of Ways and Means conceded: "That [the bank] adds facilities to trade and commerce generally . . . will not be questioned." The Bank held one-third of all deposits and specie in American banks, and made one-fifth of all bank loans. Loans were made to merchants, manufacturers, farmers, stock traders, corporations, the national and state governments, and to foreign governments as well. The question is: how vital were those loans to the economy? How much was the Bank missed as a source of capital for business expansion?

It mattered very little as far as transportation was concerned. In 1817 John C. Calhoun proposed that $1.5 million paid by the Bank to the federal government be parceled out to the states for internal improvements. This Bonus Bill narrowly passed both Houses of Congress only to be vetoed by James Madison. Thereafter, the states assumed the burden of financing what the federal government would not.* New York State borrowed $7 million for the Erie Canal. Between 1826 and 1834, Pennsylvania spent $10 million for a system of canals between Philadelphia and Pittsburgh.

---

*However, the 150-mile canal from Georgetown to Cumberland was financed by the state of Maryland ($7 million), the terminal cities ($1.5 million), and the federal government ($1 million).

Illinois piled up a debt of $11 million, and Ohio one of $27 million. Michigan's debt for internal improvements, prorated by population, amounted to $53 for every man, woman, and child.

During the canal-building era, fully 75 percent of all canal investments was made or sponsored by government, and in 1840 the burden of the states reached the staggering sum of $200 million. The Bank of the United States included a proportion of these securities in its portfolio. For example, and most notably, Biddle advanced money to the Chesapeake and Delaware Canal Company, accepting its stock as collateral. He also loaned money to individuals who wished to subscribe to certain canal offerings. But the percentages were insignificant. Most of the purchases were made by English citizens looking for low-risk, high-return investments. They recognized the profits that America's capital scarcity yielded, and they regarded state securities as extremely safe investments. The most one can say is that the Bank of the United States, like all other banks, acted as a middleman, or conduit, for these funds.

Certainly the absence of a central Bank in the 1840s had no apparent effect on railroad capitalization, which amounted to well over $1 billion in the decades prior to the Civil War. Cities, counties, states, and later the federal government, either by monetary gifts, stock purchases, bond guarantees, or land grants, financed about 25 percent of the cost. The other sources were private and abundant. French, German, and English capitalists invested a considerable amount. But the largest share was held by Americans, and Eastern banks were especially generous subscribers once it became evident that railroads were profitable ventures.

If transportation did not draw upon the Bank's resources, a wide spectrum of many other business activities did. Yet the impact of the removal of the Bank as a factor in the American economy was negligible. Part of the reason is that from the 1820s to the early 1850s there was little need, few demands, and thus scarcely any interest in interregional investments. Were the reverse true, the Bank, with its resources, its currency controls, and its branch system, would have been the natural leader of investment capital on a national level. But investors preferred to put their capital to work within their region. In New England, for example, the cotton and woolen textile industries were well supplied with funds by local residents who used their own accumulated capital from commerce or agriculture. The boot and shoe industry was financed with no outside capital. The larger iron firms usually had recourse to a partnership of wealthy investors. These private sources were supplemented by local bank facilities which—at least in the North— were substantial, well regulated, and perfectly adequate to meet the capital requirements of the region.

Even Bray Hammond admits that "a democratic, dynamic, and competitive expansion of business" characterized New York, both city and state, and he ascribes it in large part to its Safety Fund System. "This measure . . . was of great practical and political importance," writes Hammond. "It made the banks of the state a system not only strong and worthy of public trust but congenial to the Albany Regency. It gave the people of New York a source of credit which usefully supplemented the Erie Canal as a source of wealth." In Massachusetts the Suffolk System, a model of sound banking practice, supplied industry in that state with credit at low interest rates and provided the public at large with paper money of reliable, predictable value. It was not uncommon for textile manufacturers to sit as bank directors, to be on the boards of insurance companies, and to have holdings in ancillary enterprises. Their investment practices were guided largely by personal relationships and local requirements. In short, the national Bank was considered as a foreign competitor by many Northern bankers, and unnecessary as a financial regulatory agency. Between 1827 and 1829, the total business of its Boston branch declined from $4,150,000 to $629,000. The Bank was still powerful enough to create a temporary panic among New York, Philadelphia, and Baltimore businessmen by the sudden curtailment of loans in 1833, but was fundamentally superfluous as a source of capital for industry.

The student should bear in mind that the economy was not yet truly national in character, and that local banking organization was in tune with the ends of investors. "The first and second Banks of the United States," writes an economic historian, W. Elliot Brownlee, "were premature in conception. . . . New England and the Middle Atlantic states, where demands for capital investment were most abundant, developed orderly banking structures long before the establishment of a national banking system during the Civil War."

Similarly, the long-term needs of Western industry were provided for locally. Cyrus McCormick, for example, the largest producer of reapers, built his Chicago factory by pooling his personal capital with that of some partners (and then used the firm's profits to buy them out). Early meat-packing companies were financed the same way. Flour-milling was conducted on too small a scale to call for external capital. What the West required and what the Bank provided were short-term loans for trade, inventories, and crops. From 1828 on, the Bank not only increased its total loans but increased the Western proportion of those loans to 50 percent by 1832. During that period the four branches at New Orleans, Nashville, Louisville, and Lexington did four-fifths of all exchange business in the West—and still there were calls for more funds. The "demand for money," reported the cashier of the Cincinnati branch, "is enormous." Poor crops in 1831 and 1832 caused farmers and middlemen to ask for loan extensions, creating a chain reaction of requested postponements. "To add to our difficulties," the director of the Nashville branch informed Biddle, "we had a very short crop of cotton, so that our own drafts, predicated on the crop and payable at New Orleans, could not be paid out of the crop." "Nothing but the indulgence of the bank," the Louisville branch wrote in confirmation, "and a full year's products of the country" could relieve the pressure.

In other words, a substantial proportion of Bank business was in the West. This was both acknowledged and appreciated by many Westerners who supported the recharter of the Bank or its replacement by a comparable institution—all of which is contrary to the traditional view.

Textbook writers usually quote Thomas Hart Benton's salty words: "All the flourishing cities of the West are mortgaged to this money power. They may be devoured by it at any moment. They are in the jaws of the monster! A lump of butter in the mouth of a dog! One gulp, one swallow, and all is gone!" The fiction is that Westerners—politicians, farmers, and speculators searching for easy money—denounced the Bank. The fiction is compounded by portraying Andrew Jackson as the chief executor and political beneficiary of this Western anti-Bank legacy.

But the Bank changed the attitudes of Westerners. In St. Louis the *Beacon,* which was established in 1829 with Thomas Hart Benton's support and dedicated to "the people" who "expect and demand of General Jackson the *reform of all abuses,*" came out flatly against the Bank veto in 1832. A proadministration paper, the *Cincinnati Republican,* warned that "a National Bank is important to the prosperity of the West." In a study of *Biddle's Bank,* the scholar Jean Wilburn writes: "These people were very short of capital and lacked a currency. For the most part they bought and sold through New Orleans and needed a ready and stable market for their bills of exchange. Only the Second United States Bank with its system of branches . . . could fulfill this need."

A recharter of the Bank in 1832, one is led to speculate, would have had a negligible impact upon canals, railroads, or other internal improvements, upon industrial growth, or upon the business cycle. Only Western farmers and middlemen in need of short-term capital would have been better served, since they were so dependent upon the Bank. But even for them the crisis of the Bank's disappearance was temporary. By the 1840s Eastern capitalists were regularly investing short-term funds in Western centers, and some farmers turned to equipment manufacturers for their intermediate credit needs.

If the failure to recharter the Bank was a minor issue, at least in the total picture of American economic development before the Civil War, the same cannot be said for its political ramifications. Ironically and unwittingly, the Jacksonians brought into being a system of corruption and special privilege which was the very basis for their attack upon the Bank. In a word, the power vacuum created by the Bank's destruction was filled by buccaneer capitalists who lobbied, bribed, schemed, and manipulated large numbers of congressmen in ways Biddle never imagined.

It is true enough that the Bank paid off various congressmen for their support. "I believe my retainer has not been renewed or *refreshed* as usual," Daniel Webster reminded the Bank. "If it be wished that my relation to the Bank should be continued, it may be well to send me the usual retainers." To W. B. Shepherd, a North Carolina representative, Biddle wrote that a loan's repayment depended "exclusively [upon] your own convenience." Senator George McDuffie, the South Carolina nullificationist, was permitted to borrow $100,000 on the security of a mortgage, though such loans were expressly against the Bank's policy. Davy Crockett of Tennessee, who boasted that he could "whip my weight in wild cats, hug a bear too close for comfort, and eat any man opposed to Jackson," changed his political loyalties between 1827 and 1833. His Bank loan was personally extended by Biddle when it appeared that the buckskin congressman would default. Congressman Gulian Verplanck of New York obtained a loan even though Robert Lenox, a merchant of that city who served as one of the Bank's directors, advised against it. "You know the existence of this institution must depend on the opinion entertained of it by those who will before long be asked to continue its charter," Biddle reminded Lenox. "If a proper occasion presents itself of rendering service . . . so as to convert enemies to friends, we owe it to ourselves and to the stockholders not to omit that occasion." All told, the Bank made loans to members of Congress as follows:

1829	$212,346	34 members
1830	$192,161	52 members
1831	$322,199	59 members
1832	$478,069	44 members
1833	$374,766	58 members
1834	$238,586	52 members

These figures, however, are deceiving. First of all, many of the loans were genuine, backed by collateral bearing normal interest rates, and repaid on schedule. Not all, not even most congressmen were as morally corrupt as Daniel Webster. Secondly, loans did not always convert enemies to friends. Senator John Forsyth of Georgia owed the Bank $20,000 he could not repay, yet remained a staunch supporter of Andrew Jackson. The father-in-law of Governor William L. Marcy of New York was desperate for a loan—this information came from Henry Clay to Biddle, who suggested it be made since "the desired accommodation would have the best effects." Probably Biddle made the loan. Yet Governor Marcy did much to help break the financial pressures Biddle exerted upon businessmen in 1833. Colonel Richard "Tecumseh" Johnson of Kentucky, as well as his brother, had their debts suspended by the Bank. Yet Johnson remained firmly opposed to recharter. Even historian Arthur M. Schlesinger's hostile account of the Bank admits that "there was not much correlation between the size of the loans and the intensity of the devotion to the Bank."*

Many of Biddle's banking favors would be called, in twentieth-century parlance, "public relations" rather than bribes. Whatever the label, Biddle believed the cause was just and the means legitimate. His motivation was to strengthen the Bank and to make it indispensable, independent, respected, and ultimately neutral in the political wars of the nineteenth century. In no way can his actions be likened to those of the money men who scrambled for influence and control after the demise of the Bank.

At first their natural cupidity was checked by a reluctance to become involved in national politics. Some, of course, immediately used their connections to obtain favors. Thomas Ellicott, president of the Union Bank of Baltimore and a trusted friend of Secretary of the Treasury Roger Taney, had been a leading spokesman in the fight against the Bank of the United States. The Union became a depository of government funds, a "pet," and within a matter of months Ellicott withdrew those funds for his private speculations. By 1834 he was hailed before a Maryland court. Cornelius W. Lawrence, a Democratic congressman from New York and a confidant of Taney, vigorously supported the qualifications of a Wall Street bank in which he owned stock, the Bank of America. He wrote its president, George Newbold: "With the Secretary of the Treasury no bank stands higher than the Bank of America, and no officer of a bank higher than yourself." Newbold regularly extended favors to Democratic politicians and support to other "pet" banks. No speculation was involved in these financial transactions. But the substantial federal deposits permitted the Bank of America to increase its loans and profits dramatically.

Perhaps the best example of what one historian has labeled "the stereotype of the self-seeking personal influence peddler" was Reuben M. Whitney. He acted as a paid middleman between the Treasury and the "pet" banks, especially for the Girard Bank of Philadelphia. In return for his services and to maintain the federal deposits it enjoyed, the Girard Bank made unusually large loans to Whitney's brother.

---

*Biddle also made loans to newspapers, hired writers, and ran up a considerable bill with printers for articles and pamphlets favorable to the Bank. Jackson complained that Bank funds were being used to buy up "the whole press of the country." Biddle defended his policy as educational: "I believe that nine-tenths of the errors of men arise from their ignorance—and that the great security of all our institutions is in the power, the irresistible power, of truth." Biddle overestimated the capacity of the public to read long and abstruse essays on banking.

By the 1840s, as financier Jay Cooke later remarked, "it was a grand time for brokers and private banking." Elisha Riggs, John Ward, William W. Corcoran, John J. Palmer, and many others, some representing English and European banking concerns, came to Washington to lobby for deals, favors, contracts—in a word, profits. Biddle's actions had been guided by some sense of national responsibility; the new breed, with few exceptions, subordinated all other interests to their own particular economic concerns. Of course, they would have bridled at such a statement. They equated self-interest, class interest, and national interest. Thus no moral dilemmas intruded. No guilt nightmares surfaced. As shrewd and ambitious businessmen, they merely were taking advantage of what President John F. Kennedy once termed "the pressure of opportunity." For example, William W. Corcoran's "pecuniary transactions with politicians," writes his biographer Henry Cohen, "ran the gamut of bribes, joint interest, commissions, loans as political *quid pro quo,* and loans and agencies as routine business." Throughout he "never failed to take a high moral position." Corcoran was involved with Texas bonds (see Chapter 6), Arkansas bonds, Mississippi bonds, Mexican indemnities, federal mail subsidies, Indian claims (substantial profits here), Florida debts, the Illinois Central railroad, town loans, real estate speculations in Wisconsin and Minnesota, War Department contracts for arms, telegraph lines, as well as land sales both to and from the government.

The roster of local and national politicians who were paid in cash, land, or stock was long indeed. "I am not disposed to extend my services for pure patriotism," one advised another. "If this town on Lake Superior is to be so much benefitted they can afford to give some lots to you for valuable services. . . . This of course is sub rosa."

By the mid-nineteenth century, men like Corcoran viewed themselves as America's builders, expansionists, and visionaries who helped turn villages into booming cities. Some have concluded that their grafts and corruptions were a socially bearable price, a beneficial lubricant, an intricate part of the energy and creativity they contributed to American growth. That may be, but what began in the 1840s was a prelude to the "great barbecue" of corruption in the post–Civil War decades. One might argue that a national Bank might well have participated in the barbecue. Rechartered in 1833, it might have become too powerful, a super-corporation buying up the votes of legislators in wholesale quantities and always seeking the main chance of profits for its stockholders. As a quasi-public institution, however, the Bank would have been subject to rigorous periodic reviews by Congress. Private banks were not.

Economically, the Bank was not vital as a source for capital expansion. The remarkable growth of the 1840s and 1850s occurred in the absence of a central banking institution. Politically, however, as the *de facto* fiscal agent of the United States government, the Bank might have become a watchdog of national finance. It could not have stopped what was inevitable. But it might have curbed the worst excesses of corruption between unscrupulous businessmen and obliging politicians—a result, one assumes, that Andrew Jackson would have approved.

SUGGESTED READINGS

W. Elliot Brownlee, *Dynamics of Ascent: A History of the American Economy,* 1974

Ralph C.H. Catterall, *The Second Bank of the United States,* 1902

Henry Cohen, *Business and Politics from the Age of Jackson to the Civil War: The Career Biography of W.W. Corcoran,* 1971

James L. Crouthamel, "Did the Second Bank of the United States Bribe the Press?" *Journalism Quarterly 36,* 1959

Lance E. Davis, "Capital Immobilities and Finance Capitalism: A Study of Economic Evolution in the United States, 1820–1920," *Purdue Faculty Papers in Economic History, 1956–66,* 1967

J. Van Fenstermaker, *The Development of American Commercial Banking,* 1965

Thomas P. Govan, *Nicholas Biddle,* 1959

Bray Hammond, *Banks and Politics in America From the Revolution to the Civil War,* 1957

John T. Holdsworth and Davis R. Dewey, *The First and Second Banks of the United States,* 1910

Walker Lewis, *Without Fear or Favor: A Biography of Chief Justice Roger Brooke Taney,* 1965

George Macesich, "Sources of Monetary Disturbances in the United States, 1834–1845," *Journal of Economic History 20,* 1960

John M. McFaul, *The Politics of Jacksonian Finance,* 1972

Fritz Redlich, *The Molding of American Banking: Men and Ideas,* 2nd ed., 1968

Robert V. Remini, *Andrew Jackson and the Bank War,* 1967

Arthur M. Schlesinger, Jr., *The Age of Jackson,* 1953

Walter B. Smith, *Economic Aspects of the Second Bank of the United States,* 2nd ed., 1969

Esther R. Taus, *Central Banking Functions of the United States Treasury,* 1943

Peter Temin, *The Jacksonian Economy,* 1969

Jean A. Wilburn, *Biddle's Bank: The Crucial Years,* 1967

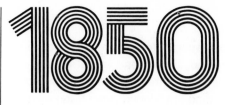

What If the Compromise of 1850 Had Been Defeated?

The Constitution is built upon the presumption that humans are naturally factious, and that society is divided into contending groups seeking political power. By balancing one faction against another, the Founding Fathers hoped to prevent any single interest from seizing and maintaining control of the national government. "In the extended republic of the United States and among the great variety of interests, parties and sects which it embraces," James Madison explained in *The Federalist,* No. 50, "a coalition of a majority of the whole society could seldom take place on any other principles than those of justice and the general good." Blacks and Indians might quarrel with Madison's assessment, with good reason, but he did not have them in mind. He meant that white Americans must live by consensus: that the Constitution was a device of national fusion to keep Americans from the unbearable alternative of civil conflict.

If consensus was the theory, compromise was the practice, and Americans became masters of the art. Whether the issue was Western lands, assumption of state debts, congressional representation, protective tariffs, or internal improvements, American politics operated mainly by way of accommodation rather than confrontation. The system worked well, since the country was rich, the people were optimistic, and what a vested interest sacrificed for the sake of harmony on one occasion it could regain on another. Differences among optimists rarely become irreconcilable conflicts.

The most difficult subject to compromise, however, because it was so complex and involved human and moral dimensions, was slavery and slave-related issues. The three-fifths clause, the return of runaways, and the provision regarding the African slave trade were the result of sectional hard bargaining at the Philadelphia convention. Without it there would not have been "a more perfect union." Some decades later, the problem of slavery extension into the Louisiana Territory evoked a brief but harsh debate before the Missouri Compromise of 1820 was enacted. Thus legislative compromise was woven into the American system by the basic law of the land and by experience. It became exalted, almost sanctified, and those who opposed it were labeled as extremists and fanatics. Yet compromise over slave-related issues often left a residue of bitterness, of distrust, and of anger that one section benefitted at the cost of the other. Thus Northern legislators frequently complained that the three-fifths clause was inequitable; and Southerners, that obstructions to the return of runaways made a mockery of the Constitution. Compromise seemed to postpone slave issues, not resolve them, and they returned to haunt the country, larger, more strident, more explosive than ever before. Such seemed to be the situation in 1850 when the two sections quarreled over the territorial spoils of the Mexican War.

Four years earlier, a Pennsylvania Democrat, David Wilmot, had introduced a proviso to exclude slavery from any territory to be acquired from Mexico. Twice it passed in the House only to be defeated in the Senate, and on numerous other occasions it was reintroduced, sparking venomous exchanges between legislators. The issue threatened to break apart both national parties. In the North, "Conscience Whigs" and "Barnburner Democrats" abandoned their traditional political allegiances and joined with ex-Liberty party members to form the Free Soil party. In the South, 180 delegates from nine states met at Nashville to plan a common sectional strategy. Most Northerners were not abolitionists, but they were determined that slavery should be contained where it was. That determination was composed of the following elements: dislike of the economic characteristics of slavery, racist opposition to the spread of the black population, and moral disapproval of the institution itself. Most Southerners were not secessionists, but they insisted that each citizen had a constitutional right to take slaves into the territories, and considered the willingness of the federal government to uphold this right to be a test of the government's good faith. Northerners were committed to bringing California in as a free state. Southerners swore that California—conquered mainly by soldiers from their section—would come in as a slave state or not at all.

The walls of Congress resounded with threats of secession and vindictive personal denunciations. At one point in 1850, Thomas Hart Benton of Missouri rose from his senatorial desk and strode toward the speaker,

Henry Foote of Mississippi. Foote drew and cocked a five-chambered revolver to defend himself. "I have no pistols! Let him fire!" Benton shouted. "Stand out of the way and let the damned assassin fire!" One by one, different politicians offered what they regarded as fair settlements of slavery problems, but none could obtain majority support. The spirit of concession, which had so frequently and so effectively operated in past crises, appeared bankrupt.

Then, in the winter of 1850 and in the twilight of his life, Senator Henry Clay pled once again the cause of moderation. Clay took pride in and carefully cultivated his image as "The Great Pacificator." Now he proposed a five-part package, "an amicable arrangement of all questions in controversy between the free and slave states." California would enter the Union as a free state; the Southwestern regions would be organized into territories by legislation that neither permitted nor excluded slavery; the Texas boundary with New Mexico would be drawn in the latter's favor, and Texas compensated by federal assumption of its preannexation debts; the slave trade, though not slavery itself, would be prohibited in the District of Columbia; and a new and more powerful fugitive slave law would be enacted guaranteeing Southerners the return of their runaways.

One cannot read Clay's speech without being impressed by its evident sincerity, its skillful defense of compromise, and its patriotic grandeur. "I implore, as the best blessing which Heaven can bestow upon me upon earth," he ended, "that if the direful and sad event of the dissolution of the Union shall happen, I may not survive to behold the sad and heartrending spectacle." Another voice, no longer resonant but nevertheless spellbinding, joined in support. Daniel Webster, on March 7, addressed the Senate "not as a Massachusetts man, nor as a Northern man, but as an American." "I speak," said Webster, "for the preservation of the Union. Hear me for my cause." Yet one must ask: Was compromise the wisest strategy in 1850? Was it not inequitable to tie California's admission to other issues? Was it not time to call a halt to sectional blackmail? The President of the United States, Zachary Taylor, thought so and set his course in direct opposition. He did not go as far as Senator William H. Seward of New York, who pronounced all legislative compromises to be "radically wrong and essentially vicious," and he certainly disapproved of Seward's appeal to "a higher law than the Constitution." But Taylor discerned elements of weakness, of escalated controversy, in an omnibus measure that both sections might accept rationally but neither could live up to emotionally.

Most historians have dismissed Zachary Taylor as an able general and a bona fide hero of the Mexican War but untrained for and largely incompetent as President. His 16-month administration has been judged "below average" in a poll of scholars. A noted authority writes that Taylor's elevation to the presidency "was no boon to the Republic." Another concludes that his opposition to the Compromise of 1850 was grounded "in an almost childish jealousy of Clay." Still another assumes that while "Taylor was suspicious of the men and measures involved in the Compromise, it is difficult to believe that he would have stood out against them." His motives, abilities, and judgments are all impugned. Clearly the palm of history has gone to Clay and Webster.

Perhaps Taylor's lack of charismatic qualities have led so many scholars to a negative view. He possessed neither oratorical genius nor political shrewdness—that was not his style—but approached national problems as he did military ones: directly, resolutely, and confidently. It would have been expedient for Taylor to side with his fellow Whigs, Clay and Webster. Virginia-born and Louisiana-bred, a slaveholder with Southern interests, Southern friends, and Southern ties—his son-in-law was Jefferson Davis —Taylor could have accepted the compromise and received a rousing endorsement from his own section. What opprobrium was leveled at the compromise by Northerners would have attached to Webster, as in fact it did. Instead, convinced that his own position on slavery in the West was just and equitable, Taylor remained fiercely independent and impervious to all political coercions. "It is fortunate that we have a man of pluck at the head of affairs in the present juncture," a reporter for the *Portland* (Maine) *Advertiser* wrote with approval. "Whoever else may become alarmed, General Taylor will not. The country may repose in this conviction."

What was Taylor's plan? Simply put, he believed that California should immediately enter the Union as a free state. The discovery of gold had multiplied its population, transforming squalid villages into booming towns that were administered haphazardly—sometimes under military law, common law, or lynch law. Instead of passing through a territorial stage, Taylor urged California settlers to proceed directly to statehood. In September 1849, a Constitutional Convention of 48 delegates, including many transplanted Southerners, assembled at Monterey and unanimously agreed that slavery should be prohibited. In fact, as the chaplain at Monterey later recalled, "there was no sign of the amazing importance of that decision, so easily reached in that little, far-off town." The state constitution was duly ratified—approximately 12,000 affirmative to 800 negative—a temporary state capitol selected, and a governor chosen. To delay California's admission or, even worse, to associate it with slave-related issues, Taylor felt, was ill-considered and unjust. Thomas Hart Benton said as much on the floor of the Senate: "I am opposed to this mixing of subjects which have no affinities. . . . [California] has washed her hands of slavery at home, and should not be mixed up with it abroad."

Secondly, Taylor sought precisely the same treatment for New Mexico. He had dispatched Lieutenant Colonel George A. McCall to Santa Fe with specific instructions to aid the movement to statehood. In due time, a convention was held and an antislavery constitution adopted. "Slavery in New Mexico," the convention resolved, "is naturally impractical, and can never in reality exist here." In July 1850, the constitution was ratified, approximately 6,800 in favor to 40 opposed. The fact that proslavery Texans laid claim to the eastern portion of New Mexico and threatened an armed invasion did not deter Taylor. He was prepared to send reinforcements and accept the consequences of war. (Taylor never did like the high-spirited and aggressive character of Texans.) Even Horace Greeley, editor of the *New York Tribune* and an opponent of Taylor in 1848, agreed that the President was taking "the only right course."

The President's plan was not designed to precipitate conflict, however, but to minimize it by leap-frogging from the military jurisdiction of California and New Mexico directly to statehood, without an intervening territorial stage. The federal government could administer territories, of course, which is why so many different proposals were debated in Congress: Wilmot's Proviso, a 36°30′ line to the Pacific, popular sovereignty, and so on. But the federal government had no authority over slavery in the states. Thus, Taylor's tactic would immediately remove a divisive area of congressional hassling. All other slave-related issues should be avoided, Taylor believed, at least in the heavy atmosphere of 1850. Surely they should not be coupled to California and New Mexico. "With a view of maintaining the tranquillity so dear to all," Taylor advised Congress, "we should abstain from the introduction of those exciting topics of a sectional character which have hitherto produced painful apprehensions in the public mind."

Henry Clay maintained that silence was no answer to the "bleeding wounds" of America. In a sarcastic speech, he rejected Taylor's plan as being too simplistic, an ostrichlike approach that would plunge the nation into war. There was the matter of fugitive slaves, of the slave trade in the District of Columbia, and of Texas claims in New Mexico, which only his compromise could settle amicably. Clay's speech, a spectator noted, "alluded to the policy of the administration . . . in terms of mingled scorn, contempt, derision, hate, and inflexible opposition."

Taylor wrote no long addresses or expositions in defense of his stand. He never answered Clay's challenge. But others did, especially a perceptive journalist, James S. Pike, who attended the debates and tried to convince his readers that the proposed compromise was unnecessary and dangerous.* Concerning the problem of fugitive slaves, Pike wrote that the law

---

*Pike's ideas reflected the views of many Northerners. He was both an abolitionist and antiblack. In 1860 he favored letting the South secede in peace. Later he suggested an apartheid-type solution of penning up all blacks in a few isolated areas of the South. In 1873 he wrote *The Prostrate State* dealing with black rule in South Carolina. But in 1850 his position on compromise was similar to Taylor's, a position history texts have neglected to evaluate.

"has remained untouched on the statute-book through all the changes and mutations of parties and administrations, slumbering in profound and undisturbed quiet during the whole period, and never before dragged from its repose to the light of day by even that vigilant guardian of the public welfare, Mr. Clay himself." It was best to let that subject "sleep the sleep of death in the musty records of a past century."

Concerning the proposal to abolish the slave trade in the capital, Pike wrote: "It is the merest burlesque and mockery that ever occupied the grave attention of sensible men. An abolition which is nothing more nor less than drawing away a putrid carcass from before a gentleman's mansion to leave it to fester and pollute the atmosphere of some less aristocratic neighborhood. It needs to be buried, not removed. Pass the law proposed, and not a manacle falls from the limbs of a single human victim, and not a slave less will be sold in the American market."

Concerning the bill to pay Texas for relinquishing its New Mexican claims, Pike called such claims "spurious," "preposterous," and "atrocious," and designed to extract money from the federal government. "The almighty dollar is an object with everybody," Pike insisted. "It is especially an object with Texas. Texas has a great deal of land and very little money. She would like to finger ten or a dozen million of Uncle Sam's six per cents, in the way of barter, for some of her acres, especially for those demesnes to which she has really no equitable title whatever. I do not speak at random when I say that Texas is ready, willing, and anxious to sell out her claim to New Mexico."

Finally, Pike warned that Clay's course spelled disaster for the Whig party. "Can a party stand with its leading men pulling openly in different directions on a great question of public and party policy?" Pike asked. "It will not take a thimbleful of brains to answer the question. . . . The Whigs have elected General Taylor as President, and unless they stand by him and his policy they are doomed, and the administration is doomed. . . . The president's plan is simple, just, wise, beneficent, unexceptionable, tranquillizing, harmonizing to all sections. It will save the integrity and nationality of the party. No reasonable man can deny it."

As the debate in Congress raged on, neither position could command a majority. All the magnificent oratory had little effect upon the deep-seated prejudices of legislators. Most of the support for Clay's compromise came from the Democratic and Southern side of Congress, but it had no real possibility of enactment so long as Taylor was President. Webster's speech changed the mind of not a single Northern Whig. However one totes up the votes for compromise, it was insufficient, certainly not enough to override the potential of Taylor's veto. There the matter stood, stalemated, with party lines dissolving and reforming, torn between old fealties and new ideologies, when Zachary Taylor died on July 9, 1850.

Five days earlier, he had munched on green apples, sat for hours under a broiling sun listening to Independence Day speeches, strode sweating through the Potomac flats, and then consumed a large quantity of raw fruits washed down with cold milk and water. The diarrhea and vomiting that followed did not seem initially alarming—dozens of prominent Washingtonians had similar symptoms for similar reasons—and Taylor was treated with calomel, opium, and quinine. Intermittently he sucked on ice, which did not help matters. He was bled and blistered, which helped even less. The fever mounted, and Taylor's condition became critical. The attending physicians diagnosed his illness as "cholera morbus," but the best evidence is that Taylor died of acute gastroenteritis probably due to contaminated water or milk.

His death was a national calamity, not recognized at the time but more apparent with each passing year. Clay's compromise was passed, piecemeal, through the efforts of Stephen A. Douglas, only to break down as Taylor had suspected it might. The law abolishing the slave trade in the capital accomplished little. An infamous "slave pen," a yellow house located between the Smithsonian and Capitol Hill, was closed. Nor could slaves be transported into the District for the express purpose of being merchandised. Otherwise, slaves were bought and sold as before, and newspapers carried numerous advertisements and announcements of the sales agreements.

The law compensating Texas was readily accepted, as Pike had predicted, and served to enrich bond speculators who lobbied for it. The banking firm of Corcoran and Riggs received over $420,000, an enormous sum for that period. (On the night of March 7, following his famous speech in defense of Clay's compromise, Daniel Webster received a gift of $6,000 from William Corcoran.)

But that part of the compromise which exacerbated rather than allayed sectional animosities was the Fugitive Slave Act. Northern mobs committed numerous acts of violence to stop its enforcement. In Boston and Syracuse, fugitive slaves were rescued from federal marshals. In Pennsylvania a slave hunter was murdered. In Wisconsin the state supreme court declared it unconstitutional. Other Northern state legislatures passed personal liberty laws to render the Fugitive Slave Act a nullity. As Taylor had feared, and Pike had articulated, the Whig party disintegrated and vanished in a few years. The Presidents who succeeded Taylor—Fillmore, Pierce, and Buchanan—were not without talents, but each lacked his fortitude and his vision. It was in truth a blundering generation. Under the popular sovereignty doctrine, the territory of Kansas became a bloody battlefield. John Brown's raid at Harpers Ferry ignited Southern fears, touching off a witch-hunt for subversives. Few were found, but hundreds of innocents suffered. The compromise may have delayed civil war for a decade, but when war finally came it lasted four years, took the lives of 620,000 soldiers, and bequeathed a legacy of Southern bitterness and Northern demands for retribution.

"If General Taylor had lived," Daniel Webster confided to Henry Hilliard of Alabama, "we should have had civil war." Undoubtedly Webster was right, since the Texans were at the point of invading New Mexico. Mass meetings held in Austin and San Jacinto demanded the use of force. The bellicose governor of Texas, Peter Bell, responded by calling a special meeting of the legislature to obtain its consent. In early July 1850, the news that 2,500 Texans would probably march on an American force of 600 at Santa Fe shocked the capital. No internal crisis in American history had ever reached such proportions. "The first federal gun fired against the people of Texas, without authority of law, will signal freemen from the Delaware to the Rio Grande to rally to the rescue," Representative Alexander H. Stephens of Georgia warned in his usual effeminate tones. "The cause of Texas will be the cause of the entire South. When the 'Rubicon' is passed, the days of this Republic will be numbered."

Had Taylor lived, there is no doubt that he would have met force with force. A Philadelphia newspaper reported that "southern ultraists invaded his sick chamber" to threaten a vote of censure if Taylor persisted in his determination to send additional troops to Santa Fe. Humphrey Marshall of Kentucky, Charles Conrad of Louisiana, and Robert Toombs of Georgia —Whigs who had supported Taylor's candidacy—came away from the White House rebuffed. They reported that Old Zach was obstinate, and that there was "no longer any hope" for the Union. A decade later, Abraham Lincoln would agonize over a similar problem—the reinforcement of Fort Sumter—and come to a similar decision, despite the advice of some cabinet officers to the contrary. In 1850 Taylor's secretary of war, George W. Crawford, said that he would not sign an order to American military forces to resist Texas jurisdiction in New Mexico. Taylor was unperturbed. He stated that he "would sign it himself."

Some scholars believe that the South might have won if war had broken out in 1850. They point to the widening margin of Northern economic superiority over the next 11 years in manufacturing, railroad mileage, the value of real and personal property, pig-iron production, population, and so forth. By Lincoln's time, the North possessed an enormous advantage in military potential over the South. But how much advantage did it need? In 1850 the North already outstripped the South substantially in every industrial category. Not counting the border states, the North led in the number of manufacturing establishments: 93,700 to 16,700; in the annual value of manufactured products: $843,387,000 to $79,157,000; in railroad mileage: 13,100 to 3,300; in pig iron: 422,000 tons to 54,000 tons; in population: 13,400,000 to 7,200,000.

This statistical superiority would have had a telling effect if a civil war in 1850 had involved the entire nation and been fought with wholesale ferocity for a number of years—which was not likely. There were significant distinctions between conditions in 1850 and those in 1861 which lead one to conclude that an earlier war would have been more limited in bloodshed and shorter in duration. The Southern extremist cause would have been crushed decisively at a fraction of the human cost and without the tragic aftermath of Reconstruction. Why? What is the justification for such a speculation?

First, by the time Lincoln became President the Southern position had hardened considerably. Frederick Douglass put it best when he said that "the South was mad. They had come to hate everything which had the prefix 'Free'—free soil, free states, free territories, free schools, free speech, and freedom generally." The attitude of the imperial South, Douglass reported, was "haughty and unreasonable and unreasoning." In 1850 such was not the case. Certainly the fire-eaters of the lower South did not speak for the thousands of moderates who would not be pressed into a war over New Mexico. Slavery could not thrive there anyway. These Unionists would have either remained discreetly neutral or sided with Taylor.

Second, Lincoln was a Northerner, elected completely by Northern votes, and Southerners felt that he was being imposed upon them. His position on slavery was disturbing to them. On the one hand, he called it a moral wrong, a blight upon the land; on the other, he promised that the federal government would not interfere with slavery in the states. Southerners put no credence in these promises and were, in fact, obsessed with the notion that Lincoln was an abolitionist. By no stretch of the imagination could the same be said for Taylor. He was a Southern slaveholder and, though opposed to its extension, he would brook no interference with slavery in the states. "So far as slavery is concerned," Taylor wrote, "we of the south must throw ourselves on the constitution and defend our rights under it to the last, and when arguments will no longer suffice, we will appeal to the sword if necessary." He would "be the last to yield an inch."

There were these differences as well: in 1861 many Southerners believed that the federal government would not support a costly war to prevent secession; in 1850 there was absolutely no doubt that Taylor would, and that his determination would rally all Unionists behind the flag. In 1861 the Democrats had split, and the Republican organization was restricted to the Northern states; in 1850 the Democrats and Whigs had serious problems, but each still functioned as national parties. In 1861, after Lincoln ordered supplies to Fort Sumter, four more states (for a total of 11) joined the Confederacy, but West Virginia remained loyal, as did Delaware, Kentucky, Missouri, and Maryland; in 1850, given the circumstances, the probability is that none of the states of the upper South would have seceded.

The steps toward war might well have commenced with a fiery address of

Governor Bell to the Texas legislature in August. Bell had fought at San Jacinto and Buena Vista, served as a Ranger, and was reputed to be the most pro-Southern of competing Texas politicians who vied for that honor. His firm stand against the federal government was heartily approved by Texas voters in 1849 and again in 1851. Without a doubt, the legislature would have voted overwhelmingly to send troops to Santa Fe. Concurrently Bell would have requested and received military aid from the deep South. In fact, when the crisis was merely brewing, Governor John A. Quitman of Mississippi had promised to send 5,000 hand-chosen troops to fight on the side of Texas. One county in South Carolina (Kershaw) resolved "that the course which the General Government is pursuing towards the sovereign State of Texas is insulting and degrading to the South, and should be resisted 'at all hazards and to the last extremity.' " Public meetings in other parts of South Carolina, as well as Mississippi, Georgia, and Alabama, passed similar resolutions. "These speak the voice of the South, now upheaving and in commotion," an admirer wrote to Bell, "and thank God it is so."

Whether Taylor would have left the capital to lead American forces personally—he stated that he would do so if the flag was attacked—first blood would have been shed in the Southwest. Once the crisis moved from academic arguments over slavery extension to a shooting war involving the Union, a whole new psychology would have come into play. Taylor would have called for volunteers, as did Lincoln, and a whirlwind of patriotism would have swirled throughout the North. ("Now we have a country again," Ralph Waldo Emerson wrote in 1861. "Sometimes gunpowder smells good.") Stephens of Georgia had informed Secretary of the Navy William B. Preston that "if troops were ordered to Santa Fe, the President would be impeached." Preston asked: "Who will impeach him?" Stephens answered: "I will if nobody else does." But with a war, with the fate of the Union at stake, Stephens' flippant words would have become truer than he had thought. Relatively few would have sided with Stephens. Congressmen and other government officers from the deep South who favored secession would have submitted resignations and returned home.

Even as soldiers marched, another Southern convention would have convened at Nashville to consider secession. One can well imagine the bellicose speeches for rebellion, the pleas for union, and the last-minute unavailing attempts to find some kind of compromise. For many, the decision would have been agonizing, but at best no more than seven or eight states of the lower South would have joined the second Texas rebellion.

Joel R. Poinsett of South Carolina had predicted that the North would win the Civil War of 1850. He had refused to be a state delegate to the first Nashville convention on the grounds that it might adopt measures which "will lead to immediate civil war." Such a war, he informed a friend, would "probably terminate in defeat and humiliation," and he would not "by any act of mine aid in the perpetration of our own destruction." There is no reason to describe imaginary armies fighting in imaginary battles. One must agree with Poinsett, however, that the end result would have been a quick and humiliating defeat of the seceding states. The prestige and political power of Taylor, a celebrated hero, would have risen to the level of Andrew Jackson's two decades earlier. Surely the idea of compromise would have been dropped. Few congressmen would have been willing to appropriate funds to Texas, a rebel state, even with lavish bribes. Probably California would have been admitted as a free state by 1852.

What is often obscured by the heat of debate is the fact that large numbers of Southerners agreed with Taylor. Back in December 1849, 29 conservative Whigs and one Union Democrat of the Georgia legislature signed a statement that it was unjustifiable to oppose California's admission as a free state. Others who shared this opinion had been intimidated by public opinion to remain silent. With military defeat, however, and with the extremist cause squelched, these moderate voices would have been heard throughout the South.

One can also speculate with some assurance that New Mexico would have been admitted to the Union along with or shortly after California. Many knowledgeable Southerners understood that a war over Texas claims in New Mexico could not alter fundamental geographical truths. In 1847 John A. Campbell of Alabama advised John C. Calhoun that a political disaster for the South would follow the annexation of Mexican lands: "The territory is wholly unfit for a negro population. The republic of Mexico contains a smaller number of blacks than any of the older colonies of Spain and tho' this is not conclusive yet it is a persuasive argument that negro labor was not found profitable." Of course, there would have been die-hard secessionists even in defeat, zealous as ever in their spurious dreams of a slave empire stretching to the Pacific. But defeat would have pierced the dreams for many, lanced the tumor of secessionism, and restored a sense of reality to national debates.

If our speculation thus far appears to be reasonable, it follows that Taylor's war would have had profoundly different consequences than Lincoln's.

The Civil War of 1861–65 resulted in the physical devastation of the South. Eyewitness accounts describe a land of ruins and desolation. Between Richmond and Washington it was "like a desert." Charleston was a city "of vacant houses, of widowed women, of rotting wharves." Along the path of General Sherman's march, it "looked for many miles like a broad, black streak of ruin." The manpower shortages and loss of markets laid waste much of Southern agriculture. Industries were crippled. The banks were bankrupt. What is not so well known is that the Civil War retarded Northern growth. Contrary to popular belief, the war neither inaugurated nor spurred the American Industrial Revolution. The loss of the large Southern market for its manufactured products and the depletion of its labor supply by military demands actually caused Northern labor productivity to *decline*. All significant economic indicators were lower for that decade than for any other in the nineteenth century.

Moreover, the Civil War of 1861–65 bore the fruit of Reconstruction, and it could not have been otherwise. Lincoln was a towering figure, but neither his words imploring charity and justice nor the lesson of his assassination could erase the hatreds born of fratricidal conflict. There were too many empty chairs, too many vacant bedrooms, too many maimed, and too many ill-treated at infamous prisons such as Andersonville.

A decisive victory in 1850 and a speedy return to normalcy, on the other hand, would scarcely have disrupted the growth pattern of the American economy. In 1851 the products of American technology were displayed at the Crystal Palace Exhibition in London and came away with a hundred prize medals. The inventiveness of American artisans impressed foreign visitors and, in the manufacture of products involving the use of precision instruments, the United States already outstripped all industrial nations. The South was also booming, since world prices for cotton continued to climb. A short war would not have impaired national prosperity and might even have served to emphasize the fact that the economies of both sections were neatly complementary.

Taylor would have been reelected in 1852 and could have named his successor four years later. Instead of unstable administrations wrestling with the psychological strains imposed by the Compromise of 1850, a strong coalition of Whig Unionists would have directed affairs on a completely pragmatic basis. Northern and Southern moderates would have joined to resist extremist solutions. They would not have permitted "bleeding Kansas" to develop, to fester, and to interfere with economic growth. Instead of vindictiveness and divisiveness, confidence, optimism, and enterprise would have marked American society. The Democrats would not have been tainted with treason. No military rule would have been imposed upon the South. There would have been hard arguments over taxes and tariffs, railroads, homestead acts, banking, and internal improvements at federal expense, but with the slavery issue removed and a modicum of political wisdom, these issues could have been legislated in a logrolling package. In short, the nation could have resumed its briefly interrupted course of happy compromise between contending economic interests.

In still one other crucial respect, Taylor's war would have had a significantly different result than Lincoln's: there would not have been any abolition of slavery. It is a matter of ironic fact that Lincoln had no intention of taking such an action. One wing of the Republican party did badger him to use his war powers to abolish slavery, but Lincoln felt such a policy would violate the Republican platform and antagonize some of the border states, pushing them to the Confederate side. "My paramount object in this struggle," wrote Lincoln, "*is* to save the union, and is *not* to save or destroy slavery." Nevertheless, under constant pressure from the radical Republicans, Lincoln in 1863 issued the Emancipation Proclamation, which actually ordered freedom for slaves only in those areas in which the President had no real authority. Some radicals thought Lincoln should have made a more courageous and forthright statement. Democrats, on the other hand, thought Lincoln had acted hypocritically by yielding to the demands of the radicals:

> "Honest old Abe, when the war first began,
> Denied abolition was part of his plan;
> Honest old Abe has since made a decree,
> The war must go on till the slaves are
>   all free.
> As both can't be honest, will someone
>   tell how,
> If honest Abe then, he is honest Abe now?"

Yet posterity remembers Lincoln as the great emancipator, and the Civil War became, in the eyes of many, a noble conflict. Surely Taylor would never for a moment have considered an emancipation proclamation. Quite the contrary. He would have made a strong and reassuring statement that slave property in the states would be afforded every constitutional protection by his administration. Thus, had the Civil War started in 1850, the North would have been victorious, the human cost would have been minimal, the Union would have been strengthened, and the economy would have continued its steady pattern of growth—but the blacks would have been kept in slavery. Whether such results would have been preferable to those America experienced from 1861 to 1865—that is, whether the gains in human freedom justified the cost in human lives—involves a moral calculus which is properly left to the conscience of each individual.

SUGGESTED READINGS

William C. Binkley, *The Expansionist Movement in Texas, 1836–1850,* 1925
William N. Chambers, *Old Bullion Benton,* 1956
Avery Craven, *The Coming of the Civil War,* 1957
Louis Filler, *The Crusade Against Slavery, 1830–1860,* 1960
Herbert D. Foster, "Webster's Seventh of March Speech and the Secession Movement, 1850," *American Historical Review,* January 1922

Loomis M. Ganaway, *New Mexico and the Sectional Controversy, 1846–1861,* 1944

Philip M. Hamer, *The Secession Movement in South Carolina, 1847–52,* 1918

Holman Hamilton, *Prologue to Conflict: The Crisis and Compromise of 1850,* 1964

Holman Hamilton, *Zachary Taylor, Soldier in the White House,* 2 vols., 1951

Allan Nevins, *Ordeal of the Union,* 2 vols., 1947

Roy Nichols, *The Stakes of Power,* 1961

James S. Pike, *First Blows of the Civil War,* 1879

Robert R. Russel, "What Was the Compromise of 1850?" *Journal of Southern History,* August 1956

Glyndon G. Van Deusen, *The Life of Henry Clay,* 1937

Glyndon G. Van Deusen, *Thurlow Weed: Wizard of the Lobby,* 1947

Whites and Indians—Was There a Better Way?

There has never been a simple answer to the question: What policy should the national government follow regarding the Indians? The problem perplexed the British crown, and occupied much of the time of every American President in the first century of our national existence, from Washington through Jefferson, Jackson, and Lincoln.

The issue was always how best to displace the Indians, with least cost and risk to whites. There was never any single policy for achieving this in the pre–Civil War era. The national government, like trappers, land agents, and state officials, tried various policies. These included land purchase, treaties with promises of continuing aid and territorial respect for tribal reserves, gifts, bribes, and, of course, war. There were costs to be paid no matter what the policy or mix of policies, but the Indians were nonetheless irresistibly displaced by advancing white populations with superior technology.

The Civil War brought no pause in white pressure upon Indian lands, as the 1860s and 1870s saw a spreading conflict over control of the Great Plains.

Again the federal government was involved in Indian policy as treaty bargainer where negotiation would accomplish sufficient displacement, and as a source of armed power where it would not. The Homestead Act of 1862, with promise of free transfer of a quarter section of public domain to settlers, encouraged the surge of westward-bound whites. The 1870s were a running brush fire of conflict, as whites overran Indian reservations which seemed to the white mind so empty and poorly utilized. The Sioux of South Dakota, promised a secure reservation in an 1868 treaty, encountered George A. Custer's cavalry in 1874 running interference for a horde of miners. The Sioux killed Custer in 1876 at the Little Big Horn, but were eventually overwhelmed. Stockmen and settlers invaded the Wallowa valley of the Nez Percés in Oregon, defeating Chief Joseph's braves after brilliant resistance in 1877. The Utes of Colorado experienced the same story—pressure from miners, Ute resistance, violence, entry of the United States army, and defeat. The Poncas of Nebraska were shuttled from the Sioux reservation to Oklahoma, and suffered greatly from starvation and disease.

War had always been an occasional element of federal Indian policy, but very few whites believed that it was the best way to handle the matter. The strife of the 1870s between Indians and whites thus produced much soul-searching on the issue of Indian relations. On the white side, a sizable reform movement developed with its center of gravity in the East. The Indian Citizenship Association of Boston grew mainly out of the Ponca disgrace, and counted as members novelist Helen Hunt Jackson (author of *Century of Dishonor,* 1881) and Massachusetts Senator Henry L. Dawes. Philadelphia was the site of the Women's National Indian Association, established in 1879, and of the Indian Rights Association organized in 1882. Reformers had a humanitarian purpose, and sought the best way to aid the Indian in the admittedly tragic circumstances of his encounter with an advancing civilization of superior technology and numbers.

Historian Wilcomb Washburn concludes that several main policy alternatives presented themselves in the years just after the Civil War, as whites moved rapidly westward. The first alternative was to invade tribal reservations without compunction, killing the aborigines when they resisted. The second alternative was to scrupulously observe treaty rights and the territorial integrity of Indian lands. The first was abhorrent to those large numbers of Americans who held Christian and humanitarian principles. These whites were more numerous than the Poncas, Utes, and Sioux would have been inclined to believe. If the United States was to have a permanent policy, it must not simply be extermination—so believed a substantial element of the white population. The second alternative might have been preferred by Eastern humanitarians, but almost without exception they accepted the irresistible quality of white expansionism. In some way the Indians must be led to yield land to whites and still survive.

This left only the invention of a new role for the Indian, one that would enable him to live on after the loss of much of his land and the disruption of his culture, which on the Great Plains was chiefly nomadic. Here entered the idea of shifting the Indian from communal landholding to severalty landholding—individual property ownership in the traditional white fashion.

If Indians could be led to adopt severalty landholding, they might then learn the arts of agriculture, and adaptation to the rest of white cultural life would follow. Indians would not have to be killed; they would gradually be converted into farm families and assimilated into the American nation as citizens. As the Commissioner of Indian Affairs wrote in 1879 in recommending a draft law establishing severalty for Indians: "The government is impotent to protect the Indian on their reservations," and so the allotment of tribal lands to individual families was the only means by which "the race can be led in a few years to the condition where they may be clothed with citizenship and left to their own resources."

The underlying assumptions here were, of course, old and deeply rooted. Jefferson had best expressed the American faith in an agrarian freehold as the basis for all political democracy and social progress. The idea surfaced as naturally when the Indian's future was considered in the post–Civil War years as when the fate of the ex-slaves was a central issue. That the ex-slaves did not get their "40 acres and a mule" as a passport to assimilation, while the Indians were to get their 160 acres, was not for lack of public faith in the redemptive power of the freehold. It was because the Indians already held the land that was to be allotted to family heads.

Indeed, the Indians occupied more than enough land for a generous allotment of title in severalty, still leaving vast acres for acquisition by whites. Severalty, an apparent solution for the Indians as white civilization washed around them, was also a solution to the problem of white land hunger. Severalty was thus the inescapable and fundamental idea in the formulation of long-range policy. It was a formula that appeared to accommodate the ungovernable greed of advancing white society but also that society's abhorrence of simple extermination of the continent's original human inhabitants.

Yet there were many ways in which this policy could be devised and implemented. The one we know best is the road in fact taken. After a decade of discussion, the General Allotment Act (or Dawes Act, after its principal sponsor, Senator Henry Dawes) was passed in 1887, based upon the sort of logic advanced by former Secretary of the Interior Carl Schurz, who said that "the enjoyment and pride of the individual ownership of property is one of the most effective civilizing agencies."

The provisions of the act may be readily summarized. When the President decided (advised, of course, by the bureaucracy—in this case, the Bureau of Indian Affairs) that a tribe was ready for allotment, each head of family would receive 160 acres, and single persons lesser amounts. To prevent the Indians from selling their freehold to a beguiling white as the Manhattan Indians sold a certain island for approximately $24, the Dawes Act prohibited transfer of title for a 25-year period. During this time the government would act as trustee. The period might even last longer, if the

President chose. But when the trust period was over, Indian lands individually held could be sold by their owners, who were given citizenship at the time of allotment. The 25-year wait did not entirely bar whites from gaining title to Indian lands, of course, for this would have been intolerable to impatient settlers. Only individual allotments could not be sold during that time. Tribal lands beyond the acreage required for allotment were available for sale, from the passage of the act in 1887, at the President's discretion. The funds from such sales were held in the Treasury for the tribe, and the interest was used by the BIA for its work. Large reservations would thus be broken up, and the Indians would necessarily end their nomadic ways and become tillers of the soil on the Yankee model.

The results of the Dawes Act were not, to put it mildly, as had been predicted by its sponsors. Indian lands beyond those needed for allotment were sold at a rate that, by the 1930s (when sales were discontinued), had reduced the total from 140 million acres to 50 million, or by almost two-thirds. This appeased white land hunger to a considerable extent, but it stripped the tribes of much of their best hunting, grazing, agricultural, mineral, and forestry holdings. Of course, a principal goal of the act had been to weaken the tribes, and this was successfully accomplished. The prime cause was the reduction of Indian land holdings, along with the steady pressure of white culture and of BIA administration upon all aspects of Indian life. With their religion, speech, dress, skin color, and history denigrated by the surrounding civilization, Indians on 160-acre freeholds or those remaining in tribal communities did not become sturdy Jeffersonian yeomen. They became instead, in President Nixon's words, "the most deprived and most isolated minority group in our nation," falling behind all other racial and ethnic groups in income, health, life expectancy, and other indices of social situation.

While the white population doubled in the years from the Civil War to the 1930s, the Indian population barely held its own, and entire tribes disappeared. By the 1960s the Indian population was growing again after 300 years of decline, and racial survival was not an issue.* Yet every Indian child was born to an unpromising future. A study in the 1960s showed 72 percent of reservation Indians earning less than $3,000 annually, and approximately 40 percent were unemployed. Indians were 20 years behind the rest of America in median years of schooling, 20 years behind in life expectancy, and 24 years behind in infant mortality. "Left to their own resources," as Carl Schurz had recommended in 1879, the Indians had not become assimilated. If anything, they had become decimated.

---

*Data are poor, but there were probably 260,000 Indians in 1887, 525,000 in 1960, 800,000 in 1970, and perhaps 1 million today.

This failure of the Dawes Act to provide for successful assimilation became inescapably clear by the 1920s, and another reform movement began to build up pressure for change. The Indian was voted citizenship in 1924 (from 1887 to 1924, citizenship came only with land allotment to an individual Indian), and the famous Meriam Report of 1928 publicized a devastating critique of both BIA administration and its underlying assumptions. President Herbert Hoover's administration made some policy reforms, but the Dawes Act was still official policy. Then in 1934 President Franklin D. Roosevelt signed the Indian Reorganization Act (IRA), proclaimed an Indian New Deal, and appointed reformer John Collier head of the BIA, the agency Collier had criticized for a decade.

Collier's ideas and the operating philosophy of the new Indian policy of 1934 were a sharp departure from the past. To halt the erosion of the Indian economic base, land sales were ended. Indian tribal customs and culture were now to be respected and nurtured. Reservation schools would tolerate and even teach Indian languages and culture. "Indian societies," Collier wrote, "must be given status, respect and power . . . . The land, held, used and cherished in the way the particular Indian group desires, is fundamental to any life-saving program." Tribes would be granted new constitutions and given enlarged powers of self-government. Indians were to be advanced in the BIA service; more money was to be channeled to Indian aid and to a new program of land purchase. The Indian New Deal was a complex mix of more federal aid and less federal control, a blend of liberal commitment both to social welfare and to invigorated political participation of disadvantaged groups.

The old Dawes era idea of early assimilation into an agrarian individualistic mode was repudiated. The IRA eased that pressure, and Collier asserted, at the hearings upon his nomination to head the BIA, that assimilation now had to be on the Indians' own terms and in their own good time. In his writings, Collier made it clear that he saw as many reasons for whites to adopt some Indian values as the other way around. Indians, he argued, were in many ways superior to whites— "in public spirit, in rhythm, in joy of life, and in intensity realized within quietude. . . . These superiorities will be masked by an apparent inferiority until their group as a group moves into status and power. Then the mask will fall away." The new Indian policy was based upon a very new vision of the Indian participating permanently in American life, not as an absorbed individual but as a member of a distinct and permanent racial subgroup held together by some combination of the old customs.

The Indian New Deal marked a policy shift so abrupt that it was, not surprisingly, temporary. After passing the 1934 act, Congress balked at appropriating the funds Collier thought necessary to carry on BIA land-purchase efforts and to improve reservation programs. World War II broke the momentum of the broader liberal reform movement of which the IRA was comfortably a part and, even before Collier's resignation in 1945, Congress and the BIA began to turn away from the act's guiding principles. Collier, in the words of Harold Fey and D'Arcy McNickle, had led "a broad attack upon poverty, educational backwardness, health service deficiencies, bureaucratic control, and dependency" while head of the BIA between 1933 and 1945. He left when the pendulum was swinging back in the other direction.

Twenty years after the IRA, in 1953, Congress passed, and a conservative President (Dwight D. Eisenhower) signed, House Resolution 108, setting a new goal of early "termination" of federal responsibilities in Indian life. Sentiment for termination had been strong in Congress since the late 1930s, in fact, and Collier and his successors up to Dillon Meyer (1950–53) fought rearguard battles against hostile congressional committees who found the Indian way of life "communistic" and wanted the BIA to stop nurturing such cultural affronts to the American way of life. HR 108 simply codified the resurgence of the old Dawes-era assumption that early and complete assimilation was the correct federal policy, whatever the consequences.

But too much time had passed, too much had been learned for the old assumptions to return in unimpaired force. After HR 108, some tribes were quickly terminated whether or not they requested it or seemed ready for it—the Klamaths in Oregon, the Menominees of Wisconsin, the Poncas of Nebraska, the Wyandottes and Ottawas of Oklahoma, and others. The effects were almost uniformly disastrous—valuable timber and mining resources plundered by whites, the end of BIA schooling and community services, desperate poverty, and intensified social disorganization. These developments slowed the drive for termination. Even Eisenhower's secretary of the interior, Fred Seaton, was forced to admit in 1958 that:

> It would be incredible, even criminal, to send any Indian tribe out into the mainstream of American life until and unless the educational level of that tribe was one which was equal to the responsibilities which it was shouldering.

John F. Kennedy's secretary of the interior, Stewart Udall, appointed a task force that recommended once again a more active BIA role in preserving Indian assets and shifting program emphasis away from termination. These strides back toward the Collier–New Deal approach were accelerated under Lyndon B. Johnson, and Richard Nixon's 1970 message on Indian affairs marked the official acceptance by American conservatism that the federal government bore unique responsibilities for the careful, lengthy, and inevitably expensive nurturing of Indian cultural strength.

Nixon urged Indian self-determination within a special federal relationship, and—without mentioning that as legislator he had supported HR 108—specifically repudiated the idea of termination and forced assimilation.

Today, federal policy has returned to the letter of the New Deal approach and, to some extent, also to the spirit. But some residue of the pre–New Deal attitudes remain within the federal bureaucracy, and Indian spokesmen complain that Congress has yet to provide the resources necessary to carry out promises made by Presidents Johnson and Nixon in recent years. Clearly the United States has not yet found the solution to "the Indian problem." In January 1975, Congress established an American Indian Policy Commission to conduct a comprehensive review of policy and to recommend appropriate changes.

Yet if the policy record is mixed, there has emerged a remarkable consensus that unites the vast majority of interested Indians and whites; this consensus confirms the Collier and not the Dawes analysis of the Indian future within a white society. Virtually every writer on American Indians and virtually every informed witness before contemporary congressional committees regards the reversal of policy in 1934 as having been highly desirable in principle, and regrets that the spirit and the letter of the IRA were not given a decisive and sustained trial. For the Indian to live decently and successfully in modern America, as Collier in his own way understood, Indian group life and communal ways must be the respected base from which native Americans move into a better future. The surrounding white society may condemn these ways as being "communistic," and may want the reservation Indian to come into town with a deed to individual property so that he may be made an offer he cannot refuse. But the Collier–New Deal policy would put a sympathetic government firmly between the Indian and such pressures, protecting his culture and his resources from premature cries for assimilation. This special time of wardship must be helpful and not paternalistic in spirit, must permit substantial tribal self-determination, and must last for that indefinite time until individual Indians choose to abandon gradually the old ways out of cultural self-confidence rather than inferiority and economic desperation.

This, in broad outline, was the Collier idea, endorsed today wherever one turns, by anthropologists, self-styled Indian experts in politics and private life, and by most Indians themselves. It is a dream of separateness with no terminal date, of tribal independence—within the larger union—that is free from all cultural and even political pressure, yet an independence underwritten by massive federal economic aid. A moment's thought exposes the unlikelihood that a policy of such subtlety and internal tension could be fully implemented by a democracy. And, indeed, the Indian New Deal was never adequately put into practice. From the beginning, when Collier faced hearings upon his nomination as BIA head, some congressmen did not like the open-ended nature of the new reforms. Collier was forced to admit that he did not know how long the period of transition for the Indians might be. He apparently anticipated an almost indeterminate period when Indians would live in relatively isolated clusters amid an entirely different civilization. During that time, the controlling civilization and its government must not insist upon assimilation; indeed, the only way to facilitate it was to nurture the native culture and appear not to care when or how the conversion to modernity would occur. To achieve assimilation, the white government must not aim at it. It must, in fact, work to preserve Indian culture intact, trusting to Collier's conviction, paradoxical though it seems, that only strong cultures blend readily into others.

Executing such a policy required of the federal government a subtle, dichotomous role. Government must aid the native American in many ways, providing health, educational, and general social services while acting as a buffer against surrounding commercial and cultural pressures from whites. Yet at the same time, this government with a crucial welfare mission must reduce bureaucratic controls to a minimum, while encouraging tribal self-government and the habits of political participation.

It was a difficult assignment that was never given a sustained trial. As an ideal, however, it has attracted the admiration of most students of the subject—both Indian and white. Could this policy in some broad way have been tried much earlier, perhaps in 1887, eliminating the tragic 50-year experiment with the Dawes policy? Indeed, would not a reversal of the two policies have produced better results? Given a 50-year period under the IRA-Collier idea of respect for Indian culture along with a sufficient land base for tribal survival, might not the Indian community have been ready for gradual integration into white society somewhere toward the middle of the twentieth century? This tantalizing idea draws strength from a contemporary understanding, wrung from hard experience, that integration of different ethnic groups and races into Anglo-Saxon American life comes most painlessly—as with the Jews or the Irish—when the group is permitted an extended period of relatively separate cultural life within the nation, building a base of identity and self-confidence from which individuals may gradually choose increasing degrees of cultural assimilation into the dominant culture.

Let us examine this prospect for the light it throws upon the making of the first formal and comprehensive Indian policy which bore Dawes' name. Here we will develop some serious doubts that the more enlightened Collier approach could have come first. The 50 tragic years of Dawes-era Indian policy, from the 1880s to the 1930s, take on a certain inevitability. There will also be some doubts about the Collier approach itself, which today so dominates the discussion of Indian policy that even President Richard Nixon—who supported HR 108 in 1953—endorsed it.

The debate about federal Indian policy has been endless, a sad reminder of the intractability of the problem. But after passage of the Dawes Act in 1887, it did not seem to contemporaries that the issue need continue to vex us. Extended discussion and experimentation over a half-century, particularly intense argument from 1879 to 1887, had produced a comprehensive policy with broad support. On reviewing the debate, it is surprising how few really viable options there were amid all the passionate clamor.

Notice the fundamental assumptions that commanded unshakable majorities, and how little room they left for maneuver. Every working assumption of the white community in the late nineteenth century supported a policy of peaceful, orderly, but incessant assault upon separate Indian cultural existence. On this there could be no extended debate, even though a rare individual occasionally saw it differently. From the beginning, when whites encountered Indians at Jamestown and Plymouth, there had been in the white mind a conviction of cultural superiority, reinforced continually by technological mastery. Whites knew that they represented "civilization," an unmitigated good. Indians were barbarians, a primitive people whom history and the Almighty had intended to yield and vanish as a culture. As Thomas Jefferson had said in 1824:

> where . . . progress will stop, no one can say. Barbarism has, in the meantime, been receding before the steady step of amelioration; and will in time, I trust, disappear from the earth.

It was clear that by barbarism he meant not merely primitive frontier conditions for early explorers and settlers, but Indian civilization. "The backward will yield," the ex-President wrote in 1812, "and be thrown further back. . . . We shall be obliged to drive them, with the beasts of the forest into the Stony mountains." An historian of the late eighteenth century expressed this general sentiment more grandly:

> The savage has had his day . . . . His nation and race must cease to exist, and . . . his mighty forests must finally bow to human strength . . . . His agonies, at first, seem to demand a tear from the eye of humanity; but when we reflect, that the extinction of his race, and the progress of the arts which give rise to his distressing apprehensions, are for the increase of mankind, and for the promotion of the world's glory and happiness . . . we shall be pleased with the perspective into futurity.

There was, of course, a better fate the Indians might choose, if they would. Jefferson advised them in 1808:

> Let me entreat you therefore, on the lands now given you to begin every man a farm, let him enclose it, cultivate it, build a warm house on it, and when he dies let it belong to his wife and children after him.

Here the door of agrarian democracy opened to white civilization, and where Jefferson would advise the Indian to take it, the Dawes Act would codify it as the only escape from extinction for the native American.

If anything, the course of the nineteenth century had strengthened these assumptions of the inevitable displacement of all Indian civilization by a superior race and culture. Historian Reginald Horsman has shown how white attitudes toward all societies on the borders of an expanding United States became even more aggressive as the era of "manifest destiny" opened in the 1840s. "Confidence in American institutions," in Horsman's words, "reached new heights" during the expansionary era of the Mexican War, and the assumptions of cultural superiority of earlier days were even more virulent for the rest of the nineteenth century. An association of whites in Cheyenne, Wyoming, wrote in the 1880s:

> The rich and beautiful valleys of Wyoming are destined for the occupancy and sustenance of the Anglo-Saxon race. . . . The same inscrutable Arbiter that decreed the downfall of Rome has pronounced the doom of extinction upon the red men of America.

Indian policy in the 1880s would be shaped in a climate devoid of significant dissent regarding these assumptions.

In such a climate, the Collier–New Deal approach was politically out of the question. Whites would take Indian lands and condemn Indian culture, and it would not occur to more than a tiny minority that this in itself was questionable. Discussion was possible only on timing and methods. The native civilization was not conceded any right to independent existence. Why should it deserve it, even wish it, when a superior civilization had arrived in history's good time? It would take four or five decades after the Dawes Act for different assumptions about cultures to gather any significant following.

The Anglo-conformity idea, as Milton Gordon tells us in *Assimilation in American Life* (1964), had, by the beginning of the twentieth century, yielded some ground to the slightly different Melting-Pot theory, which saw all ethnic and racial groups blending eventually into one new American type. But even the Melting-Pot theory assumed that distinct, non-Anglo-Saxon groups would disappear into a higher breed. To provide the Indian, among other nonwhites, with a theoretical justification for extended separate existence, it was necessary to develop a guiding cultural theory quite different from the Anglo-conformity or Melting-Pot ideas, which jostled together for dominance as the twentieth century opened. This new theory eventually arrived in the second decade of our century, and began to slowly edge its way toward acceptance. It was to be called Cultural Pluralism, and emerged from the writings of John Dewey, Norman Hapgood, Randolph Bourne, and Horace M. Kallen. It flourished in the settlement houses of the progressive era, where Jane Addams, for example, devoted displays and evenings of study to the learning of the folk cultures of Chicago's immigrant groups. But it was Kallen who gave Cultural Pluralism its most ringing expression, writing first in a 1915 article, "Democracy Versus the Melting Pot" in *The Nation.* He talked of "the union of the different . . . . A democracy of nationalities, . . . a multiplicity in a unity, an orchestration of mankind."

By the 1930s, the new outlook on non-Western cultures which Kallen had named Cultural Pluralism was strong enough in the intellectual life of the United States so that Collier's experiment in a new Indian policy could actually be given legislative form and a qualified trial. Nothing of the sort was conceivable in the 1880s. During that time, not only did the general public unquestioningly assume that Anglo-Saxon civilization should sweep all others before it, with the blessing of God and destiny, but the experts in anthropology and Indian civilization usually agreed. Major John Wesley Powell, that peerless explorer of Western lands and later head of the Smithsonian Institution's Bureau of Ethnology, testified before a Senate committee that the Indian ought to be civilized as soon as possible and that "no measure could be devised more efficient for the ultimate civilization of the Indians of this country than one by which they could successfully and rapidly obtain lands in severalty." Alice Fletcher, the Boston lady whose love of Indian life had spurred her to become a self-made anthropologist of some repute, was an ardent champion of severalty laws and the shift of Indians to freehold farming.

A minority of Indian "experts," it is true, disagreed with the Dawes bill as it worked its way through the Congress. A. B. Meacham, editor of *The Council Fire* and steady friend of the Indians (although he had been shot and left for dead in the course of negotiations with the Modocs in 1873), insisted that the Indian must be allowed to adopt white ways only "when he is ready," and warned that this might take much longer than anyone anticipated. Senator Henry M. Teller of Colorado prophesied that:

> when thirty or forty years shall have passed and these Indians shall have parted with their title, they will curse the hand that was raised professedly in their defense . . . and if the people who are clamoring for it understood Indian character, and Indian laws, and Indian morals, and Indian religion, they would not be here clamoring for this at all.

These doubters were outnumbered and had no constructive alternative with broad appeal. They could not shift the discussion of the Dawes Act toward the entirely different approaches of the 1930s for reasons we have seen—land was wanted by an expanding society of unshakable cultural arrogance—and thus the policy talk of the 1880s turned upon lesser matters. Assuming the inevitability of the breakup of tribes and reservations, with Indian survivors pointed toward the severalty escape hatch, the disputes arose over issues such as the length of the trustee period, citizenship, and compensation. In all these matters, the humanitarian reformers put up a stiff fight on behalf of the Indians' welfare as they understood it.

They were able to secure citizenship for Indians who had received their allotment, and most of them had concluded that the rights of citizenship were not only a matter of human right but the cornerstone of Indian self-defense in the future. It occurred to some people that the Indian citizen would be easily outmaneuvered by the white citizen, and that this right would expose the red man to all sorts of exploitation of an entirely legal character, but there seemed more to recommend citizenship than to warn against it. Dawes thought that a middle ground between the risks of premature citizenship and the unthinkable alternative of no citizenship was to confer it only upon individuals taking allotments after the trust period. This was both prudent and principled, but in its final version the act expanded citizenship to all Indians who left reservations or held land in severalty, exposing a larger group to the white legal system than Dawes wished. Dawes compromised, but the alternatives in either direction were not particularly attractive and hardly pivotal.

Reformers also successfully insisted upon compensation for tribal lands sold by the government. They insisted on a 25-year trusteeship period before any individual allotments were final, a time during which Indians could not alienate their land to whites. How much more could have been achieved in a law setting forth Indian policy in the 1880s? We agree with Loring Priest, author of *Uncle Sam's Stepchildren: The Reformation of United States Indian Policy, 1865–1887* (1942), who implicitly argues that the details of the Dawes Act were about as favorable to Indian welfare as could be expected given the reformers' general acquiescence to the idea of severalty and the breakup of the reservations. Things were bound to go badly for the American Indian, for even his friends thought he should get out of the path of advancing civilization, give up his heathen ways, and become a small farmer.

So the law was passed, hailed by most contemporaries and now so widely condemned. Disillusioned historians have hinted that tougher leadership, from Dawes or somebody else, would have driven a harder bargain for the Indians. But they have not shown in any detail just what legislative alternatives were available. There do not appear to have been any important ones. There was a commanding consensus on severalty, the sale of surplus lands, citizenship, compensation, and the inferiority of Indian civilization. Perhaps some sort of Indian consent might have been provided for, but the mood ran strongly toward the firm assertion of white authority, and anyway the consent of Indian tribes was not so difficult to arrange in the face of economic dependency and social disorganization.

Historians have often tacitly admitted the unpromising legislative possibilities, and have criticized the reformers for not choosing instead to block any law at all that promised to divest the Indian of land and to infringe treaty rights. This cannot be taken seriously. The existing situation was chaotic and intolerable, with several tribal treaty rights being variously violated by those whites whom reformers considered the worst—those physically pressing hard against Indian lands. The pressure, not only for land but for one national policy, was irresistible. In fashioning a national policy, the inevitable could at least be brought about in an orderly way, and in the process something could be salvaged for the Indian. Also, it was no small added inducement that the high costs of a confused federal Indian administration could be reduced and ended by a law that promised to settle the problem in 25 years.

But if the Dawes Act had to be passed and in essentially its final form, did it have to be administered with such an inspired combination of bad judgment and bad motives? Why not, even under the Dawes statute, something closer to the Collier spirit of administration—sizable appropriations, training in self-help and economic development, bureaucratic protection against premature allotment and excessive sale of surplus lands, and respect for Indian culture?

Something like this possibility may seem to have entered the minds of the reformers themselves. Many of their contemporaries accepted the idea of sustained governmental supervision of Indians in a transition period, even though such a paternalistic role in a sense ran quite contrary to the central assimilationist thrust of the Dawes Act. Secretary of the Interior Henry Teller said in 1884 that the order of policy should be "education, preparation, first; lands in severalty and citizenship afterward." His successor, Lucius Q. C. Lamar, equally understood the need for federal protection after the general principle of allotment was accepted: "To set him [the Indian] free from tribal reservations, tribal religion, and the supervision of the government . . . would, by destroying the Indians, violate the moral obligation under which this nation rests to protect the Indians, to ameliorate their condition. . . ." Dawes and other reformers always agreed. The Massachusetts senator had said in 1882 that "200,000 savages who cannot read a word of any language or speak a word of English . . . cannot be set up in severalty and left to stand alone any more than so many reeds." How did he overcome such doubts to sponsor severalty legislation? By providing for the 25-year trustee period. This was the reprieve written into the legislation, a saving administrative flexibility designed to ease the doubts of those who knew very well that the severalty policy they urged was sure to bring disaster if immediately implemented. In short, reformers knew their policy to be correct in the long run but disastrous in the short run, so it would not be put into immediate effect. Time would be provided, in addition to administrative machinery—the Bureau of Indian Affairs—with a vague mandate to use that time to good effect.

The time was not well used and, in any event, was not enough. Presidents after Grover Cleveland, and their secretaries of interior and BIA bureaucrats from top to bottom, were aggressive advocates of land sales, and tended to find reasons why Indian tribes were ready for severalty rather than evidence that they were not. Much tribal "surplus" land was sold prior to the end of trusteeship, and very few tribes were ready for allotment when the waiting period had run out. A generation of "education" had no ameliorative effect. Indian property was leaching away in a great flood, as tribal lands were sold or individual allotments came under local property taxes and were forced upon the market. Tribal life continued to wither from the once-proud independence of the eighteenth century toward the impoverished disorganization of the twentieth.

Were Dawes and the reformers foolish to have imagined that 25 years of federal trusteeship would give the Indian a better-than-even chance to make the great transition to Jeffersonian citizenship? Certainly they were wrong, and tragically so. One is struck by the almost universal lack of serious thought about the portion of the Dawes policy upon which they placed such weight, the administrative role of the BIA in preparing and protecting. In part, the reformers did not think deeply about the administrative assignment because its difficulties would have qualified their enthusiasm. They did not want to think much about how hard the task would be. Heirs of abolitionism, they were holding a huge revival, talking and hoping for another major social reform without facing the sobering difficulties under the surface of the problem. Perhaps this is not forgivable. But in retrospect, there are many reasons why this self-deception was easy and predictable.

What would have been required to make the period of federal trusteeship a protected staging ground in which Indians could develop the capacity to participate successfully in the life of white society? Even yet, we do not know exactly. But if we may assume from the now narrowing gap between Indian and white economic and social indicators that 90 years of federal policy have finally discovered a formula with some successful features, perhaps we may list the needed ingredients. Collier himself described them. First there was time. A wise federal bureaucracy must stall for time, prevent the sale of tribal lands, and resist individual allotment. During that time, it must respect and nurture Indian culture, and provide education in the modes of Western life in a facilitating but not coercive way. It must fend off political pressures from whites eager to exploit Indian resources. It must spend substantial sums (the federal government at the end of the 1960s was spending $5,500 annually upon every Indian family on reservations in the United States) and have endless patience. In addition, the bureaucracy must shoulder this enormous burden of social management in a fashion that encouraged self-confidence and democratic independence in the wards who were being helped.

If this broad strategy is, in fact, the only path to a successful trustee relationship between government and Indians, the Dawes generation never came close to grasping it. These Americans were innocent of the attitudes underlying such a strategy and never dreamed of the effort and time that it would require. The federal government prior to 1887 had never attempted anything remotely like the special assignment in wardship over the Indians; the single exception was the Freedmen's Bureau, an aborted attempt at a social welfare role which had not been carefully studied and from which almost nothing had been learned. The ruling attitudes of the late nineteenth century were, in fact, entirely opposed to what we call social-welfare activities by the central government. Individuals were supposed to stand on their own two feet. If they required aid, let private charities provide it. Not until the 1930s would the American political climate permit a large-scale commitment by the national government to the permanent care of the weak and disadvantaged. Even then—even *now*—it is a federal activity that many regard as folly and that everyone concedes to be far more difficult than had been thought a generation or two ago.

Thus, in voting for the Dawes Act, the reformers were not assuming a staggering assignment in social welfare which they would later shirk. They were a generation that did not believe in such a governmental assignment. The national government had no helping tradition of that kind, no trained people ready for the task. The administrative reprieve written into the act was no such thing. It was merely a gesture, a 25-year delay that no one had thought through in any positive way. About all that the reformers had considered in connection with the government's assignment was the necessity of appointing "men of good character" as BIA agents. Neither history nor the individualistic social philosophy of the day had prepared any white group to make anything at all of the government's administrative opportunity. Indeed, Dawes himself probably reflected the opinion of many who voted for his reform act in his view that the new policy would mean an early end to government interference and bureaucracy— "all this machinery," as he called it. His notion of the period of trusteeship was not a positive vision of aid, but a short time during which the Indian would advance quickly toward independence and the government could get out of the Indian business. "I have come to the conclusion that the quicker he is mingled with the whites in every particular the better it will be," Dawes said in 1886.

For Dawes and most of his generation, it was not the government that would help the Indian if he needed it, but private groups. Helen Hunt Jackson assured the readers of *A Century of Dishonor* (1881) that once the government passed a law prohibiting whites from stealing Indian land outright, "time, statesmanship, philanthropy and Christianity can slowly and surely do the rest." She, Dawes, and others expected too much from these elements in American society. Philanthropic and humanitarian groups dedicated to Indian welfare were to become weaker after the 1880s. Not until the 1920s would there again be another surge of public interest in the Indian question sufficient to stir some reform. This cycle of reform sentiment lasted until World War II, and then it too waned, leaving the Indian again with his familiar and inept protectors, the BIA.

"Red Power," the organized political power of the Indians themselves, might have changed the history of federal Indian policy if it had existed from the beginning. But Indian political organization did not begin in any significant way until the formation of the American Indian Congress in 1945. In this, the Indians were somewhat behind other racial and ethnic minorities. Chicanos began to organize for political action in the late 1920s and 1930s, and blacks with the formation of the NAACP in 1909. In all cases, there was a considerable gap of time between initial organization and the buildup of significant community cohesion and political influence. The American Indian is only now beginning to exert effective group pressure upon the federal bureaucracy and public opinion, and even with more white sympathy than at any previous time, it is not clear how long it will take to alter policy significantly in directions favorable to Indian welfare.

The evidence we have reviewed leaves us little room for concluding that a better bargain could have been driven on behalf of the American Indian in the 1880s. Friends of the Indian, not to mention Indians themselves, may find this a pusillanimous judgment. But we know much more today, in the 1970s, than was known at any previous time about the government's capacities as an agent of social reform, and our expectations are correspondingly modest. Some things the government can do—wage wars, stimulate scientific research, and encourage economic growth. But these and other achievements of the State are, one notes, reinforcements of things the society was ready or eager to do in any event.

Sadly, the national government has proved to be much less potent in redirecting citizens from well-established habits, values, and ideas. It committed itself (after a fashion) to racial justice, to a second Reconstruction, in the 1950s. The going has been slow and progress disappointing. Deeprooted social arrangements are terribly difficult to alter, especially if they involve racial or ethnic prejudices and social differentials. If one lists the social reforms that the national government probably *cannot* accomplish except with agonizing slowness, fulfilling the Declaration of Independence for black people may come to mind first, but incorporating the Indian into American life on the same terms of equality must rank with it as a task of staggering difficulty.

Is such a statement meant to imply that federal Indian policy cannot even now really benefit the Indian? No one sensitive to the rhythms of history would agree. Things change. "Assimilating" the Indians on terms that ensure the health of all parties to the transaction was a task so formidable in the 1880s and for years afterward that it *would* be bungled. The 50 years that passed between the Dawes Act and the IRA were not simply a gap. They were necessary to produce gradually the different conditions required for an intelligent revision in policy. These different conditions included the easing of white land hunger by the sale of 90 million acres of tribal lands, more tolerant and pluralistic anthropological and cultural assumptions, and the distressing evidence of the demoralization of the Indian minority under the Dawes approach. Even these changes, requiring 50 years, improved policy and administration only a little. More time was required, with more changes in underlying American racial attitudes.

Today, Indian policy is in ferment. President Nixon's Indian message of 1970 was squarely in the Collier tradition, and congressional committees give a sympathetic hearing to Indian complaints. Appropriations are on the increase for Indian education and economic development, the sum spent on all Indian affairs doubling in the decade of the 1960s alone. If current levels of spending are not enough they will probably be raised, although the $5,500 spent annually upon each reservation family is an impressive sum. The BIA now promises a vigilant protection of Indian resources, and even more tribal self-determination. No other group in our society currently has the same level of federal subsidy support, along with the same independence in deciding how it will be spent.

If the Indian now enjoys an almost adequate combination of federal aid and tribal independence for the first time in the history of his relation with whites, he also coexists with a white society that has entirely converted to Collierism. Today it is the whites who doubt their own machine civilization and, among the young especially, there is a fervent admiration of things primitive. Whites disillusioned with the nuclear family and middle-class life are drawn to the Indian's communal and communistic habits. Americans repelled by environmental destruction admire the Indian's close communion with nature. Hollywood movies portray the Indian as hero. Bumper stickers proclaim the once-gallant Custer as a genocidal criminal. The American Indian meets no cultural resistance to that pride in heritage that Collier thought indispensable for group survival. The whites, whatever the Indian thinks of himself, are proud of him.

Collier taught that these were the required circumstances for success: adequate federal aid, Indian cultural resurgence, and white respect. We closely approach these requirements, if we have not quite fully arrived. Now we shall see what the Indian will choose. If there is some workable combination of white and Indian cultures, some adequate adaptation to modern culture while preserving the essentials of a heritage rooted in an entirely different way of wringing man's life from the earth, the Indian has a better chance to find it in the last quarter of this century than at any earlier time. If the fusion of two different and even antagonistic cultures can be devised by Indians moving toward white habits (or by whites moving the other way), Collier's dream will be fulfilled. It may be that the cultures will not blend, and we will have the reservations with us forever—enclaves of protected native American life in the midst of a penitent, respectful, alien culture. Either way, the United States has apparently decided to let the Indian choose, and from strength. The cost in money is modest, and the cost in white pride has already been paid.

In retrospect, it does not seem that there was any shortcut to this point, from the 1880s to the 1970s. Forced assimilation had to be tried by Dawes' generation and the two or three that followed, and there was little for the Indian to do but survive until time made it possible again for the two societies to contend on a more equal footing.

SUGGESTED READINGS

John Collier, *Indians of the Americas*, 1947
Angie Debo, *A History of the Indians of the United States*, 1970
Harold Fey and D'Arcy McNickle, *Indians and Other Americans*, 1959
Henry E. Fritz, *The Movement for Indian Assimilation, 1860–1890*, 1963
Reginald Horsman, "American Indian Policy and the Origins of Manifest Destiny," *University of Birmingham Historical Journal 11*, 1968
Norris Hundley, ed., *The American Indian*, 1974
Helen Hunt Jackson, *A Century of Dishonor*, 1881
Oliver LaFarge, ed., *The Changing Indian*, 1943
Sar A. Levitan and Barbara Hetrick, *Big Brother's Indian Programs—with Reservations*, 1971
Robert Mardock, *The Reformers and the American Indian*, 1971
D. S. Otis, *The Dawes Act and the Allotment of Indian Lands*, 1934
Loring B. Priest, *Uncle Sam's Stepchildren: The Reformation of U.S. Indian Policy, 1865–1887*, 1942
Francis P. Prucha, ed., *Americanizing the American Indian: Writings by the Friends of the Indian, 1880–1900*, 1973
Alan L. Sorkin, *American Indians and Federal Aid*, 1971
Wilcomb E. Washburn, ed., *The American Indian and the U.S.: A Documentary History*, 4 vols., 1973
Wilcomb E. Washburn, ed., *The Assault on Indian Tribalism: The General Allotment Act of 1887*, 1975
Wilcomb E. Washburn, *The Indian in America*, 1975

CHAPTER
8

1917

What If the United States Had Remained Neutral?

Our century has been preeminently an era of war—repetitive, frequent, and twice worldwide in scope. Science and technology perhaps come to mind before war as forces transforming society, as does their byproduct, an explosion of human population. But these are sustained human activities. What intermittent force, what episodic common experience has so decisively shaped twentieth-century life as has war?

For the United States, the experience of war most distinguishes the nineteenth from the twentieth century. A transforming science and technology, along with economic and population expansion, characterized both centuries. The second was different only in the degree and scope of change, not in the basic forces at work. But we think of the nineteenth century now as peculiarly a time of isolation from the necessity to arm and defend the nation. The Civil War was the only major exception, and the little conflicts of 1812, 1846, and 1898 only underline the general rule. In the nineteenth century, preparations for war, reflections upon war, the people who professionally conduct war, and war itself—these were not permanent and obtrusive shapers of American development as they have become in our own time.

How different our own century—era of two world wars and an interminable Cold War, of a series of armed interventions around the world, and of an overhang of terror from weapons raining down from the sky. The necessity to wage war or be ready to wage it has altered our society in ways we still struggle to clarify and understand.

103

Economics is an advancing science, yet where modern war is concerned economic analysis deals with exceptionally rough data and clumsy conceptual tools. Other disciplines meet similar obstacles in estimating the impact of war. But the effort is made, and the results are instructive. The first of the world wars of the twentieth century engulfed isolationist America only toward its end in 1917, yet scholars have pondered, quantified, and sifted its apparent impact upon our society in a substantial literature.

Of course, we must begin our accounting with war's foremost byproduct and one of its goals, human death. For Americans, the most salient result of intervention was 170,000 deaths due to combat, with 24,600 more people permanently and totally disabled. This was a higher cost in blood than we had anticipated, even if it was a trifle compared to the 20 million Europeans killed from 1914 to the end of the war in 1918.*

The dollar cost of the war to the United States was estimated by Yale economist John M. Clark at $33.5 billion in direct expenditures by 1920, leaving aside pensions and debt service. Then one must add the lost productive potential of those serving under arms or in defense production, even though these were routinely added to the growing gross national product figures. This war-related, and hence "wasted," activity is estimated by Clark at 20 million "person years, or more than half of one year's normal gainfully employed manpower for the country as a whole." All of this must be accounted social loss, against which economists set off the unmeasurable gains for economic efficiency through simplified and standardized production methods learned during the war, and an equally unmeasurable stimulus to general productivity. The cost of the war was not paid out of a static GNP, but out of one that climbed from an average of $40 billion in the period 1912–16 (the data are poor) to $79 billion by 1919. Clark offers the following summary judgment:

> Have we been richer or poorer than we would have been if the War had come as it did, but we had remained neutral? . . . It is possible, though far from certain, that the peak of our post-war prosperity was not only the highest in our history but higher than anything we should have experienced if there had been no war. But it is also morally certain that the depressions of 1921 and 1930 cut deeper than any that would have occurred if the War had not disrupted the economic life of the world. . . . The balance sheet of the War probably shows a loss, though this may not be susceptible of proof.

---

*Some say that the 400,000 influenza deaths in the United States during the winter of 1918–19, from a particularly virulent strain of the disease which was exported from European trenches, should also be attributed to the war.

On balance, the war was clearly a drain upon lives, energies, time, and resources. We are today more sensitive to the latter category than ever before, yet no scholar has attempted a calculation of the waste of war in terms of American metals, minerals, petroleum, or soil fertility.

War also alters behavior and values, areas that present even more difficult problems of measurement. There was a school of thought prior to World War I, with Friedrich Nietzsche perhaps its leading philosopher, that believed war to be good for humanity. It allegedly brought out the manly, virile qualities in a population becoming effete. It taught sacrifice, courage, and cooperation. There is no need here to explore the vast European literature, written during and after World War I, that reveals how wrong was the anticipation of the war's benefits. The trenches did not prove a school of elevated feelings. It is reasonable to assume that those who were naturally brave, or in whom war brought out bravery, were the first to die, leaving the human race somewhat shorter in bravery genes than before. Nietzsche did not live long enough to reflect upon the issue.

In the United States, the briefer war experience had an impact upon collective behavior and values that was less profound but that seems to have generally followed European patterns. At first, good things appeared to happen. There was an upsurge of patriotic feeling, a willingness to sacrifice personal interest for the common good. A strong sense of national unity was everywhere evident. These feelings, however, did not last long. The war was short, in any event—at least the portion of it we experienced—and the subsequent peace was disappointing to Americans. Yet even before the settlement at Versailles, the American mood had begun to turn sourish. It was all very well to talk of unity and the common good, but Americans were soon unhappy with each other. A substantial minority of citizens opposed the war itself, and they had to be corrected or silenced by their neighbors, by vigilantes, by local government, and finally by the national government operating under the new Espionage Act of 1917 and the Sedition Act of 1918. In behavior and values, conformity waxed and tolerance waned.

In other ways beyond the drive for loyalty to the war effort, there arose internal tensions. War mobilization lured many black people northward for industrial work, and the mingling of the races in new competition for jobs and housing led straight to the more than twenty race riots that marred the year 1919.

We have not the space here to discuss these war-encouraged divisions, which so often set native Americans against recent immigrants or people of a different color, and brought conflict between nervous conservatives and the dissenting cluster of war resisters, socialists, and labor organizers. War did not bring Americans together to work as one. Toward the end of 1918, through 1919 and well into 1920, its chief and obvious effect was to exacerbate nativism and economic class schisms. Its apparent long-range impact upon behavior and belief was probably to accelerate further the modern distrust of God, idealism, and even human nature. It enhanced the tendency to live more for the moment than the Victorians had done. These are difficult changes to measure, let alone to assess. Certainly by the ruling ethical standards of the day, the war did not teach Americans to be "better," but to be a little bit worse.

Historians know more, or at least have written more, about the impact of World War I upon American politics and government than upon character and behavior. When the war began in 1914, the United States was in the second year of the reform presidency of Woodrow Wilson. A broad and multifaceted movement for social reform had preceded the Wilson era, working changes at local and state levels and culminating in Wilson's election to the White House in 1912. Historians are not agreed as to whether progressive reform was thoroughly transforming American life, making it more democratic and just, or whether reform measures had been superficial in their impact. But it is generally agreed that the first Wilson administration saw the gathering of 20 years' reform pressures in the nation's capital, and the President had by 1916 put himself at the head of most of them. Important reforms were enacted with his support, and more were in prospect on the eve of American involvement in World War I. In 1913–14 Wilson's leadership had helped to reduce the tariff and to create a Federal Trade Commission and a central bank. In 1915 the President began to adopt an even more expansive philosophy of governmental action, pressing for advanced social legislation of the sort Theodore Roosevelt had urged in the 1912 campaign—federal wage and hour laws, invigorated conservation measures, and agricultural credit.

Where progressivism was headed, no one could be sure. No major expansion of welfare legislation was in prospect, but progressives thought that the regulatory apparatus established since 1906, if given a few more years of sympathetic nurture, would live up to all their hopes. Thus, while progressivism at the national level in 1916–17 achieved most of its legislative goals (although not yet woman suffrage or a thorough overhaul of the federal tax structure), much work remained to be done. To the Left of this progressive ferment, the socialists grew in influence, buoyed by Eugene Debs' nearly one million votes in the 1912 presidential race.

The war both blunted progressive reform and redirected it. Yet this happened in ways that were not at once obvious or anticipated. "Reform," of course, meant many things to many people. It is remarkable how Woodrow Wilson had been able, by 1916, to embody and articulate most of its goals. He spoke for most of his generation in pledging to break up monopoly power in economics and boss rule in politics, to stop the apparent advance of materialism and division in society, and to keep alive the possibility of middle-class standing for the poor. These were large enough assignments for peacetime. War made them even more difficult.

Wilson himself sensed this when he made the decision for intervention in 1917. He somehow knew that, as Richard Hofstadter put it in *The Age of Reform* (1955), "war has always been the Nemesis of the liberal tradition in America." To Wilson, the illiberal potential of war mobilization seemed relatively simple. War would put the businessmen back in their positions of power. "Those we had unhorsed," he once put it, would come back to dominate the government and, having neutralized it, the entire economy.

Wilson was exaggerating the extent to which the progressive legislation enacted under Theodore Roosevelt and himself had "unhorsed" any segment of the business community. But he was certainly right that the necessity to mobilize for defense would put an end to the antitrust impulse, and would bring businessmen to Washington to control the key agencies of taxing, spending, and regulating. To the extent that Wilsonian progressivism had been a crusade to reduce the threatening power of the huge corporations and financial institutions, the war stopped it in its tracks. This much Wilson had foreseen. Big business could hardly be attacked and broken up when the armed forces required the fruits of mass production and when the very governmental agencies managing the mobilization were filled with businessmen who had come to help out in the emergency.

The record does not show, however, that Wilson anticipated the other ways in which participation in the war would shatter the reform efforts his generation had mounted. Its first impact was to create that sense of national unity and purpose, of community over individual interests, that reformers had wanted from the beginning. These feelings of solidarity were intense, but they were also brief. Very soon the pendulum swung the other way, and what people were most aware of was not solidarity but the woeful lack of it. The predominantly Anglo-Saxon middle class became concerned that society was not sufficiently united behind the war effort; the government shared these feelings and even took the lead in fostering them. Nativist fears went on the rise, as we have seen. Superpatriots went out in search of "hyphenated Americans" to subject to loyalty checks, teachers to fire, or labor organizers to intimidate.

People who are worried about dissenters and lend their energies to drives for greater intellectual and political conformity are too busy for serious efforts to clean up slum housing, reform the city charter, pass a minimum wage law, or attend to the other activities of prewar reform. It is true, as Allen Davis has argued, that progressive social workers and housing reformers found their roles expanded during the war, organizing the training camps and providing housing for war workers. But public support for the wide range of progressive-era reforms of the social welfare variety dissipated very quickly as war preoccupied American energies, and only a few reformers found the war a time of rapid progress along the old lines.

The war wounded the reform spirit in other ways. It redirected idealism from America's internal problems to the world stage. Then, in its own time, it helped to discredit all forms of idealism when the Wilsonian world crusade produced so little lasting benefit for democratic goals. "A pervasive cynicism became the spirit of an American generation," wrote historian George Mowry. "Faith had been squeezed out of the intellectual environment as juice from an orange, faith in . . . the most hallowed American institutions." If Mowry put it a bit too strongly (he was writing in 1940, under the shadow of another involvement in a world war), most scholars have agreed that the war experience raised crippling doubts about the very foundations of contemporary democratic theory—that the public was essentially rational, that government intervention was inherently benign, and that Americans united in common purpose could make a better world. Certain facts mocked these tenets of faith—the hysteria of wartime repression and the postwar Red Scare, the irrationality of trench warfare, and the shockingly low physical and mental condition of the mass of recruits as they came forward for processing.

Doubts about human nature, democracy, and democratic governments helped to turn the postwar mood unreceptive toward any notions of resumed domestic reform. Some disappointed liberals blamed President Wilson, whose lofty rhetoric had raised hopes too high, and whose leadership of the progressive elements at home had been both erratic and feeble. But Wilson could not single-handedly have prevented the conservative turn in American political life and thought after World War I. Today we know that every twentieth-century war has been followed by a season of reaction, in which conservatives come to power on a mission of reversing recent social changes. In requiring an exceptional community effort in pursuit of victory, war ensures a resurgent individualism and privatism that make postwar liberal reforms unlikely. It may be correctly pointed out that wars also stimulate radicalism to some extent, in "breaking the cake of custom" and in awakening the democratic spirit; yet it remains true that in America the Right has benefitted more from postwar climates than the Left. This was true in 1919, again in 1946, in 1953, and in 1969 after the Vietnam War had reached its crest.

Thus the decision for war in 1917 was, among other things, a decision to call off the progressive movement, although Wilson's cabinet certainly did not discuss the decision in those terms at its final meeting on the issue in late March 1917. How long the reform era would have continued without involvement in World War I is impossible to say. It had been in progress for a generation, and there were already signs of the exhaustion of the reform impulse at state and local levels. Yet we must remind ourselves that the cyclical pattern of reform-reaction in American politics has been closely tied to war, and may not be as predictable as our history suggests. Students of the Wilson administration know that his second term promised, in many ways, to be more liberal than his first. There was still much creative and innovative potential in the progressive coalition in 1917 when international issues eclipsed domestic ones. Without the involvement in war, the eventual return of conservative government would very likely have been less decisive than it was in 1921, when Warren Harding led a weary nation back to business as usual.

One result deriving from belligerency that Wilson very much did intend was the permanent alteration of America's place in the world. Indeed it was altered, although not exactly as Wilson had meant. What he had in mind was for his country to assume her proper and God-given leadership of the world. This was to be done chiefly through the power of American ideals. We would teach the world how to practice political democracy. We would also take the lead in political internationalism, joining with other nations in a form of world government sufficiently strong to prevent war while leaving nations sovereign. Beyond elevated ideals and leadership in a League of Nations, American world influence would naturally rest upon economic power. Wilson understood this, and told many business audiences that they, too, had a role to play in America's destiny as exporters of goods for sale. He was, however, primarily interested in the export of ideas and institutions.

We entered the war, and our world position did sharply change. The ideas that Wilson articulated so brilliantly made a brief and intense impact in Europe in 1918–19, then faded in importance as hard terms were struck at Versailles. A League of Nations emerged from the peacemaking as the core of Wilson's hopes, but America would not join. Our role as a world power, at least as a diplomatic and military force, was brief and soon renounced. Our (Wilson's) ideals flared and then dimmed, and the nation declined its new international political role. The 1920s found America isolationist still, except for the Caribbean, where we remained as we had been before the war— vigorously involved. On the whole, Wilsonians were disappointed and frustrated men in the 1920s, when the shape of things finally emerged. Perhaps, as some scholars argue, the whole brief experience of participation was a school for internationalism, moving Americans toward their eventual world role. The handful of internationalists of the 1920s and 1930s would have found the evidence for this view very flimsy indeed. They had labored in vain, so it seemed.

What had changed most decisively and permanently was America's economic, rather than her political, role in the world. The war made us a creditor nation, and shifted the world's financial center from London to New

York. This, of course, was something that would have happened in any event, probably by the late 1920s or the 1930s. American exports had been expanding for decades and, in every year since 1888, had exceeded imports. This favorable balance of merchandise trade was joined after 1908 by an excess of capital exports over inflowing investments. The dynamism of the American economy wrote upon the wall our future place as the world's banker and leading trader. The war greatly accelerated this development, both during our neutrality period and then more rapidly during our belligerency.

This seemed a great thing to Americans who noticed it, a matter to be placed on the positive side of the ledger in our accounting of the war decision. Yet it turned out to be no simple blessing. As George Soule was to write in his economic history of the decade from 1917 to 1929:

> The former debtor position of the U.S. was thus dramatically changed to a creditor one, and American producers became accustomed to a large export surplus financed on credit. Few gave any thought at the time to the question of how these loans were to be repaid or what would happen to exports when the stream of foreign lending stopped. It was not until later that people began to be aware of the difficult problem of transferring payments for the Allied debt. The controversy that subsequently arose concerning this matter and the long train of misfortunes set in motion by postwar readjustment were not foreseen.

Thus the war brought the United States greater economic power and what appeared to be a favorable ledger-book position, but these advantages were to do us little good. During the 1920s, the United States assumed that it could export both goods and capital forever, in excess of returns the other way. This we called a "favorable" set of balances. Ignorant and inexperienced where world economic leadership was concerned, we made too few and too feeble efforts to rationalize world trade relations prior to the Crash of 1929, and these we made outside the League of Nations structure. The collapse of world trade after 1929 helped to deepen the Great Depression that gripped the industrialized world until another war brought a form of rescue.

These developments arose when America intervened. With no intervention, some of them would not have happened at all; most would have occurred later and with less devastating effect. Most of the results of our decision to intervene thus appear, in retrospect, to be regrettable. But there are, as always, some positive consequences as well. The war may have promoted efficiency in American industry and transportation, at least in particular sectors. In the making of dyes, for example, and optical glass, our being cut off from Europe stimulated a rapid advance in domestic technology. Another useful byproduct of intervention, in the eyes of some writers, was the upwelling of patriotism and self-sacrifice in a society normally dedicated to individual gain.

William Waller, writing with 20 years' hindsight, qualified his main judgment, that "the effect of war upon institutions and upon human life is undeniably bad," with the view that participation in World War I had challenged static institutions and bureaucracies with beneficial effect. He could not document the point. But William Leuchtenburg made an impressive case, in a celebrated essay published in 1964, that the war mobilization experience had taught Americans many lessons that the New Dealers were to recall when they took over in the emergency situation of 1933. This nurturing time for national economic management—perhaps even for planning—was depicted as a clear gain by an historian writing in the 1960s. Perhaps, in today's climate of distrust of "big government," this World War I strengthening of the muscles of government will not seem a happy development. On this point there will be less agreement than when Leuchtenburg wrote. In any event, the national government did not go on, after the war, to practice the arts of economic management, so that any benefits from the experience of mobilization were deferred until considerably later.

We should also note that during the war many blacks left the South and many women left the home for defense work, even military service. This trend, like others, predated the war but was enormously accelerated by it. Leaving the rural South and leaving the kitchen—these must be seen as steps toward eventual emancipation. Blacks in the North began to assume the habit of voting that was to earn them, gradually but inexorably, the attention of the national government and produce the civil rights legislation of the 1950s and 1960s. Women gained 100,000 new jobs in the munitions industry, tripled their numbers in iron and steel, and expanded their participation in the professions and clerical trades. But they lost most of these new jobs when the armies demobilized, and by 1920 women's participation in the labor force was actually lower than it had been in 1910 (it declined from 20.9 percent to 20.4 percent). As historian Constance Green wrote: "The brief interlude . . . which some enthusiasts heralded as launching a new era for women in industry came and went with astonishingly little permanent effect upon women's opportunities." More important was the suffrage granted to women by constitutional amendment in 1919, a reform that came when it did because of the wartime emphasis on the rights of human beings and on broad public participation in the great crusade.

The principal benefit of our belligerency we have not yet discussed, and that is of course the defeat of Germany. Wilsonian rhetoric led the public to expect much more than that from the war—such as vindication of the rights of humanity, making the world safe for democracy, ending war, and so on. These did not materialize in any obvious way, but we *did* defeat Germany.

Was this not an unquestionable benefit? This is obviously a problem of awesome dimensions, and one understands why no scholar has explored it in an extended way. As it was, the victorious Allies got a settlement out of their victory, which helped to cripple Europe economically by the end of the 1920s, solved none of the intranational or international problems that had produced World War I, and lay the essential groundwork for another, more horrible war in 1939. This record has little appeal. One may put it positively and say that the defeat of Germany in 1918 gave the Atlantic community 20 years of peace, but this sad comment is not satisfying. Could there have been a better future the other way—if America had stood aside and let European events take their course? Options fan out like the headwaters of the Rhine. The Germans would have forced some sort of settlement upon the Allies, who were very weak in mid-1917. Most promising to the United States would have been a peace without a clear German victory, to temper their postwar gains and to maintain some balance of power. More probably the French would have collapsed, and a clear-cut German victory would have followed. The rest of Europe would not have enjoyed the hegemony of Kaiserian Germany. The historian Fritz Fischer and others have told us of the Germans' incredibly expansionist war aims, and all of Europe knew of the Teutonic arrogance of that vigorous nation. But Kaiserian Germany was at least not fascist, and there remained within it some elements of democratic political life, which might have flourished better after a victory than they did during the Weimar era after bitter defeat.

Victorious in some substantial way in World War I, would Germany have launched World War II? These speculations lead to many imponderables. Not every reader will agree with us that they add some slight additional weight to the negative side of the scales when the costs and benefits of American intervention in 1917 are weighed.

Do we speculate upon a turn of events that could not reasonably be thought possible? Here we may be fairly certain. A noninterventionist course for America was neither impossible nor even very difficult. The circumstances of the time permitted American policy-makers to make a different set of choices.

We may recall the major decisions that Wilson made on the road to intervention—a long one, with many twists—and the circumstances that shaped his performance as chief executive of a neutral country. When the war broke out, there appeared to be no decisions for him to make. The war was far away and, to Americans, it was pointless—a barbaric irrelevancy. Let the Europeans settle it, as they were expected to do one way or another in about six months. These were virtually every American's first reactions when the war commenced. Certainly they were Wilson's views.

Yet he soon had choices to make, as we were a maritime power engaged in trans-Atlantic trade. The British began to impose an ever-tightening blockade of the Axis powers to intercept goods intended for Germany which Her Majesty's government classified as "contraband" by an unprecedentedly broad definition. In this and other ways, the British began a series of violations of American neutral rights to which the Wilson administration was forced to respond. To foreshorten a long and complex story, the Americans officially complained but never pressed so hard as to endanger relations with England. At the same time, credits and then loans by private banking firms were permitted by the government, so that Anglo-American trade steadily forged an ever more substantial ligament of sympathy and common interest.

Perhaps there was no sharply different policy that could have been adopted where Britain was concerned, although some of Wilson's contemporaries thought there was. British violations of our rights were irritating but they cost no lives. The public was less than outraged. Hurt feelings were buffered by Anglophiles in the President's circle of advisers and by timely British concessions to American pride. Impoundment of ships and cargoes was never pressed to the point of justifying a breach of diplomatic relations. Dealing with Britain was not where Wilson had to make his major choices.

These hard decisions came where Germany was concerned. Blockaded and threatened with economic strangulation, the Germans built an undersea navy and turned it loose, in February 1915, upon all shipping bound for England and France. American rights were immediately challenged in the most shocking way, her citizens being killed in a series of submarine attacks upon Allied and even neutral vessels. An American was killed when the *Falaba* was sunk on March 28, more American lives were lost in the sinking of the *Cushing* and the *Gulflight* some weeks later, and on May 7 the huge Cunard liner *Lusitania* went down from one German torpedo, taking 1,198 lives, 128 of them American.

Wilson struggled to find a way out of an admittedly untenable position. He could not simply do nothing. Press reports of American deaths at sea would eventually bring humiliation upon the head of a nation that endured such affronts without response. Ex-President Theodore Roosevelt was already raising loud criticism. There were two broad paths for Wilson to follow. A neutral nation could hope to arrange an alteration of the rules of war on the seas, so that its citizens and trade were treated with reasonable consideration; or it could unilaterally decide to keep its citizens out of harm's way by giving up travel in whatever areas the mighty antagonists of Europe chose to define as war zones.

Woodrow Wilson chose to explore the former path, and one emphasizes the word *chose,* as there were in the years 1914–17 no forces in the American political or constitutional landscape strong enough to force him one way or the other. The making of foreign policy was a presidential responsibility under the Constitution, as Wilson himself had written in *Constitutional Government in the United States* (1908) in his role as a leading constitutional scholar:

> One of the greatest of the presidential powers . . . [was] his control, which is very nearly absolute, of the foreign relations of the nation. The initiative in foreign affairs, which the President possesses without any restriction whatever, is virtually the power to control them absolutely.

This has an imperious sound, but was not far from the truth. Not once in the years 1914–17 did Congress effectively challenge either the President's right to control foreign policy or any specific policy he selected.

Obviously no President had an entirely free hand. He could not, at any time between 1914 and 1916, have secured a declaration of war, for example—on either belligerent bloc. Another foreign policy he could not undertake (in 1919–20) was official adherence to the League of Nations, although bad tactics and ill health spoiled reasonably good chances here. But between the two paths of policy previously outlined—either the search for altered and tolerable forms of oceanic warfare or the decision to forego travel in the war zone—Wilson was free to choose. There would have been some grumbling either way, but Congress—which was under Democratic majorities—would not have overruled him. As for "public opinion," it was poorly formed on international issues, and tended to be quite deferential to the executive on international issues. In the American system, the boundaries within which foreign policies may be formulated are exceptionally wide, especially when the President is articulate and politically astute. The public is relatively well organized to influence domestic policy, but knows less about international affairs, is less confident of its judgments, and is poorly organized to participate in debate. Presidents are expected to lead. This was true in 1914–17 as it has been before and since.

Yet how was Wilson to arrange a more humane practice of naval warfare between belligerents who fought, or so they assumed, for their very survival? He began at once, acting with imagination and tenacity. In the spring of 1915, at Secretary of State William Jennings Bryan's suggestion, he proposed a *modus vivendi* by which Britain would allow noncontraband into Germany and cease her misuse of neutral flags and the arming of merchantmen, while Germany was to observe cruiser rules in submarine warfare. Cruiser rules meant adequate warning before attack so that civilians could take to life boats, or a ship could surrender. Germany appeared to agree to the *modus vivendi,* but Britain found the proposal unacceptable and the idea dropped from discussion.

Then came the *Lusitania* sinking, and Wilson decided that basic neutral rights were at stake. He began a series of stern notes to Germany which, by summer's end, had forced the Axis to lift their unrestricted submarine campaign and observe the rules of cruiser warfare, which spelled futility and often death for submarine crews.

Wilson had thus forced a major change in the conduct of naval warfare. But he quickly realized how high the cost had been. Should the Germans change their minds at any time and resume the earlier tactics, the United States would have little choice but to break off relations, arm her ships, and accept the risky role of armed neutrality. The President tried throughout 1916 to escape from the corner in which he had become trapped by the combination of global events and his own decisions. He tried to persuade the British to take all but token armaments off merchant ships, and was rebuffed. He dispatched his aide, Colonel House, to Europe in order to explore opportunities for a mediated peace. To cut short a tangled story, neither side was interested in an armistice and negotiations until it had achieved the upper hand and could dictate terms. In December 1916, Wilson issued a public appeal to the belligerents, asking them to state their terms for peace. In January, he offered himself as an impartial mediator in a speech which called for "a peace without victory." It was too late. Germany had decided upon the resumption of unrestricted submarine warfare on January 9, the new tactics to commence on February 1. For two more months, Wilson resisted a declaration of war. But there were sinkings, tensions rose, and on April 2 he asked Congress to join the conflict on the Allied side. There was a brief but heated debate, then an overwhelming vote to enter the First World War.

Had there been any other reasonable alternatives open to Wilson along the way? There were several, and they all lay along that other path that Wilson had rejected—modifying American use of the seas rather than modifying the conduct of the belligerents' naval war. Two measures that were politically possible would probably have been enough to preserve neutrality throughout the long conflict: the elimination of munitions from trade with Europe, and a passenger ban.

The ban on munitions was proposed by Senator Gilbert Hitchcock of Nebraska as early as December 1914. It was a policy adopted by Denmark, Sweden, Italy, the Netherlands, Spain, and Norway, all without any apparent national humiliation. The ban would have altered Germany's perception of the impact of American trade, perhaps also her impression of the tenor of our neutrality. It would have somewhat eased the pressure for unrestricted submarine warfare, and aided Wilson's effort to emerge as an acceptable mediator. By itself, the munitions ban would only have ameliorated, without eliminating, the basic source of conflict between the United States and Germany, which was a trade running predominantly to the

Atlantic Allies. Removing munitions from that trade was not only possible, but useful in the search for a truly neutral position. To end the trade entirely would have been more useful in that direction, but one can hardly call it a plausible policy. Thomas Jefferson had tried an embargo on trade a century before, in another great European war, and the economic dislocation of that policy had set up political pressures that no President could long endure.

In addition to a munitions embargo, there might easily have been established a passenger ban on travel in the war zone. After the *Persia* was sunk in January 1916, the principal congressional reaction was anger—but not at the Germans. The irritation was directed at an American policy that encouraged citizens to travel where they endangered both their own lives and the nation's noninvolvement. The Gore-McLemore Bill to prohibit passenger travel into the war zone had instant and overwhelming support in both Houses. Only by a supreme effort did Wilson beat it back. His reasons were both moralistic and constitutional. Rigidly and with some passion, he insisted that to withdraw unilaterally from American citizens one right that they had formerly enjoyed would cause the whole fabric of international law to crumble.

This startling idea may be understood only if one was raised, as was Wilson, in a Presbyterian parsonage. Other neutral nations had banned passenger travel in the war zone without the collapse of international morality. To this unusual objection to the Gore-McLemore Bill, Wilson added the consideration that the making of foreign policy was a presidential rather than a congressional responsibility. If he allowed the bill to pass, it might be seen as a signal that Congress was now empowered to take occasional initiatives in foreign policy. Something may be said for this view, but not very much. Most contemporaries thought Wilson's views extreme, and felt that he could easily have accepted the passenger ban without damage to national honor, international law, or the Constitution. A passenger ban would have eliminated that loss of American life which so inflamed German-American relations. With this and the munitions embargo, neutrality in the long ordeal of war would rest upon much firmer foundations.

Unlike earlier occasions examined in this book, our speculations this time suggest that history might have been very different with a change in a few decisions by essentially one person. Moments of this sort do not occur too frequently in history. When they do, decisions about war are often involved. One thinks easily of other such occasions—John Adams holding out against war in 1798–99, and Kaiser Wilhelm of Germany deciding the other way in 1914.

What if America had not joined the Great War? The costs that were paid would not have been paid, nor the benefits accrued. Another set of gains and losses would have replaced them. Perhaps it is merely the present-mindedness of a war-weary (and Cold-War weary) generation that inclines us, members of that generation, at least, to prefer the road not taken. It leads toward events that may be reconstructed only in the imagination, with fragments of facts from the past. One imagines an extended era of internal social reform, the absence of death, and the avoidance of that waste of resources, that enfeeblement of moral idealism, and that repression of dissenters in wartime America. And all that is lost on the other side of the ledger of war are those fleeting moments of moral exhilaration at Wilson's splendid cause, some experience at closer cooperation, and some crude lessons in managing the economy. The situation was open for an alternative future, not vastly different from the one we lived, but different enough to stir the imagination.

SUGGESTED READINGS

W. Elliot Brownlee, *The Dynamics of Ascent: A History of the American Economy,* 1974

John M. Clark, *The Costs of the World War to the American People,* 1931

Allen F. Davis, "Welfare, Reform and World War I," *American Quarterly 19,* Fall 1967

Otis L. Graham, Jr., *The Great Campaigns: Reform and War in America, 1900–1928,* 1973

Charles Hirschfeld, "The Transformation of American Life," in *World War I: A Turning Point in Modern History,* ed. Jack Roth, 1967

George Kennan, *American Diplomacy, 1900–1950,* 1950

Lawrence Klein, "The Role of War in the Maintenance of American Prosperity," *Proceedings of the American Philosophical Society 6,* 1971

William E. Leuchtenburg, "The New Deal and the Analogue of War," in *Change and Continuity in Twentieth Century America,* eds. John Braeman et al., 1964

Arthur S. Link, ed., *The Impact of World War I,* 1969

Ernest R. May, *The World War and American Isolation, 1914–1917,* 1950

George Mowry, "The First World War and American Democracy," in *War as a Social Institution,* eds. Jesse D. Clarkson and Thomas Cochran, 1941

Keith Nelson, ed., *The Impact of War on American Life,* 1971

Horace Peterson and Gilbert Fite, *Opponents of the War,* 1957

George Soule, *Prosperity Decade: From War to Depression, 1917–1929,* 1947

William Waller, "War and Social Institutions" in *War in the Twentieth Century,* ed. William Waller, 1940

What Would the 1930s Have Been Like Without Franklin Roosevelt?

Roosevelt's absence from the stage of history almost became a matter of fact. On at least two occasions, FDR slipped through narrow passages on his way to his epochal presidency. A slight change at either of these two points would have kept him from the presidency in 1933, and thus assigned him a minor place in history.

One of these points came at the Democratic nominating convention in the summer of 1932, when Roosevelt very nearly lost the nomination. Ahead on the first roll call, he gained only 16 votes on the next two counts and appeared to have lost momentum. Only desperate maneuvers by his supporters and a good deal of luck brought the Texas and California delegations over to FDR before his own coalition splintered. It had been a close decision for Roosevelt's backers, and different decisions by only two people would have ruined his chances. Texas Congressman John Nance Garner withdrew as his state's favorite son in the middle of the fourth ballot and allowed his votes to go to FDR. William Randolph Hearst, publisher and eccentric whose overriding fear was of American entry into the League of Nations, threw the California delegation to Roosevelt while the fourth ballot went on, in order to block the rising challenge of the internationalist Newton D. Baker. There is unanimous agreement among scholars that Hearst's judgment on convention politics was correct, whatever his wisdom on international relations. If Roosevelt had not taken the nomination on the fourth roll call, his support would have fragmented and Baker probably would have been nominated.

If nominated, Baker surely would have been elected. It was the Democrats' year. While Baker almost became President through the events of November, three months later a bullet almost put Garner in the White House. In mid-February 1933, just days before Roosevelt's inauguration, he was riding in a motorcade in Miami, Florida. Joseph Zangara stepped forward shouting, "Too many people are starving to death," and fired five shots at Roosevelt from a range of about 35 feet. A woman in the crowd josiled his arm, and he missed Roosevelt, hitting Mayor Cermak of Chicago, who was riding in the President-elect's car, and two bystanders. Cermak died, and Zangara told a judge that he regretted killing the wrong man. Garner was the Vice-President-elect, and he would have been inaugurated on March 4 if Zangara had not failed in his mission.

What difference would it have made? The depression was four years old in that 1932–33 winter, unemployment stood at an incredible 25 percent of the work force, and the GNP was half the 1929 figure. It was the most profound crisis of American society since the Civil War. There had been some violence before that winter, some marches by unemployed men who broke into rioting, some armed farmers preventing mortgage foreclosures, and of course the government's use of tanks and troops to break up the peaceful assemblage of veterans in Washington, D.C., in August. Worse troubles seemed ahead. The Farm Holiday Association in the Mid-West threatened more violence in the spring if prices did not improve. Farm spokesmen predicted "a revolution in the countryside in less than twelve months," and while they may have exaggerated for political effect, a number of scholars have estimated that violent social upheaval was not outside the realm of possibility.

President Hoover clearly had no answers and could only counsel patience. But what was the nation to wait for, and for how long? Forty years earlier, in another painful depression, people had waited with remarkable fortitude for an act of God or some natural upturn in the economy. President Cleveland, when asked in 1894 what the government ought to do about unemployment, replied in some astonishment that the government was not supposed to do anything about it. God had sent it, and He would end it in His own time. This was the view of the great majority of citizens, apparently. A few people disagreed—some workers and farmers—but most Americans did not then expect government to address their economic problems with remedial policy.

By Hoover's time, the public attitude in these matters had changed significantly. The idea that government should be an active participant in national progress had worked its way deep into the history and the collective mind during the progressive and World War I years. Hoover himself certainly did not believe that the government had no responsibilities when the Great Depression came. He was active. But, in time, it was apparent that he would not go beyond a certain point that was sharply etched in his own mind but slightly vague to observers, a point where government ceased being the organizer of voluntary responses to depression and became coercively involved in manipulating recovery.

Wherever this point lay, it was reached by Hoover very early. He then found himself fighting a Democratic Congress that wanted the government to do more, backed by a public whose angry cries (or was it only the cries of lobbyists and organized groups?) for help made Congress seem sometimes laggard and slow. Congressional majorities wanted federal relief, inflation, regulation of stock exchanges, and a dozen other departures. Hoover used the resources of the presidency and a tough set of personal convictions to resist what was proposed. He would not inflate or spend his way out of the depression; but he had no other ideas from mid-1932 to the end of his term.

People were waiting for either the economic system or the political system to produce a remedy. Hoover's administration appeared to have chosen mainly to refrain from political solutions in favor of natural economic recovery.

In a remarkable display of patience, the American public gave the economic system four years to heal itself and only then turned to a different party in what looked like a signal to the government to try a political solution. If the political system worked, it would bring forward, through the slow processes of campaigning, nomination, and election, a man with broad support and appealing, successful ideas. If it did not, despair toward basic institutions would reach critical proportions.

The political system produced Franklin D. Roosevelt. People who approve what he subsequently did are fond of saying that the American political system worked. In Britain, there was an ineffective coalition government which no one remembers for any kind of success, and in France there were a series of destabilizing changes of regime which produced only one man of ability—Léon Blum—but gave him no time and no majority. America brought forward FDR and the New Deal, reinvigorating both the economy and the processes of democracy.

However, it is well to remind ourselves of what the American political system *almost* produced. But for a publisher's decision, the election of 1932 might have chosen President Baker. But for an assassin's aim, the system would have produced President Garner. And what difference would it have made?

First we ought to recall Roosevelt's record during the New Deal years, from 1933 to 1938 or 1939, when the European war precipitated an entirely new set of problems. He presided over many changes, which might be separated into those affecting the economy and those affecting the political system. In the former category, we remember that the New Deal assigned the government responsibility for direct relief of unemployment; regulated stock exchanges, agricultural production, labor-management relations, and wages and hours in industry; expanded its regulation of natural resources, banks, transportation, communications, and food and drugs; thrust the government into power production and regional development with the TVA; and made the tax system more progressive.

Stated in these summary ways, the New Deal appears to be quite a substantial agent of economic change. We may add to the list of changes the alterations in the relationship of people to their national government, and in the political system itself. These include an enlargement of the power of the presidency relative to the other branches; the Supreme Court's abandonment of an obstructionist position vis-à-vis governmental economic regulation; and the realignment of parties, leaving the Democrats as the new majority party with a marked attraction for middle- and lower-class voters, blacks, Jews, and intellectuals.

Changes of this scope were difficult for contemporaries to assess. Americans of a conservative bent thought that a revolution had occurred. Everywhere a businessman turned, it now seemed, he met the government. It regulated the minimum wages and maximum hours he could offer his employees, showed an interest in his prices and the quality of his goods, taxed away his incentives, and circumscribed his plans for expansion by threats of antitrust action. The money it took from him it gave away to those who did not, or probably would not, work. Or so it seemed to many business spokesmen, who etched their complaints into the contemporary record in speeches, trade journals, and letters to congressmen. Capitalism, after the New Deal, would never be the same—nor would the American character. Behind it all was essentially one man, a President who would probably stay in office forever, playing class against class, winning votes with expensive social programs, and cutting constitutional corners to gain his leveling ends.

That the business community generally felt this way about the New Deal convinced Roosevelt himself, most contemporary liberals, and the first generation of historians that something close to a revolution must, indeed, have taken place. The outcry from wealthy people and the surge of voters to the Democrats suggested that power and wealth had been redistributed significantly. Time has permitted more careful study and much reflection, and historians are now more aware of the limited nature of New Deal reforms than it was possible to be when the passions of political conflict still ran strongly. Wealth and income were not much redistributed, business

1933: What Would the 1930s Have Been Like Without Franklin Roosevelt?

123

regulation stabilized rather than transformed the economic structure, and poverty was only marginally reduced. The corporation, that institutional center of our contemporary American capitalism, was not so threatened by the new regulatory and welfare state, the new Democratic party, and the new militant labor movement as had been feared and claimed.

So perhaps it is best to describe the New Deal, as William Leuchtenburg has done, as a "half-way revolution," and even then the degree of social change is perhaps stated too strongly. Yet few eras of social reform—and the New Deal only lasted about five years—had touched American life at so many points and left so substantial a mark. Herbert Hoover and like-minded conservatives would never forgive Roosevelt for what he did to American government and capitalism. Norman Thomas, the eloquent leader of American socialists, ruefully admitted that Roosevelt had ruined the socialists' chances by making just enough changes in capitalism to ease it through its greatest crisis. Whatever they thought, these spokesmen of Left and Right, the electorate returned Roosevelt for four terms and put his party into a commanding position for more than a generation.

In all of this there was, of course, the interaction of impersonal forces and individual influence. If we eliminate Franklin Roosevelt from the scene, who would have exercised the most potent single influence—that of the President? The analysis is easier than it might appear, by half, for Hoover and the Republicans were, in combination, as nearly an unelectable option for national leadership as any ever nominated by a major party. Hoover perhaps had more of a chance to be returned than William Howard Taft in the three-cornered race of 1912, but not significantly more. No, the variable of individual leadership in the White House, for the years after 1932, would be controlled by the Democratic party. That party would also control both Houses of Congress.

What were its traditions and inclinations? Today only the older generation of Americans will remember what a conservative institution the Democratic party was in the depths of the depression in 1932. It was a struggling, usually out-of-power, Southern-dominated party whose only successes in national politics for half a century had come under Wilson and Cleveland. It was not associated with a belief in strong national government, but tended rather to assert states' rights. Its congressional leadership was chiefly rural and Southern; the other base of the party was in a few big-city machines where the Irish vote was strong. The urban constituency of the Democrats was a minority within a minority party, despite New York Governor Al Smith's encouragingly successful appeal to urban-immigrant voters in the 1928 presidential campaign. The labor movement officially preferred neither party. Most industrial workers still voted Republican. The Democratic party in 1932 most emphatically was *not* the party, nor the hope, of the downtrodden, the common man, the worker, the Negro, or the child of recent immigrants. Neither was the Republican party, but it attracted most of the votes from every broad economic class.

Why should the Democrats have been seen as the agents of social reform? Long ago, in 1896, the party had nominated William Jennings Bryan, and he had attacked wealthy bankers and monopolists. But he did not win, and three tries for the presidency had mellowed him into a moderate spokesman for rural social values, with diminishing quarrel with the economic system. Woodrow Wilson made the party a reform instrument for a short season, but the Wilsonian domestic program was remarkably limited—it urged antitrust activism, free trade, and banking reform. Even this amount of reformist energy drained away from the party by the beginning of the 1920s, leaving it to nominate candidates and write platforms that almost matched the Republicans for conservatism. Three years of depression did not change the Democrats' basic ideas. Their senior managers wrote a platform in 1932 which reaffirmed the old truths, that what the country needed was reduced federal spending, a balanced budget, states' rights, lower tariffs, banking reform, a sound currency—and repeal of the Eighteenth Amendment.

The big men at the convention, the party's "leaders," the handful of available candidates for the unusually precious nomination, were as follows: apart from Roosevelt, there was the wealthy corporation lawyer from Cleveland, Newton D. Baker; the speaker of the house from the town of Uvalde, Texas, John Nance Garner; former New York governor, Al Smith; and the reactionary governor of Maryland, Albert Ritchie. Only Roosevelt, of the entire group of leading candidates, had anything in his recent record to suggest ideas and impulses more venturesome than those in the jaded 1932 platform. The party was financed almost entirely by a few wealthy New Yorkers, most notably financier Bernard Baruch and industrialist John J. Raskob. They had helped to erase the party's 1928 debt, and had shaped the party's "don't disturb business" strategy after 1930 when it controlled both Houses of Congress. The platform of 1932 made a few gestures toward the old Bryanite heritage, with talk of the federal regulation of exchanges and stricter banking controls, but bankers gave 25 percent of the 1932 party treasury, suspecting that the fire had gone out of these ideas. Roosevelt was the riskiest candidate in the eyes of the party's wealthy Eastern wing and, after all, he was a wealthy man. The rest—Baker, Smith, Ritchie—were known to be staunch defenders of the rights of property. Indeed, corporations paid the salaries of both Baker and Smith, and Ritchie was the most conservative candidate in the field and (with Smith) would join the anti-Roosevelt Liberty League in 1935. Garner was something of an unknown quantity to the Eastern wing, but he had not sponsored any radical

1933: What Would the 1930s Have Been Like Without Franklin Roosevelt?

125

legislation or even a new idea in his House career, which went back to 1903.

So to a comfortably fixed American in the summer of 1932, the economic system may have been threateningly out of control, but the political system was behaving in reassuring ways. Hoover was in the White House and, if the election in November replaced him with a Democrat, it would be one of a number of tested and quite acceptable men. The Democrats began their convention balloting in Chicago on June 24, and Roosevelt was almost stopped. Garner had support in only two states, and Smith, with the second highest total, had proved to his party that a Catholic could not win a presidential election. As historian Elliot Rosen has shown, a fourth ballot would have seen the convention swing to a familiar party elder who had not campaigned in the primaries but was available as a compromise, Newton D. Baker.

On reviewing his background and social philosophy, a New Deal or anything like it seems unlikely, at least with any degree of presidential cooperation. Baker was born in West Virginia of a Southern family, and recalled his father's stories of fighting in Jeb Stuart's cavalry. He moved to Cleveland as a young lawyer, joined crusading reform Mayor Tom Johnson and was himself mayor of the city from 1912 to 1916. Wilson made him secretary of war, and he returned to law practice in Cleveland when the Wilson era was over.

By 1932, Newton Baker had put in 12 years as a corporation lawyer, was quite affluent, and gave no sign of any of the old reform urgings that had led him to challenge things as they were back in Tom Johnson's day. His clients in the 1920s were the utility companies, large Eastern banks, railroads, and insurance companies that the progressives had once fought. Baker was heard to say that labor had too much power in America, and he favored the open shop. The only element of American life that he wanted to change after 1920 was the decision not to join the League of Nations. Baker was a consistent internationalist. In 1932 his support came from those who liked the idea of another Wilsonian of sorts, but a mature and predictable one. Baker had something of Wilson's rhetorical gift, expressing a lofty and somewhat abstract idealism that was intended to move educated folk, not the masses. He was honest, and during the war had demonstrated intelligence and good administrative abilities. He agreed with the Eastern financial wing of the party that the depression ought to be fought with sound money and a balanced budget, and by a President with both Cleveland's and Wilson's strength in resisting the wild schemes that crisis times engendered among the poor and in populist-infected rural areas. Roosevelt, who had been a younger administrator in Washington during the war and had many opportunities to observe Baker, respected his abilities: "Newt," he said privately in 1932, "would make a better President than I would."

Baker was not nominated. But had he been chosen, would the unparalleled pressures bred of economic crisis have galvanized this trim, self-controlled lawyer into a liberal innovator? We only know how he actually reacted to the New Deal from his Cleveland office, and he was an early and steady critic. Through most of 1933, he suppressed his doubts about the whirlwind of New Deal legislation, but party loyalty soon ran thin and by the end of the year the Cleveland lawyer was a New Deal opponent. He wrote in 1934 that the country had turned its back on self-reliance, and that equality was conquering liberty. "As a 19th century liberal," writes his biographer C. H. Cramer, "he believed in little government," and was disturbed by New Deal bureaucracy, deficits, and the militancy of labor. "In Baker's phrase," summarized Cramer, "the voracious centralist government of the New Deal was 'eating us up!' "

As a lifetime Democrat, he could not bring himself to openly join the Republicans in 1936, but he was known to be thoroughly disaffected with the new liberalism until the day he died in 1937. The New Deal, he had said in 1936, "had no philosophy and no principles." Until the end, he thought none of it had been necessary, and remained a critic of unionism, redistribution of wealth, and social experimentation—virtually everything the New Deal had stood for at its cutting edge.

⁂

Roosevelt just managed to amass the necessary two-thirds of the delegate votes on the third ballot, and Baker receded into insignificance. Nobody paid much attention to the old Democrat's complaints, or reflected upon how closely his views had come to the White House. Roosevelt's running mate in 1932 was the man who had abandoned his own candidacy, House Speaker John Nance Garner. Had Zangara killed FDR that February, would Garner have led the way to some sort of New Deal? To the extent that the answer turns upon Garner's philosophy and character, again the probable answer is no.

Garner was raised on small farms in West Texas, moving in 1892 to the little town of Uvalde, near the Rio Grande. His formal education was meager, but he prospered as a lawyer, and his political instincts were sufficiently acute to enable him to win sixteen consecutive terms in the House of Representatives, beginning in 1903. Of course, the competition was not stiff in Garner's thinly populated district, and he rarely had any opposition. In the House, he rose as the leadership always had, not by merit but by accumulating seniority and playing by the rules. "His career," wrote journalist John Carter in a contemporary sketch, "is based upon the obituary column and the power of inertia."

On the surface, Garner appeared to some to be a bit eccentric, giving rise to some suspicion among people who did not watch him operate in Congress that "Cactus Jack" might harbor a few radical ideas. He told preposterous Texas stories, was salty and profane in speech by Eastern standards, and wore odd hats given him by a Texas publisher. He went to bed early and thus exposed himself to no Washington social life, and this somehow enhanced the air of unpredictability about him. He was known to be devoted to late-afternoon sessions with bourbon and branch water, poker, and a few cronies from the Hill.

Garner was a great admirer of Woodrow Wilson and a firm believer in New Freedom Democratic principles as the average Southerner understood them: party loyalty, low tariffs, regulation of banks, and strict construction of the Constitution. "One of the classic miscalculations in American political history," observed FDR's brain truster Raymond Moley, "was the belief in the East among bankers and businessmen in 1932 that while Roosevelt could be trusted to understand their point of view because of his aristocratic background, Garner, his running-mate, was a dangerous radical." But the rural Texan was far more conventional in outlook than FDR, and far more fixed in conservative views about executive and federal power. There was nothing experimental in Garner's nature at all, in fact. He was flexible in congressional tactics, but time would prove him an unyielding traditionalist about the role of government in American life, crisis or no crisis. His loyalties, summarized John Ezell in a biographical sketch, "in descending order, were Texas and the South, the Democratic Party, and the legislative branch of government."

Garner's 1932 candidacy had not rested upon broad support for his principles, admiration for his record, or enthusiasm for his program for meeting the depression. Nobody knew very much about any of these subjects, and the latter did not exist. He was Texas's favorite-son candidate, for brokerage purposes. Also, he had somehow attracted the support of eccentric publisher William Randolph Hearst, which gave him California's votes. His supporters cited his ability to "lead" the Democratic forces in the House, although the record of a Democratic-controlled Congress in the crucial 1930–32 term had been almost entirely obstructionist.

His views, when announced, tended to be appealingly simple. "The great trouble today," he was quoted as saying in 1932, "is that we have too many laws." In 1932 he made news by proposing a national sales tax to balance the budget, an idea both economically ignorant and socially regressive. Along with balancing the budget, Garner spoke once or twice about an expanded public-works program, and never explained—probably never saw—the contradiction. On Prohibition, at least, he was consistent; he liked whiskey and thought it ought to be legal to use it. As Moley said in the 1930s, "His mind was like a field sparingly planted." If he had succeeded to the presidency in March 1933, he certainly would have been ill-prepared. While FDR spent the previous 12 months gathering his collection of professors and lawyers as a brain trust, Garner was drinking bourbon with old friends in the Capitol who had as few ideas as he did about how the depression might be ended.

How President Garner would have handled the responsibilities of his office we cannot know, since Zangara's erratic aim mercifully spared the country that experience. But we know how Vice-President Garner regarded the unfolding New Deal. Outwardly he was cooperative, for party loyalty was an article of faith with him, and a Democratic President expected a Democratic Congress to enact his program even if it contained much that individual legislators neither understood nor liked. With the rest of the Southern Democratic leadership, Garner supported all the measures of the early New Deal.

His doubts increased, however, as time went on. He did not like the scale of the relief effort and the 1935 Wagner Act giving labor the right to bargain collectively; he criticized continual federal deficits, and was firmly against the Court Plan and executive-branch reorganization in 1937. The New Deal brought to Washington an entirely new kind of person that Garner did not trust or find congenial—the college-educated young lawyers and social workers, who were Eastern, urban, and often Jewish, and who hatched so many of the radical schemes that gave the New Deal its radical reputation. Like most Southern Democrats, Garner was not happy to see the administration court the labor and black vote, as Roosevelt did so successfully in 1936 and after. A seasoned compromiser and party man, Garner never aired his objections publicly, but it was an open secret that the Vice-President was no New Dealer after 1935, and that he was kept on the ticket in 1936 only to avoid the embarrassment and disharmony of a change. Like Newton Baker, the Vice-President from Uvalde voted for FDR with the utmost reluctance, disliking much of the New Deal and confessing to friends that the party from 1933 to 1936 had taken directions that he would never approve.

Baker and Garner never talked together in the 1930s, and would not have enjoyed one another's company. They were very different temperamentally, the one educated, urbane, and a Protestant minister's son who did not drink; the other a rumpled, even slightly seedy West Texan who enjoyed all the normal vices of legislators (except fast women). But in a few moments' talk about political trends, they would surely have discovered a broad agreement in principle over what the New Deal had done wrong and what the Democrats ought to be doing to meet the challenge of the 1930s. While their administrations would have differed in style and in some small details, they would have brought government by the established Wilsonian leadership and according to old, tested principles. Both would have been more fiscally conservative than even Roosevelt, and would have yielded less to relief spending and other expensive social programs. A lower tariff would have occupied a more central place in administration efforts. Banks and stock exchanges would have been further regulated by any Democratic

1933: What Would the 1930s Have Been Like Without Franklin Roosevelt?

129

regime, but this would have almost exhausted the zeal for social or economic restructuring had Baker or Garner been in charge. Business confidence would have been a central commitment under Baker; even Garner, who had no corporations in his district and did not come into contact with business executives in his life's routine, seems to have believed always that recovery came only when businessmen invested.

That would have been basically the outline of a Democratic government from 1933 to 1937 under either of these old Wilsonians: free trade, balanced budgets, and banking reform, then wait for an essentially sound economic system to right itself.

That, at least, would have been a conservative Democratic President's program. Powerful political currents would have pressed the administration toward more activism. There are probably three policy areas where Baker or Garner—even Hoover—would have been literally forced to accept some governmental programs for which they had some distaste. With one-quarter of the work force unemployed, federal aid to local government for relief was inevitable. Indeed, the Democratic platform had promised it. But the federal role in it could have been minimized and the scope of relief kept small. A cold reception would have been given in the White House to the ideas of people like Harry Hopkins for a federally administered program such as the Civil Works Administration (CWA) of 1934 or the Works Progress Administration (WPA) that lasted from 1935 into the war.

Also, something had to be done for agriculture. Roosevelt decided upon production controls; about the only alternatives were the 1920s McNary-Haugen plan for dumping abroad, and inflation. Quite likely, some system of production controls would have been forced upon Baker or Garner. Then there was the matter of inflation. Some minor inflation of the currency was almost inevitable, with the money supply having shrunk by 25 percent in the four years after 1929. Baker would have resisted it strongly, but Garner less so. Neither man, and no national government including Roosevelt's, would go very far down that road. But some gestures probably had to be made.

With these concessions to popular pressure, we may imagine the outlines of a conservative Democratic administration. The deep banking crisis of 1933 would come and would have been weathered in much the same way. Then the country would have been given a program of fiscal conservatism, banking and exchange regulation, and tariff reduction, as well as, more grudgingly, a small public-works effort, some federal aid to local relief, some sort of production controls for agriculture, and some minor concessions to inflationary sentiment. It would have been a remarkably deflationary program, producing less economic recovery than the New Deal was able to manage.

There would have been no buoyant, charismatic personality in the White

House to sustain the hope that all would be well. Senator Norris would not have found a receptive presidential ear for his plan for a multipurpose development of the Tennessee River valley. Rexford Tugwell would have remained harmlessly at Columbia University rather than put to work organizing new communities, a tenant resettlement effort, and national planning. Blacks would have found no Eleanor Roosevelt to speak for them at the centers of power, and no Harry Hopkins or Harold Ickes to insist that there be no discrimination in programs under their charge. There would have been no Civilian Conservation Corps—Roosevelt's own invention—surely no effort to build that astonishing shelterbelt of trees in the Great Plains, and less presidential interest in conservation in general. Washington would have been a less interesting town and the government engaged in fewer tasks than the New Deal proposed (and probably administering them better). Major pieces of social legislation would have been ignored, opposed, or vetoed—the Wagner Collective-Bargaining Act, Social Security, and the tax reforms of 1935–37. As a result, the major shift of working-class votes toward the Democrats would have been greatly reduced.

In speculating upon these matters, it appears that Roosevelt and his New Deal had a more decisive psychological and political impact than an economic one. Economists are unable to agree on whether a conservative administration, determined to reassure the business community and balance the budget, would have impeded recovery or facilitated it. Keynesians argue that such a deflationary federal fiscal policy would ensure continued depression, and that private investors, however reassured, could not overcome an incorrect fiscal strategy. But a few economists have insisted that recovery would have come more promptly if New Deal reforms and antibusiness rhetoric had not spoiled the investment climate. The issue is technically complex, and informed opinion splintered. We may most safely assume that a conservative economic policy would have produced about the same result as Roosevelt achieved, if not worse. We incline toward the adjective *worse.* When FDR made a major effort to balance the budget in 1936, a recession came swiftly a year later. Baker and Garner would have been in that predicament much earlier, in all probability. But even if their economic success only matched that of the New Deal, a solicitude for business neutralizing their deflationary fiscal strategy, the difference in psychological and political results looms large. Roosevelt did not get the country through the Great Depression by ending it; the 1929 GNP of $104 billion was not reached again until late in 1940, and when the election of 1936 was held the GNP was struggling up to a very depressed total of $82 billion. He got the country through it by enhancing a very modest economic record with a stunningly attractive personal performance. No contemporary matched his skills in reassuring the public that something was being done and that, if it failed, something else would be done, and that things would

1933: What Would the 1930s Have Been Like Without Franklin Roosevelt?

131

work out. Without FDR's personal warmth and popularity, along with the array of New Deal agencies and laws that were at least trying to respond to the needs of every group, the Democratic party's 1933–36 record would be difficult to defend when election time came.

By mid-decade, the electorate had moved decisively to the Left. FDR, after an initial hesitation, moved with them in 1935, sponsoring labor and social legislation, progressive taxes, antitrust measures, and the WPA. Few of the Democratic elders, certainly not Baker or Garner, had the liberal leanings, the experimental temper, or the political skills to attract a Leftward-moving electorate back into the Democratic party and accomplish the major realignment that took place in the 1930s. The new, urban-based majority party that carried 46 states in 1936 was a peculiarly Rooseveltian achievement; Smith's 1928 campaign had initiated this shift of urban and younger voters to the Democrats, but it was the New Deal that confirmed and extended the shift. Under different leadership, of one of the conservative elder statesmen of Wilsonian Democracy, stubborn deflationary policies would have combined with a political style either too urban upper-class (Baker) or too rural Southern (Garner) to permit the grand new liberal coalition that FDR put together. The political consequences of a different presidency might easily have been sufficiently explosive as to bend the course of history.

Radicalism was on the increase in America at mid-decade, severely testing even Roosevelt's abilities to contain it. As usually happens, social unrest did not coincide with the economic cycle. At the lowest level of the depression, in 1932–33, there had been some scattered violence in the corn belt, in Harlan County, Kentucky, and in the District of Columbia when Hoover mismanaged the dispersal of the Bonus Marchers. But it was not until the economic upturn began that lower-class militancy reached the levels that made the 1930s seem to some people "the Red decade." Discontent in the industrial labor force made 1934 a year of strikes and unionization. By 1936 the AFL had failed to accommodate the militancy of workers and the new CIO was expanding in the mass-production industries. The labor movement tripled in size between 1933 and 1940—from 3 million to 9 million members; unionization for the first time reached the auto and steel industries, and surged into the agricultural work force that harvested crops in California and along the Eastern seaboard.

Labor militancy caught the New Deal somewhat by surprise, but Roosevelt took up a sympathetic position and managed to remain on friendly terms with labor's leaders and rank and file. But the New Deal was too modest a reform package to satisfy millions of others, and there was never a year when radical political movements did not flourish to the administration's Left. The socialists, having polled nearly 900,000 votes in 1932 behind Norman Thomas, expected that the 1930s would prove to be their decade. The communists were active and full of hope. American radicalism, however, tended to flow toward non-Marxist parties and leaders. Upton Sinclair, the novelist who had long been sympathetic toward society's underdogs, stunned the California Democratic party by taking its nomination for governor in 1934 and very nearly carrying the state on a platform of ending poverty through cooperative economic enterprises. Governor Floyd Olson of Minnesota declared that if capitalism could not be cured of depressions, "I hope the present system of government goes right down to hell," and openly called himself a radical. Huey Long, senator and boss of Louisiana, stumped the country in 1934–35 with a loosely defined program for sharing the nation's wealth, and built an organization claiming between 5 and 7 million members. A Catholic priest in Royal Oak, Michigan, Father Charles E. Coughlin, mobilized millions of people through weekly radio broadcasts and in his National Union for Social Justice. His twelve-point program expressed resentments against banks and the present economic system, and called for vague but radical-sounding reforms.

Long and Coughlin were able speakers, and their success in mobilizing millions of people was, to some extent, written off as a personal achievement of demagogues whose oratorical skills were exceptional. But the astounding success of a 67-year-old retired doctor from Long Beach, California, Dr. Francis E. Townsend, was bedrock proof of the volatility of public sentiment. Townsend promised to rescue all the elderly from poverty through a program of $200-a-month pensions, and his Old Age Revolving Pensions, Ltd., spread from California all the way to Maine and so frightened congressmen that the House would not risk a floor vote against his patently unworkable scheme.

The leaders of these spontaneous mass movements with their various demands for government intervention against hardship and injustice did not at once set themselves against the New Deal. They tested public sentiment in the first year, and gave the administration time to indicate its direction and strength. Then in 1934, each of the three major mass leaders broke with FDR, denounced the New Deal as too conservative, and took a path that pointed toward a third-party effort in 1936.

Roosevelt, as we know, took these and other signs as proof that public sentiment wanted a more reformist government in Washington, and he moved to break the momentum of the gathering forces of radicalism in the summer of 1935. His own rhetoric became more antibusiness; he endorsed collective bargaining through the Wagner Bill, holding labor to the New Deal; and he sponsored social insurance to undercut Townsend, and a tax on wealth to neutralize Long. In his 1936 campaign, he welcomed the hostility of the wealthy.

1933: What Would the 1930s Have Been Like Without Franklin Roosevelt?

133

All of this was brilliant politics. It aided Roosevelt's bid to retain lower-class support, when an assassin shot and fatally wounded Huey Long in September 1935. A third party did emerge—the Union party of 1936—based upon the Townsend and Coughlin movements and the remnants of Long's Share Our Wealth organization. But its candidate (William Lemke) was uninspired, FDR too popular, and the new party took not a single electoral vote. The socialists, too, lost strength, falling from 887,000 to 187,000 votes. For the rest of the 1930s, some radical third-party opposition to the New Deal continued to appear, most notably in the 1938 Progressive party formed by the LaFollette brothers in the upper Mid-West. But Roosevelt and his program had pulled most reform-oriented voters back into the Democratic party.

Whether the millions of common people with bleak prospects were making a mistake when they rallied to FDR—beguiled mostly by charm and patchwork repairs when more radical changes in the economic and political systems were all that would help them—is a question beyond our interests here. Undeniably it was Roosevelt and his program that eased the two-party system through the 1930s without a radical challenge. Roosevelt himself claimed that he had saved capitalism in the United States by making only necessary changes, and some weighty authorities have agreed. Norman Thomas, who headed the socialist resurgence in 1932 only to be routed in 1936 with about one-quarter of his 1932 vote, was asked what happened to socialism in a decade when its prospects had seemed so bright. His response: "It was Roosevelt, in a word."

Without him, one imagines the Democrats being led by one of the old Wilsonians, inspiring no more confidence than that other stubbornly conservative Wilsonian with no popular touch, Herbert Hoover. More radical people and parties would inherit the wind. One beneficiary would have been Norman Thomas and the socialists, who had a coherent program for recovery. If the Democrats had appeared as inept as did Hoover and his party, the socialists would have enlarged their role in American politics.

But the majority of the American public was wary of socialism for reasons that have entertained and, to some extent, eluded scholars for years. The increase in socialist influence would probably have been limited to a larger presidential vote, along with some socialist mayors and congressmen. To have them participating in American governance at all would be significant, a return to the peak reached by the party in 1912 behind Debs' leadership. But it is difficult to foresee how far this socialist growth would have developed, and easy to perceive that this was a long-term matter, depending upon America's relation to the European war of the 1940s. In the 1930s, disgruntled American voters were sure to turn more readily to more native solutions, to a third party with a strong populist tone.

Does our contemporary mind resist the idea of a powerful third party eventually replacing one of the ancient two? The Democrats and the Republicans are not written into the Constitution. Established major parties have failed and vanished before, and the 1930s was a crisis time with many of the conditions for that sort of upheaval. One way that a third party could have emerged from the discontent was behind Huey Long, whether there was a Roosevelt or not. Long, of course, was shot and killed. But recall how he was feared by intelligent observers for just this potential.

He was not always taken seriously, at least at first, because he had a pudgy face, a hillbilly twang, and outlandish manners. But Huey Long had a brilliant mind, an almost totally retentive memory, and an appetite for power that his Louisiana opponents had underestimated to their great regret. When he promoted himself to the United States Senate in 1932, he was the acknowledged dictator of Louisiana politics, his power rooted in a political machine built with ruthless tactics and also upon the loyalty of the poor classes in the state who benefitted from his social programs. Washington wanted to regard Long as a typical Southern demagogue, a type the capital city was familiar with, but people soon found that he was different. He was brainy, restless, unpredictable, and not satisfied with merely being a senator. In a depression, his repeated encouragement to the Have Nots to take what was properly theirs from the Haves made him a political magnet.

Long broke with the New Deal before 1933 was out, largely over its tax policies, which he thought lay too lightly upon the rich. He struck out to build his own national organization, and a careful check by one of Roosevelt's aides indicated that Long might draw as many as 4 million votes in 1936 if he ran as an independent. Roosevelt thought Long the second most dangerous man in America, behind only General Douglas MacArthur. Presumably he saw one of these two men coming to power through nonparliamentary means if democratic government did not deal adequately with the depression. Long's national potential was underscored in 1934 when he raised underdog Hattie Caraway to a Senate seat from Arkansas by making a two-week tour through that state. Then he spoke to enthusiastic crowds as far away as Iowa and Madison Square Garden, New York. By April 1935, Long's office was receiving an average of 60,000 letters a week endorsing Share Our Wealth, and after one of his radio attacks on the New Deal, he received 30,000 letters a day for 24 consecutive days. His following appeared to be very largely Southern, but one could never be sure where the appeal of his redistribution-of-wealth ideas would catch fire.

There has always been doubt that Long was really an economic radical. His Share Our Wealth program included heavy taxation of the wealthy (a capital levy on fortunes over $300 million and an income tax confiscating all annual income over $1 million), and promised a job, housing, and education for the mass of citizens. "I'm for the poor man—all poor men," he told Roy Wilkins. "Black and white, they all gotta have a chance. They gotta have a

1933: What Would the 1930s Have Been Like Without Franklin Roosevelt?

135

home, a job, and a decent education for their children." This was of course demagoguery, the arousing of the masses, but Long's Pulitzer Prize–winning biographer, T. Harry Williams, concluded that Long was serious about his redistributive program even though he was careless about the economic details.

Perhaps as President (and he was headed there, quite openly; in 1935 his *My First Days in the White House* was published), he would have moved social policy decisively to the Left. Perhaps power alone was his goal, and the program would have slipped to the background. What seems more certain is that Huey Long would have governed the country with a disregard for parliamentary niceties, for legal procedures, for checks and balances, and for constitutional rights, which would have permanently altered our institutions.

He aroused bitter class animosities, and it is a difficult question whether the major threat to democratic procedures came first from Long or from his opponents determined to defeat and ruin him. Threatened with Long, Louisiana conservatives readily resorted to bribery and intimidation, and Franklin Roosevelt in similar circumstances took some early steps toward Watergate by instructing the Bureau of Internal Revenue to make Long a special target of investigation and harassment. Long responded in kind, with a special ruthlessness of his own. With him, a South American political style came to the United States—the strong popular leader, subservient legislatures and courts, a manipulated press, and the building of a political machine based on the civil service. FDR was accused of wanting and working toward these arrangements, but his movement in such directions was minor and qualified by his own aristocratic sense of sportsmanship and fair play. Long was very different, having been raised in a meaner school. In 1940, when observers thought his power would have peaked, Long would have been only 46 years old.

Without Roosevelt, and without the two doctors who did Long in—the one who shot him, and the one who botched the operation—there would have been a greatly altered political prospect in America. Even with no Huey Long, the potential was there, in the crippled economy of the 1930s, for a powerful third party with a radical-sounding program. For depression in America intensified the public impatience with the slow, deliberative processes that characterized political democracy—just as it did in Germany, Italy, Great Britain, and France. Divided government, parliamentary bickering, and obstructionist, unimaginative presidents would have extended these processes, not for four years to 1932 but for eight years to 1936. Without attempting to guess at details, we may be sure that the 1936–40 period would have greatly exceeded Roosevelt's second term in class polarization and the mobilization of mass movements of the Left and Right. Some will see in such a development the potential for a more democratic America, moved to the Left by a deep social upheaval. It would be an America entering the 1940s much farther to the Left on the world political spectrum, having revived its own revolutionary heritage.

Others will see demagoguery and confusion, the excesses of mass politics and then a reaction toward Right-wing repression. From the first perspective, Franklin Roosevelt's historic role was to deflect and co-opt the gathering forces of democratic reform and to reinforce and repair a political and economic system that deserved a thorough transformation. From the other view, Roosevelt emerges as the leader who preserved the country from the politics of class polarization and violence, and restored its faith in basic institutions. Either way, it would have been a different world without him.

Only one general outcome seems much beyond dispute. If Roosevelt had been somehow blocked from the presidency, America would almost certainly have had a President in 1940 with very different foreign-policy views from those he held. For Roosevelt was very unusual among prospective presidential aspirants of the 1930s. Most were considerably more isolationist than he. Certainly Herbert Hoover was less inclined toward intervention in world troubles where his mandate was unclear, and Garner was instinctively isolationist. Huey Long did not volunteer to fight in World War I ("I was not mad at anyone over there") and was consistently isolationist in outlook during the 1930s. Norman Thomas and the socialists took a dim view of American involvement in World War II, although they despised fascism. The LaFollettes of Wisconsin, who launched the Progressive party in 1938, were also inclined toward isolation.

Indeed, majority sentiment in both of the major parties was more neutralist than Roosevelt was, and all the third-party leaders of the era were strong in the traditional isolationism of their rural, small-town, Southern-Midwestern, middle-American constituencies. Long, Coughlin, and Townsend all expressed a distaste for European quarrels that reflected the beliefs of the desperate millions who sent them contributions and packed their lecture halls. Populism in America was historically Anglophobic and isolationist, and any third party arising in protest would have been inclined to let Britain and Germany settle their own differences. The odds were against the prospect that control of American foreign policy in 1939 or in 1940–41 would be in the hands of the interventionist Eastern wing of either of the major parties.

This foreign-policy direction as a possibility will continue to strike people differently. Some pine for it, while others shudder at their narrow escape from isolationism and eventual Nazi encirclement. This is another subject. But a world without Roosevelt, these thoughts remind us, would have been in many ways unlike the one we know: perhaps farther to the Left, even conceivably much farther to the Right than it was after the New Deal, and much more reluctant to join with the rest of the world in a war against Germany or Japan. In this instance, one man seems to have made quite a difference.

SUGGESTED READINGS

David H. Bennett, *Demagogues in the Depression: American Radicals and the Union Party, 1932–1936,* 1969

Leon H. Blair, ed., *Essays on Radicalism in Contemporary America,* 1972

C. H. Cramer, *Newton D. Baker,* 1961

Mauritz Hallgren, *Seeds of Revolt,* 1933

R. Alan Lawson, *The Failure of Independent Liberalism, 1930–1941,* 1971

William E. Leuchtenburg, *Franklin D. Roosevelt and the New Deal, 1932–1940,* 1963

Donald McCoy, *Angry Voices,* 1957

Elliot Rosen, "Baker on the 6th Ballot: The Democratic Party's Alternative, 1932," *Ohio History,* Autumn 1966

David Shannon, *The Socialist Party of America,* 1955

Bascom Timmons, *Garner of Texas,* 1948

Unofficial observer, *The New Dealers,* 1937

Frank Warren, *An Alternate Vision: The Socialist Party in the 1930s,* 1974

T. Harry Williams, *Huey Long,* 1969

The United States, Russia, and the Cold War—What If Franklin Roosevelt Had Lived?

Human ingenuity was sufficient to arrange the Cold War and to wage it, but calculating its costs has been beyond human arts and sciences. In the mid-1960s, before the Vietnam War had ballooned into the disaster it became, a government official testified to Congress that the dollar cost of the Cold War could conservatively be estimated at $1 trillion. In a 1972 essay, James L. Clayton put the Cold War's cost, from 1947 to 1971, at $1.4 trillion.

In arriving at these figures, historians totalled up the difference between pre–World War II defense budgets and those staggering outlays after 1945; plus the cost of the Korean War; and plus the many delayed costs, to the Treasury, of World War II veterans' benefits, pensions, and interest on the defense portion of the national debt. The dollar cost reflects the diversion of national resources from other things: from education, public health, conservation, public housing, or many private purchases had the government not expended the money. The diversion of resources from "civilian" goods and services to military goods and services is not the entire story. The Cold War distorted our national politics, paving the way for anticommunist demagogues like Senator Joseph McCarthy, and presenting the American Right with a potent issue with which to deflect and confuse the forces of domestic social reform. The Cold War led the government to establish and nourish not only a huge defense establishment, but also the Central Intelligence Agency (CIA), which has become so remote from public control and enamored of clandestine operations that it has acted for years as a second foreign-policy source, a strike force, and an aspiring assassin of foreign leaders. Our national police force, the FBI, rode the currents of Cold War anxiety to almost unchallenged power, and did its part in the struggle against worldwide communist subversion by harassing not only domestic communists but also student activists, Black Panthers, and Martin Luther King, Jr. It kept files on the sex lives of congressmen, senators, and those Presidents who seemed to have them. The Cold War is the tapestry against which the Vietnam War made sense to American decision-makers, as was the case with the Watergate break-in, the overthrow of the elected President of Chile, atmospheric testing of nuclear weapons, and other alterations of the traditional American way of conducting our national affairs.

An international rivalry that levied such costs and brought such social distortions upon a formerly isolated nation unburdened by standing armies, alliances, or an imperial presidency—could it possibly have been avoided? This has been a compelling issue in the literature on the origins of the Cold War. Those who have concluded that the conflict was inevitable have proceeded from a philosophy of history that stresses impersonal forces and minimizes the influence of leadership and individual decision-making in shaping the course of history. Most historians, however, have not been willing to adopt this philosophy without qualification. Individuals have *some* choices, most Western scholars feel. This assumption undergirds our legal system, our religions, and our social mores, and accounts for much of the dynamism of Western life. Men and women make history, not as passive actors in a predetermined play, but as individuals with some real alternatives. If it were not so, praise or blame would make no sense, and we are a society much devoted to sorting out our heroes and heroines as well as our culprits.

As to the origins of the Cold War, most scholars occupy a middle ground between inevitability and unfettered individual choice, blending impersonal social forces with leaders' decisions in a causal explanation. Corporals in the army, voters, and the mass of citizens in the United States or the Soviet Union had little or no responsibility for how things turned out. But powerful leaders of State made choices from among some alternatives and shaped history. Their choices were not unlimited. Their alternatives varied in number and range; to choose a costly path here often meant the narrowing of alternatives over there. But within the limits imposed by the vast sweep of global events and the structures of existing power, the wartime leaders of the great powers made the decisions that led to a Cold War between former allies.

These are the operating assumptions of most scholars. Stalin, Churchill,

Franklin Roosevelt, and Harry Truman have had to face historical writers who overwhelmingly reject the deterministic logic. In the United States, historians have naturally been most interested in our own leadership, whose State papers are the most accessible—Roosevelt, and then his successor.

One of the pivotal moments of American and world history appears to have been the death of FDR on April 12, 1945, and the shift of leadership to Harry Truman. There are many who believe that the two men were sufficiently different in convictions and talents that the course of history was sharply altered by the transfer of power. This is the argument of Roosevelt's son, Elliott Roosevelt, in a book published in 1946—As He Saw It —and of Roosevelt's friend and New Deal advisor, Rexford Tugwell, in Off Course, From Truman to Nixon (1969). It was the perspective of former Vice-President Henry A. Wallace and those liberals who left the Democratic party in 1948 to form the Progressive party. And it is a view that some scholars have adopted, among them Denna F. Fleming, David Horowitz, and Gar Alperovitz. Let us summarize and examine the case they make.

Roosevelt immodestly thought himself gifted in a special way to deal with the Soviets both during and after the war. The record offers some support for this claim. It was his government that had recognized the Soviet Union in 1933, and sent the sympathetic Joseph Davies as ambassador in 1937. The war brought a close Soviet-American alliance, cemented by the joint peril from Nazism and expressed through Lend-Lease, military consultation, and two wartime conferences (Teheran, in 1943; Yalta, in 1945) at which Roosevelt and Stalin established what appeared to be warm relations. FDR prided himself upon his ability to charm anyone, and he included the tough, suspicious Soviet leader. Indeed, at their two meetings, and in cable communication, there was candor and even some warmth.

Roosevelt's advantages in dealing with Stalin went beyond the President's open manner and adroitness in human relations. For Roosevelt was, in his own way, a man of the Left, a social reformer at home and an outspoken advocate of a reformed world order. He was internationally known as a friend of "progress," a liberal who favored democratization within nations and an end to colonialism abroad. He thus saw himself as standing between the reactionary colonialist powers of Europe and the forces of socialist revolution, symbolized so adequately in the figures of Britain's Churchill and Russia's Stalin. He would mediate a peaceful path between their conflicting instincts, between revolution and the status quo.

Woodrow Wilson had seen himself in this same role in foreign affairs during and after World War I, but he failed to establish a progressive center in world politics. His hostility toward Leninism was too great, and ill health and personal misjudgments prevented him from mobilizing the liberal-internationalist coalition he needed at home. But FDR's prospects for hewing a pathway between the conflict-laden ideologies of Right and Left appeared much better than Wilson's did at the end of the first war.

For one thing, Roosevelt was more independent of the British than Wilson had been. This was partly because of the enlarged power of the United States, and partly because Roosevelt was more genuinely at odds with the British view of the world than Wilson. While on exceptionally good terms with Winston Churchill, Roosevelt always twitted Churchill mercilessly when Stalin joined them, conspicuously adopting a neutral position to undercut suspicions of an Anglo-American bloc. Privately he was critical of British imperialism, and talked frequently of putting an end to it in the postwar world. The British, he told his son Elliott, must be taught to put their hopes in a postwar alliance of all nations, "not just in the British empire and the British ability to get other countries to combine in some sort of bloc against the Soviet Union." The President expressed a willingness to appeal, over the British government, to public opinion in order to push British policy to the Left. This vague notion showed that he had not made a close study of Wilson's mistakes. In any event, FDR made it clear many times, always in private, that the postwar world had no place for the British, French, and Dutch empires. (Of course, in his view there *was* no American empire, in the usual sense, and no need for one; we would do quite well in a world where doors were not closed to American enterprise.)

More to the point, Roosevelt also assumed that the Western European powers must acquiesce in some inevitable expansion of Soviet influence after the war. This the British, especially, could be expected to resist. They had gone to war over Poland, and Churchill had long expressed in an aggressive form the traditional British interest in the Balkans. But like it or not, the British would have to accept some changes in the world, Roosevelt believed. As he said to his son: "We're going to be able to make this the 20th century after all, you watch and see."

Thus Roosevelt as President appeared to possess the attributes required of a mediator in a postwar era of adjustment. Toward the old European colonialist powers, he had established a posture of warm cooperation, combined with a vague but persistent anticolonialism that preserved his independence. His relations with the international Left were equally promising in terms of a role as mediator. Of all the heads of advanced capitalist nations, Roosevelt was in the best position to maintain working relations with the world socialist movement.

There was, of course, a vast difference between FDR's brand of liberalism and any form of revolutionary socialism or communism. Still, he was known around the world as a social reformer whose domestic enemies had been principally to the Right, not to the Left. He repudiated communism, but showed no interest in attacking American communists as a subversive force. To him, the communists were merely a political party, a tiny one at

1945: The United States, Russia, and the Cold War—What If Franklin Roosevelt Had Lived?

143

that, and the main response of democrats to such extremist minorities should not be to hound them out of existence but to reform the social abuses upon which they thrived. The tide of Red-baiting in the United States, which caught up several congressmen in the late 1930s, never had any support from the Roosevelt administration. As for the Soviet Union, the President had always regarded it as a dictatorship of a brutal variety, but he did not think it compared for malevolence with the Nazi system. As he wrote to Pope Pius XII in 1941:

> . . . Russia is governed by a dictatorship as rigid in its manner of being as is the dictatorship in Germany. I believe, however, that this Russian dictatorship is less dangerous to the safety of other nations than is the German form of dictatorship.

The wartime alliance with Russia did not bother Roosevelt as it did the other capitalist in the Big Three, Winston Churchill, who explained the Soviet alliance to the House of Commons by saying that the peril of Hitler unfortunately required a willingness to accept the devil himself as an ally. Stalin may have been seen by some people as a paranoid Russian tyrant who could not be trusted, but Roosevelt's experience and conclusion were otherwise. "I just have a hunch," FDR wrote to William Bullitt, "that Stalin is not that kind of man. Harry [Hopkins] says he's not and that he doesn't want anything but security for his country, and I think that if I give him everything I possibly can and ask nothing from him in return, noblesse oblige, he won't try to annex anything and will work with me for a world of democracy and peace."

These were, of course, mere sentiments, uttered in a time of firm wartime alliance. Roosevelt's position in the world as a leader of moderate Leftist credentials at best did no more than to create some of the conditions for a relationship as mediator between the West and the Soviet Union. In order to hold the alliance together, an American President would need more than these advantages. The postwar settlement required hard decisions about the future of Germany, Eastern Europe, the Far East, an association of nations, and the atomic bomb. Roosevelt's instinct was to put these decisions off as long as possible, for they contained the seeds of conflict and would tend to weaken the Allies if discussed before German and Japanese power was thoroughly broken. He was rather good at this procrastination, but events nonetheless forced him to make certain preliminary decisions about the postwar world. In his record of dealing with the Soviets on postwar arrangements, there is much to support the optimistic hope that he might have steered events away from polarization and conflict.

Roosevelt understood, as well as any American could, the terrible ordeal that Russia had suffered at German hands—for the second time in the twentieth century—and that Russian security was sure to be at the head of the Allies' agenda as the peace approached. Roosevelt appears to have believed that, if Russia felt secure, there should be no reason for postwar friction. American policy could theoretically enhance the Russian sense of security by appropriate action in three major areas.

They were: postwar social and political arrangements agreed upon for Germany and for the nations along Russia's vulnerable western border; loans for economic reconstruction of the Soviet Union; and the atomic bomb. On all of these issues, the American President deferred final decision. But he told Bullitt of an intention to "give him [Stalin] everything I possibly can. . . ." Leaving aside for the moment whether a "generous" policy designed to assure the Russians of their postwar security would have minimized a Soviet-American conflict, let us review the evidence that FDR might have shaped such a policy.

Roosevelt had gradually become an advocate of a postwar successor to the League of Nations as a peace-keeping organization, but he could never get Stalin very interested in this. The Russians would join such an organization, but they placed no faith in world government as a guarantor of Soviet security. The world, after all, was chiefly capitalist and, in any event, everybody knew that the history of the League was not reassuring to nations that had reason to fear aggression. More important to Russia would be a firm mutual defense treaty. But even much more vital than such a treaty—America, one recalls, had never believed in peacetime entangling alliances—was a zone of buffer states of "friendly" (that is, Leftist) political and economic institutions closely tied to the Soviet Union. Combined with this basic change in international arrangements was the necessity for a permanent crippling of German power. These were the basic elements in the Soviet design for security.

This meant a Russian sphere of influence reaching westward to control a belt of states from the Baltic to the Balkans, and spheres of influence ran against the historic American commitment to the open door. Yet Roosevelt was a confirmed spheres-of-influence man. Many times he spoke privately to friends, diplomats, and Stalin himself of a world run by the Big Four—the United States, Russia, Great Britain, and China. The President told Cardinal Spellman in 1943, for example, that the postwar world would be divided between the four great powers: "China gets the Far East; the U.S. the Pacific; Britain and Russia, Europe and Africa." This was, of course, an odd formulation. China was a very weak "power," Latin America was discreetly not mentioned, and the whole scheme had the grand imprecision of the ideas of Anglo-American geopolitical cranks such as Henry and Brooks Adams or Halford Mackinder. Still, Roosevelt often talked this way, and whatever the geographic details, he was clearly ready to accept a rather cynical (or if one prefers, "realistic") division of the world into areas of Great Power influence. He seemed to believe that these satiated powers would then keep the peace.

1945: The United States, Russia, and the Cold War—What If Franklin Roosevelt Had Lived?

145

Here was possible common ground with Stalin. Of course, it was one thing for a President to hold the idea of spheres of influence, and another to get the American public to accept all the new arrangements that would be required in Europe in the aftermath of German defeat. America was populated in substantial part by people from Central and Eastern Europe, who would not be disinterested. There were more than 6 million Polish voters in the United States, Roosevelt reminded Stalin more than once, and there was also a free press, a Bill of Rights, and an opposition party—all the ingredients of political trouble for the administration in power when Russian expansionism had to be condoned. Yet Roosevelt thought that Russian security requirements could be met in the occupied areas; things could be worked out. He went to Yalta to begin this task in early February 1945. The agreements made there were so ambiguous where Poland was concerned that argument will go on forever. The most recent monograph on the subject, Diane Shaver Clemens' *Yalta* (1970), reaffirms an old view, that Roosevelt at Yalta essentially conceded what the Soviets would insist upon anyway: a controlling hand in the political reconstruction of this and other border states vital to their security.

The first reports from the conference were certainly full of hope. In Harry Hopkins' words:

> We really believed in our hearts that this was the dawn of the new day we had been praying for and talking about for so many years. We were absolutely certain that we had won the first great victory of the peace. . . .

This estimate was based upon the friendly mood of the conferees— American, British, and Russian—and upon the agreement as to the main outlines of a United Nations organization, upon the Soviet pledge to go to war against Japan, and upon the bargain struck concerning the future of Poland. The mood was real enough. The pledge to join the Japanese war and enter the UN was honored by the Russians. But Yalta did not settle the issue of Poland or the other border states, and here the Cold War began.

What had Roosevelt intended? It is not entirely clear. He wanted free elections, but conceded that they might bring to power a regime hostile to both Russia and communism, and he agreed with Stalin that an unfriendly government in Poland was out of the question. Two Polish governments claimed preference as the German armies were driven out: a communist group of Poles that the advancing Soviet armies picked up in Lublin and took to Warsaw, and an anti-Soviet group in London. The Russians would not even discuss a free election between the two for fear of the outcome, and they did not like Churchill's and Roosevelt's proposal of a balanced coalition. Neither did either of the Polish factions, which detested each other.

Roosevelt appeared to understand. The capitalist West had twice in a generation sent formidable armies across Poland and deep into Russia, inflicting terrible damage. The Russians must naturally have on their border a Poland whose social and economic systems were oriented toward the Russian models. How could they include the London Poles and arrange some compromise? The Yalta Accords read as follows: "The provisional government which is now functioning in Poland should . . . be reorganized on a broader democratic basis, with the inclusion of democratic leaders from Poland itself and from Poles abroad." This did not allow for a "new" coalition government, but a coalition in which the Lublin Poles were the basic foundation and certainly the dominant element. Then one would hope for the best. As Roosevelt reminded Churchill some weeks later:

> We placed, as clearly shown in the agreement, somewhat more emphasis on the Lublin Poles than on the other two groups from which the new government is to be drawn.

Admiral Leahy mentioned to FDR that the Russians could stretch the agreement on Poland all the way to Washington and back without breaking it, and Roosevelt answered: "I know, Bill, I know it. But it's the best I can do for Poland at this time." He persuaded the others to sign a Declaration on Liberated Europe, which reaffirmed the principles of the Atlantic Charter—that is, self-determination of all peoples. The Declaration called for Eastern European governments "broadly representative of all democratic elements in the population and pledged to . . . free elections." But as Roosevelt proposed no enforcement machinery beyond consultation among the Big Three—overruling his own State Department in this—Stalin probably took the Declaration as intended to help Roosevelt placate American public opinion.

The President, who conceded the Russian objection to "unfriendly" governments on her borders, accepted that nation's security fears and was willing to go some distance to ease them. This had implications in the two other policy areas we have mentioned. In addition to permitting a Soviet sphere of influence in Eastern Europe—including a neutralized Germany—there would have to be American loans for Soviet economic reconstruction, and reassurance of some kind on that exceptional new element in the balance of world power, the atomic bomb.

Russia began asking about a loan well before the end of the war. Roosevelt was receptive, and his treasury secretary, Henry Morgenthau, thought the request for $6 billion was too small. A loan of $10 billion would demonstrate our goodwill and set Soviet-American relations upon the right path. At his death, Roosevelt had made no decision about the loan, and regretted that he had not gone into it at Teheran or Yalta. The door was still open.

The atomic bomb, of course, was developed jointly by the Americans and the British; the Russians had not been drawn into the project. This issue had come up, however. Roosevelt had listened to scientist Niels Bohr, Supreme

1945: The United States, Russia, and the Cold War—What If Franklin Roosevelt Had Lived?

147

Court Justice Felix Frankfurter, and others, who urged him to magnanimously share the atomic secret with Russia to avert suspicion and a postwar arms race. He indicated general agreement with their thinking, but took no steps in that direction. This door, too, was one he had kept open but not entered. Thus American policy on basic issues affecting Soviet-American relations remained unclear in the spring of 1945 as a broken German army fell back upon Berlin. The President had indicated personal leanings toward a conciliatory policy, but had fended off final decisions until the war was over. No one could say what Congress and the public would accept, in any event, let alone what Russian policy would be. Then Roosevelt suffered his fatal brain hemorrhage on April 12, and Harry Truman became President.

Truman inherited Roosevelt's problems, but Roosevelt had used up all the time available for delay. At once the new administration made decisions that represented what the journalists call a harder line. The State Department and Ambassador Averill Harriman had for some time been urging a rebuke of Russian policy in Poland, and in Truman they found a President who listened to his official experts—as Roosevelt had not. As Ernest May writes in a brilliant discussion of the role of career diplomats in his *The Lessons of the Past* (1975):

> . . . Truman and the men around him received much of their tutoring about foreign affairs from diplomats who deliberately sought to teach them that the Soviet Union was malevolent and untrustworthy. Roosevelt had little to do with these diplomats. With some justice, he had judged professionals in the State Department to be Republicans at heart, unsympathetic with his domestic programs, and generally critical of his initiatives in international relations. In the late 1930s he began to circumvent them when dealing with European crises. Once the war commenced, he bypassed them most of the time. . . .
>
> Truman, on the other hand, assumed office with the conventional view that the State Department was and should be the principal organization dealing with foreign affairs. When he took over the oval office, the department's professionals for the first time in years found themselves . . . with a prospect of significantly affecting what a President thought, said and did.

Advice that he should distrust the Russians was, in any event, congenial to Harry Truman, who in 1941 had remarked that we should give aid to the Germans if the Russians were winning, to the Russians if Hitler was winning, and hope that the two evils would remove each other from the earth.

Before April was out, Truman had tongue-lashed Ambassador Molotov for breaking the Yalta agreements over Poland. Now the American version of that agreement was that an entirely new government was to be formed and entirely free elections held, no matter whether the resulting government was friendly to the Soviets or not. As Diane Clemens writes in her recent book, *Yalta* (1970), "Truman set out to implement the Yalta agreements by changing them." That Truman honestly thought himself to be carrying out Roosevelt's foreign policies is more evidence of how Roosevelt had used ambiguity to keep his options open. Truman had never been told by FDR that the Poles were being delivered up to a Russian-dominated future as part of the high price of postwar friendship between the two great powers. All he had heard on the subject from Roosevelt was the speech the President had given to Congress upon his return from Yalta, a speech that specifically promised an end to spheres-of-influence diplomacy.

In the weeks after Roosevelt's death, the Truman administration gathered itself for a close look at the pattern of Soviet actions in Eastern Europe, and did not like what it saw. A first response was the lecture to Molotov. Then in May, Lend-Lease to the Soviet Union was abruptly cut off. The loan request was held up, then "accidentally misplaced," and American officials let the Soviets know that economic aid would not be given in the *hope* that Russian behavior would improve, but only *after* it improved. At Potsdam in July, Truman and Churchill lowered the reparations figure that Russia could expect from Germany, and Truman gave Stalin in one sentence all the information on the bomb that an American official was ever to grant the Russians. Relations between the former allies were deteriorating quickly. Russia entered the war against Japan, but was excluded from the surrender that removed the last common enemy between communist and Western worlds. Soviet rule in Poland was firm; there were no free elections. In the fall of 1945, Truman's new secretary of state, James Byrnes, tried at two international meetings to influence Soviet treatment of Poland, Rumania, Bulgaria, and Hungary, but with no success. By March 1946, Winston Churchill announced the arrival of a Cold War in a speech at Fulton, Missouri, and Harry Truman introduced him. The policy distance between President and Prime Minister which Roosevelt had maintained had narrowed with changed circumstances and different American leadership.

Prospects of a loan to the Russians gradually evaporated. Atomic secrets were offered to the world in an American proposal offered in 1946, but in a form that required inspection of Soviet defense facilities and internal economic affairs, making it unacceptable. The future of Germany was never really negotiated between the Allies, and soon the Western allies began to rebuild German economic strength. The Grand Alliance was shattered and replaced by hostility, declarations of ideological war, and an arms race that stretches into tomorrow.

In accounting for this turn of events, American scholars have faced an obvious handicap. They have not had access to Soviet archives or leaders, and cannot do more than guess at that side of the story. American leadership has thus borne the full thrust of scholarly curiosity, appraisal, and criticism. Truman has taken most of it, for most decisions were his to make, and undeniably his policies did not achieve American ends of peace, tranquillity, and an open world. Stern talk, the loan refusal, and possession of the bomb—none of these made the Soviets malleable. They did not withdraw from Eastern Europe, did not allow free elections in Poland, probed for a foothold in Iran, and wrangled in the United Nations. Therefore, Harry Truman was criticized, often bitterly, and from all sides. To his Right, Republicans and conservative publicists argued that he had been too "soft" on the Russians. Presumably he should either have been sterner sooner or perhaps have launched some kind of preemptive war to settle affairs prior to the Soviet acquisition of nuclear capacity in 1949. Criticism of this sort hurt Truman politically during his presidency, and reinforced his tendency to distrust and dislike the Soviets and to continue to talk tough to them.

The passage of time, however, has seen most historians take on a new perspective concerning these events. Scholars rarely criticize Truman anymore (some did in the 1950s) for not being "tough" enough. They know that public opinion was in a demobilizing mood, that apart from the practical difficulties of using force against a former ally there was the moral necessity to give the Soviets a chance to convincingly demonstrate their contempt for the principles of the Atlantic Charter. Many scholars now argue, in fact, that Truman was too tough too soon, reversing FDR's conciliatory policies and replacing them with an aggressive American interference in the Soviet sphere of influence.

This view was widely expressed in the postwar era, at least on the Left. Henry A. Wallace was forced from his post as secretary of commerce for making a speech criticizing Truman's foreign policy as being too bellicose in late 1946. Many people at that time shared Fiorello La Guardia's sentiment when he said in 1947: "How we miss him [FDR]! Hardly a domestic problem or an international situation today but what we say, 'Oh, if FDR were only here!' " There were enough such people, convinced that Truman reversed Roosevelt's policies, to generate the Progressive party effort of 1948 with Wallace as presidential candidate.

The argument that Truman "reversed" FDR's policies is pushed too hard when that verb is used. For one thing, there simply can never be agreement on what Roosevelt's policies actually were. Robert Divine, in his *Roosevelt and World War II* (1969), provides equally persuasive chapters on FDR as realist and pragmatist, isolationist and interventionist. A spheres-of-influence thinker upon occasion, Roosevelt was the mover behind the Atlantic Charter. He agreed with Stalin that there should not be unfriendly governments on the Soviet border, then described the Yalta conference to Congress as spelling "the end of the system of unilateral action, the exclusive alliances, the spheres of influence . . . and all the other expedients that have been tried for centuries—and have always failed."

Would he have finally chosen a conciliatory policy? The evidence may not be evenly mixed, but it *is* mixed. It is frequently pointed out that FDR became irritated with Stalin in the last weeks of his life. He cabled the Russian dictator just days before he died:

> You must believe me when I tell you that our people at home look with a critical eye on what they consider a disagreement between us at this vital stage of the war.

On April 5, 1945, when Stalin had complained about American secret negotiations with the Germans in Switzerland and had not been satisfied with Roosevelt's assurances that no separate surrender was contemplated, Roosevelt cabled in exasperation:

> It would be one of the greatest tragedies in history if at the very moment of victory now within our grasp such distrust and such lack of faith should prejudice the entire undertaking after the colossal losses of life and material and treasure involved.

And on April 6, less than a week before he died, the President dictated this message to Churchill:

> We must not permit anybody to entertain a false impression that we are afraid. Our armies will in a very few days be in a position that will permit us to become "tougher" than has heretofore appeared advantageous to the war effort.

One report tells of the President pounding the arm of his chair just a few days before he died, exclaiming that Stalin was not living up to his promises.

Those who would find Truman guilty of a sharp alteration in policy must, then, reckon with the ambiguities of Roosevelt's record. There was a marked difference in the two men's diplomatic style and in their attitudes toward the Russians, but it was not quite as sharp as some have made out. We cannot say that Roosevelt had an endless tolerance for any tactics the Soviets thought appropriate as they consolidated their influence over areas admittedly critical to their security. All we may say is that he very much hoped to arrange the unpleasant fact of an expanded Soviet sphere of influence in terms that could be made tolerable to the American commitment to self-determination, and to politically active American minority groups. Despite misgivings arising out of the Soviet handling of Poland, FDR remained hopeful. He told journalist Edgar Snow, in early April 1945, of his "absolute conviction of his ability to get along with the Russians," and cabled Churchill that they should "minimize the general Soviet problem as much as possible because these problems in one form or another seem to arise every day and most of them straighten out." Most of them do. Yet even Roosevelt allowed for the possibility that some conflicts could not be smoothed over.

Apart from the complexity of Roosevelt's own attitudes, there are other

1945: The United States, Russia, and the Cold War—What If Franklin Roosevelt Had Lived?

151

reasons to qualify the sharp impression of a Truman shift in basic policy. Truman happened to be in charge of foreign policy as the war ended, and the threat of common enemies which had united dissimilar allies was removed. This inevitable development would have unleashed many suppressed conflicts within the alliance no matter who governed. Basic policy-making institutions around the President would have exerted the same anti-Soviet influence. State Department and military advice to the executive invariably counseled caution and hard bargaining for geographical and economic advantage. The same State Department that, in June 1945, prepared an alarming report for Truman on the dangers of international and domestic communism, would have prepared it for Roosevelt. Truman's only contribution here was perhaps to read such reports with more credulity than his predecessor did, but the steady advice of the entire national security apparatus could not simply be ignored by any President. Would not Roosevelt be moved by Averill Harriman's alarmed report, which he made to Truman in late April, that Europe was faced by "a barbarian invasion"? Also, some influence toward an open-door policy in Europe would necessarily be exerted by the economic circumstances of demobilizing America.

In 1945 the Great Depression was only five years in the past, and the problems of excess capacity which were at the root of the depression were made worse by the plant and agricultural expansion of wartime. Writers such as William Appleman Williams and Gabriel Kolko have not allowed us to forget how many American policy-makers, businessmen, and publicists were fearful of a postwar depression and saw economic expansion abroad as the only remedy. Expansionism meant conflict with Soviet exclusionary policies in those parts of Europe that had fallen behind their armies.

There would be other potent influences working in the end-of-war transition period to press American policy away from the concessions that Roosevelt wanted to give to Stalin. Reactionary moods seem invariably to follow hard upon America's wars, and a strengthened American Right would surely attack a foreign policy that seemed in any way cordial to the heartland of world socialism. The American Left was in no position to offer comparable pressure the other way. American communists were insignificant in numbers and influence, American socialists were little better off, and liberals had been politically on the defensive since the late 1930s. FDR's conciliatory policy toward the Soviets, if he had truly pursued it, would have divided the liberals anyway. Among them the ideas of Wilsonian internationalism were deeply rooted. The world should be open to trade and to the movement of peoples, goods, and ideas. Closed, autarchical systems and regions bred war and depression. FDR's anticolonialism sat well with everyone on the Left, but concessions required to nourish the Soviet friendship would have to be sold to a liberal community now more universalist than isolationist.

We must note at least one other major factor in the post–April 12, 1945, situation that would have pushed Roosevelt, had he lived, toward the "tough" line that Truman took: this was the nature of the Soviet system. A President who wanted to concede the buffer zone of Eastern European states to Soviet domination, grant reconstruction loans, and share atomic secrets would be seriously embarrassed by certain hard realities that no Iron Curtain could entirely mask. Stalinism was totalitarianism with an ugly face turned toward dissent, discussion, civil liberties, and parliamentary democracy. It was difficult to make the Stalinist regime appear attractive or "progressive." In fact, it was neither. In the border states where the Russians now exercised control, there was naturally a strong anti-Russian, nationalistic sentiment that broke through constantly, reminding outsiders of the harsh realities of Russian influence. Roosevelt may have wanted to sustain the Soviet-American alliance, but it would be impossible for him or anyone else to disguise the fact that the Stalin regime was a repellent tyranny at home, and was officially dedicated to the overthrow of capitalism abroad. Even if the Soviet State had been entirely satisfied with control of the belt of buffer nations along its border and had no further territorial ambitions, as most historians believe to be the case after the war, an American President pursuing a policy of what is today called détente would be severely taxed with charges of amorality for condoning such recent conquests by a society so hostile to freedom.

How much could a healthy FDR have done to mitigate conflicts built so deeply into the internal and external circumstances of the two great powers? Whether Russian conduct might have been significantly altered by a different approach we cannot know nor even reasonably speculate about. For the American side, a different approach is conceivable even though the odds do seem to be rather against it. What might such a Rooseveltian policy have been? How might one have explored the possibilities of what he called "generosity"?

According to revisionist scholars, Truman's errors were principally three in number. In Eastern Europe, where vital Soviet security was clearly at stake and no vital American interest was present, our policy should have been, in essence: Hands Off. Finland, Estonia, Latvia, Lithuania, Poland, Hungary, Rumania, and Bulgaria all should have been left to seek the best terms they could get from the conqueror—somewhat as was expected of Mexico, Cuba, and other Caribbean republics more or less obliged to operate within limits acceptable to the United States.

There is evidence, as we know, that Roosevelt understood these basic terms but hoped that, in frankly conceding them and in further reinforcing Soviet security by loans and perhaps a mutual security pact, he could obtain from Stalin some cosmetic concessions. Russian interference in Polish

1945: The United States, Russia, and the Cold War—What If Franklin Roosevelt Had Lived?

153

politics would hopefully be as discreet as possible, with occasional declarations of democratic intent to ease the anger of Polish-Americans. If this is what FDR hoped to arrange, it is not entirely far-fetched. In 1945–46, Russian policies in Eastern Europe do appear to have been flexible. In Poland and Rumania, Soviet rule was brutal and unyielding from the start, permitting no exercise of democratic politics; but in Hungary, relatively free elections were held, Bulgaria and Finland were allowed a substantial degree of independence, and Czechoslovakia of course had a pro-Western regime until the coup of 1948. This degree of flexibility Roosevelt hoped to encourage.

One way to do so was to have altered another of Truman's policies and grant an early loan. William Appleman Williams, in his *The Tragedy of American Diplomacy* (1959), sees economic aid as the central American instrument for moderating Soviet postwar diplomacy. He points out correctly that Roosevelt, while on record in favor of a loan, never set any machinery in motion for drafting a loan agreement. He delayed the decision, in effect agreeing with those who thought that a loan ought to be used as a *quid pro quo* to loosen up the Soviet hold on Eastern Europe. This is of course the path Truman chose, and it seems to have intensified Russian fears and widened the breach. Certainly no concessions were forthcoming. Without firm evidence either way, we may allow for a reasonable possibility that Roosevelt, pressed by Molotov for a loan in the spring of 1945, would have seen that the logic of his generous policy required a loan without strings—such as was offered to the British and French—and would have requested aid from Congress.

Roosevelt, to be consistent, would have also had to pursue a different policy on atomic energy from the one Truman selected. That the bomb would have a major impact upon international relations had been clear to everyone who knew of the Manhattan Project. As Henry Stimson, secretary of war, wrote to Truman in April 1945: "The question of sharing it with other nations and, if so shared, upon what terms, becomes a primary question of our foreign relations." Yet no one knew just how to cope with the bomb's influence should it prove as devastating as anticipated. On July 16, the bomb went off in New Mexico, and Truman went to Potsdam heartened by the new sense of power the weapon gave him but unsure just how to wield that power. He never found a way to use the bomb to intimidate the Russians, and never did so, despite the arguments of P. M. S. Blackett and Gar Alperovitz that this was much on his mind. Yet they are right that possession of the bomb encouraged the Truman administration to hope for some concessions from the Russians, and to take a somewhat firmer stand than would have been the case had American power rested only upon an army in Europe that was eager to come home.

But even if the bomb were not used, or not even "rattled" at the Soviets on any identifiable occasion, its technology remained an Anglo-American secret and the decision not to share this information was having a major impact upon Soviet-American relations while Roosevelt and then Truman thought the matter over. They knew there were risks either way. Roosevelt's intentions here are characteristically clouded. He had "briefly seemed all but persuaded," writes Herbert Feis, "to inform the Russians what we had accomplished before the bomb was demonstrated and used. . . . But Churchill had rejected this course as naive; naive because it would nullify this great weapon. . . . In September 1944 Roosevelt had abruptly changed his mind and agreed with Churchill that no knowledge about the atomic bomb project should be disclosed before a permanent policy was determined."

Two scholars have recently argued that FDR's policy on atomic energy should not be seen as one of holding the sharing option open, but of virtually closing it by deferring decision. Martin Sherwin, in *A World Destroyed* (1975), and Barton Bernstein, in an article in *Political Science Quarterly* (1975), have both pointed out that while FDR appeared to agree with Bohr and others that only sharing would head off an arms race, he did nothing to implement this view. No study group was set up to prepare recommendations for sharing atomic information, so that when FDR died the policy he left Truman was not understood to be one of open options but of *de facto* retention of the American monopoly.

These arguments are persuasive, but their force is mainly to explain why Truman decided to continue the monopoly until the extremely guarded Baruch Plan of 1946. They do not prove that FDR would have so acted. The time for his decision was at hand in the spring of 1945. If we assume a larger Rooseveltian policy choice of "generosity" to assuage Soviet security fears, a decision to share atomic secrets without a *"quid pro quo"* might well have been reached in mid- or late 1945. Indications are that a decision one way or the other would have been made that early, for FDR agreed with Stimson on March 15 that he would have to opt for either internationalization or American monopoly before the bomb was used.

What this decision may have been we can only conjecture. But the advice that he share the secrets was there in official circles if he had wished to follow it. Truman, who did not know of the bomb until he became President, at once convened an Interim Committee on Atomic Energy under Henry Stimson. The President had only four months in which to make up his mind about its wartime and postwar use. Some of the committee members— urged on by a panel of atomic scientists they had invited to help—suggested some sort of opening to the Soviets at once. This was in May 1945. But General Leslie Groves, head of the Manhattan Project, authoritatively predicted that the Russians were 20 years away from making a bomb of their own, and the President's special representative, James Byrnes, was able to persuade the committee not to recommend any immediate move toward sharing the secret. The alarmed panel of scientists pressed Stimson, and

1945: The United States, Russia, and the Cold War—What If Franklin Roosevelt Had Lived?

155

with Vannevar Bush and James Conant in support, Stimson got the committee to reverse itself in late June and urge Truman to tell Stalin about the bomb before it was dropped. This Truman did at Potsdam, in the briefest comment. But the idea of also discussing international control with the Russians had not been able to penetrate from the atomic scientists through to the inner circle around Truman. And time had run out. The bomb was dropped on August 4 at Hiroshima, and the Russians had to conclude that American policy was that of scientific and technological monopoly. It did not require paranoia to suspect that this weapon, concealed by one ally from the other, might be expected to intrude into their postwar relations.

At this point Stimson, despite age and fatigue, roused himself to see if there might yet be time to avert an arms race, and before relations became "irretrievably embittered." He had been anxiously pondering the future of the world in connection with the atomic bomb for many months, but until late summer had resisted Bush's and Conant's advice to move "directly to international pooling of all scientific research and an interchange of everything susceptible of military use." It seemed to Stimson, at least until late August, that it was "advisable to wait until we had gotten all we could from Russia in the way of liberalization in exchange." This was the familiar *"quid pro quo"* strategy, a rival to the "generosity" strategy.

The two blasts in Japan changed Stimson's mind. On September 11, the secretary of war sent Truman a memorandum recommending a striking policy risk:

> . . . unless the Soviets are voluntarily invited into the partnership upon a basis of cooperation and trust, we are going to maintain the Anglo-Saxon bloc over against the Soviet in the possession of this weapon. Such a condition will almost certainly stimulate feverish activity on the part of the Soviet toward the development of this bomb in what will in effect be a secret armament race of a rather desperate character. . . .
>
> Whether Russia gets control of the necessary secrets of production in a minimum of say four years or a maximum of twenty years is not nearly as important . . . as to make sure that when they do get it they are willing and cooperative partners among the peace-loving nations of the world. . . .
>
> For if we fail to approach them now and merely continue to negotiate with them, having this weapon rather ostentatiously on our hip, their suspicions and their distrust of our purposes and motives will increase.

Stimson did not ask that the secret of the bomb simply be handed to the Russians, but that discussions at once begin on arrangements to control the use and production of atomic weapons and explore peaceful uses of atomic energy. This was not so risky as it might have seemed. An agreement not to make any more bombs would freeze the situation, with the United States and Britain in possession of the weapon and Russia without it—even if ours were impounded under some international arrangement.

Stimson raised his proposal with the cabinet on September 21 at Truman's invitation, and the cabinet split. Representatives from the State and War Departments, Commerce Secretary Henry Wallace, and others—seven in all—supported Stimson. Secretary of the Navy James Forrestal headed a group of about equal number who favored delay or expressed firm opposition to sharing anything with the Russians. The President could have decided either way without a crisis within his administration, although the public, judging by the crude polls of the day, was not favorable to the general idea of sharing. At the least, Truman could have opened negotiations with the Russians in October, and worked to educate and reassure the public that he was being prudent and that the risks were actually greater along the apparently safe but very short path of continued monopoly.

An opening of this sort to the Soviets may or may not have mellowed their diplomacy, if taken in combination with a different position on loans and on Eastern Europe. Of course, all three of these policies would have had to survive congressional scrutiny, and senior men in Congress tended to be anti-Soviet and to instinctively regard generosity in foreign affairs as a sign of weakness. But as with loans, the road to some sort of sharing of atomic secrets was open in 1945, at least for a few steps into the dark. FDR expressed agreement with advisors who advocated going down that road, and put off his decision. Harry Truman had to decide, and did so. After the cabinet meeting, he read a memo from Vannevar Bush which urged international collaboration in the atomic-energy field, and another from the Joint Chiefs of Staff opposing it. His first move was to ask Congress on October 3 for a law retaining domestic control by the government over atomic energy—under a new agency, the Atomic Energy Commission. Secrets might be shared with American private enterprise, but only the government would be allowed "to produce or use the substances comprising the sources of atomic energy."

But what would be shared with the Russians? In the same message, Truman expressed fear of an arms race, a desire to reach international agreement to ban the use of the bomb, and the intention to begin talks with Great Britain and Canada, "and then with other nations," leading to a time when "cooperation might replace rivalry in the field of atomic power." Upon subsequent questioning, he made it clear that when "sharing" took place it would involve only scientific information, not the technology of producing the bomb itself.

The decision, then, was to go slow, to wait until the political picture was clarified abroad and at home, and thus to leave the American monopoly of the bomb hanging in the diplomatic air, regardless of whatever poison it injected into Soviet-American relations. "It was against this slower but presumably safer order," writes Herbert Feis, "that Stimson had warned in

1945: The United States, Russia, and the Cold War—What If Franklin Roosevelt Had Lived?

157

his notable memo." Truman moved ahead cautiously with an initiative to get international control of atomic weapons. But after preliminary work, the American plan was entrusted to the 76-year-old millionaire financier Bernard Baruch, in the hope that his appointment would ease conservative anxieties. The conservatives were pleased, for Baruch the capitalist proved hostile to any proposal for sharing secrets with communists if the proposal rested in any way upon "trust." His June 14, 1946, speech to the UN offered a plan that included international investigations of Soviet natural resources and the mapping of their interior, while setting aside the veto in the Security Council. All atomic research would cease, leaving the American monopoly secure while the stages of atomic disarmament proceeded slowly.

The Russians countered with an equally unacceptable plan—immediate sharing of atomic secrets and atomic disarmament, *followed* by work on appropriate controls. There had been slim chances for internationalization of atomic energy in 1946 in any case and, with the Baruch proposal and the Russian counter, any such chances evaporated. There was to be no cooperation on atomic energy, and the arms race that Henry Stimson had dreaded was to run on without check or hindrance.

Let us draw together the strands of a Rooseveltian alternative policy which might have led to outcomes less harsh than the intense international rivalry of the Cold War. A healthy Franklin Roosevelt, 63 years old in 1945, finds time running out on his temporizing style when he returns from a Warm Springs vacation in mid-April. German armies are falling back, the European war will be over in May, and victory over the Japanese is not far off. He decides to follow those conciliatory instincts that had shaped his relations with the Russians ever since Hitler struck into the Soviet Union. The President asks Congress in the spring or summer of 1945 to extend a reconstruction loan to the Russians. He agrees with Stimson and the atomic scientists, and opens talks with the Soviets on a scheme for control of atomic weapons and for international sharing of technology. All these issues are difficult to negotiate in detail and progress is slow. But the multiple evidence of American goodwill eases Soviet security fears. Stalin, reassured privately by FDR that the Yalta accords really did imply dominant Soviet influence in Eastern Europe but reminded also of Roosevelt's domestic political situation and the need for moderation, manages Polish affairs more cosmetically. More notice is taken of Russian liberality in Hungary and Czechoslovakia.

The President is told by State and War Department advisors that he is making a serious mistake in "appeasing" the Soviets regarding control of Polish, East German, and Rumanian political and economic life. He avoids

Harriman, Forrestal, Leahy, and the other hard-liners, and talks instead with men of more conciliatory view—Wallace, Hopkins, General George Marshall, and journalist Walter Lippmann. The President's policies encounter stiff domestic opposition from conservative congressmen and publicists. But he rallies the Left. A resumption of New Deal reforms reinforces a foreign policy based upon conciliation with the Soviet Union, opposition to military spending and military advice, and independence from British and French efforts to restore subservient regimes in Greece or Asia. The election of 1946 turns more clearly upon the President's liberal leadership, and returns a working majority of legislators who have generally lined up with him. A touch of isolationism in the national mind is helpful here. What Roosevelt wants is for the public basically to forget Poland and Rumania, as cynical as this sounds. Apart from Polish- and Rumanian-Americans, most people are quite ready to follow their natural inclinations and to forget about Eastern Europe. When the "Greek crisis" comes in early 1947, and the British announce that the corrupt monarchy will fall to armed insurgency without American aid, there is no Truman Doctrine, no Roosevelt Doctrine. The new Greek government, which includes a minority of communists, is recognized by the United States.

Let us stretch our imaginations just one step beyond. The American foreign-service officers who urge a United States swing toward the Maoists in China—John Carter Vincent, John Stewart Service, John Paton Davies, and others—find FDR receptive. He had always sympathized with popular movements for liberation from colonial rule—including the revolution led by Ho Chi Minh in Indochina. When Roosevelt leaves the White House in January 1949, American China policy has detached itself from the ineffective and now fleeing Chiang regime and is neutral. Months later, diplomatic relations with Communist China are commenced.

This sketchy extrapolation of certain Rooseveltian policy inclinations may serve as an alternative future. It not only did not happen, it is by all calculations improbable. While elements of FDR's career and thought point in this direction, there is much that points toward the policies Truman adopted. There is, first of all, Roosevelt's character. He had always hedged his commitments and tried to find a middle way rather than a theoretically correct way. The policies we briefly sketched would require strong leadership and the acceptance of conflict. Most presidential advisors leaned toward a hard line; most senior congressmen, at least, were anti-Soviet at the marrow; and so were most newspaper publishers. Could these influential groups have been persuaded to back a policy that acquiesced to Soviet domination of most of Eastern Europe? Perhaps. There were other voices in the country that were ready to support such a policy. But this would require vigorous, sure-footed presidential leadership.

There must also be a Russian willingness to accept the territorial gains

1945: The United States, Russia, and the Cold War—What If Franklin Roosevelt Had Lived?

159

it had made in wartime, and to present a more approachable face to the West than the scowling one it directed toward the also-scowling Harry Truman. Stalin would have to disguise somewhat his determination to prevent anti-Soviet regimes on his border. He was afraid of Western economic contacts, as his regime could not survive much exposure to Western freedoms and the Russian economy would easily be dominated by American corporations. But minimal Western economic and cultural contacts would have to be tolerated for the Cold War to be avoided. What was ultimately required, on the Russian side, was a return to the relations with the West that had obtained in the latter half of the 1930s: some trade, diplomatic contacts, muted revolutionary fervor for the overthrow of capitalism, and instructions to communists everywhere to join "popular fronts" with liberal regimes to prevent the emergence of fascism in any industrial nation.

This seems an improbable combination of events, by all odds, though not strictly impossible, with Roosevelt on the scene to catalyze the elements of a different policy. Those who are skeptical will raise a host of objections. Indeed, their case seems irresistible after 1948. Even if Roosevelt had managed to sustain his "generous" policy by leading a new surge of reform sufficient to unify a Democratic party increasingly divided by the race issue, one can find no other politician with the gifts and the inclination to lead in this way after 1948. Harry Truman, Jimmy Byrnes, Baruch, and Harriman all represented the center of the Democratic party, and we know the policies they shaped. To their Right in the party was the reactionary Southern element, people like Senator Strom Thurmond, who split off in 1948 because he wanted Truman to stop being a liberal on the race question. Henry Wallace had Roosevelt's general orientation, perhaps even had a clearer vision of an alternative foreign policy, but surely lacked FDR's political skills and reputation. Roosevelt had not nurtured younger men as successors, not much wanting premature rivals. The Democrats, desperate in 1948 in the face of Truman's apparent unpopularity, even inquired whether General Eisenhower were a member of their party.

As for the Republicans, Wendell Willkie was dead, and every national leader they offered in 1948 was talking of the need for a tougher Soviet policy than even Truman had shaped. Truman's offensive against godless communism was too defensive for even moderate Republicans. A continuation of a Rooseveltian policy in 1949 would not come from that quarter. It seems an inescapable conclusion that Roosevelt would have had no successors, and that American policy would inevitably move toward the Right in 1949 even if he had been able to suppress, until that time, the deep social pressures toward a virulent anticommunism, economic expansionism, and the militarization of foreign policy.

We know that whenever the United States was ready for a Cold War—

perhaps even a bit before—the Russians were also ready with ideological hostility, willful misunderstanding, suspicion, rearmament, and dreams of expansion and victory. So the Cold War came, and probably the alternative was only a matter of different timing. Herbert Feis summarizes this best in a memorable passage from his *From Trust to Terror* (1970):

> History, continuing his ruminations, might well have asked the winds of time: "Can these countries, with such different visions and origins as I have allowed to shape in their hearts and minds, really settle their respective claims, adjust their respective visions, and maintain a lasting friendship?" To make this the more unlikely, on one lovely day in April 1945 he broke with the tip of his finger an artery in Franklin Roosevelt's brain.

SUGGESTED READINGS

Gar Alperovitz, *Atomic Diplomacy*, 1965

Richard J. Barnet and Marcus G. Raskin, *After 20 Years, Alternatives to the Cold War in Europe*, 1965

Barton J. Bernstein, "The Quest for Security: American Foreign Policy and International Control of Atomic Energy: 1942–1946," *Journal of American History 60*, March 1974

Barton J. Bernstein, "Roosevelt, Truman, and the Atomic Bomb: A Reinterpretation," *Political Science Quarterly 90*, Spring 1975

James M. Burns, *Roosevelt: Soldier of Freedom*, 1970

James L. Clayton, "The Fiscal Cost of the Cold War to the U.S.," *Western Political Quarterly*, September 1972

Diane S. Clemens, *Yalta*, 1970

Robert A. Divine, *Roosevelt and World War II*, 1969

Herbert Feis, *From Trust to Terror, The Onset of the Cold War: 1945–1950*, 1970

D. F. Fleming, *The Cold War and Its Origins 1917–1960*, vols. 1 and 2, 1961

John Lewis Gaddis, *The United States and the Origins of the Cold War: 1941–1947*, 1972

Lloyd C. Gardner, *Architects of Illusion, Men and Ideas in American Foreign Policy 1941–1949*, 1970

Charles Gati, ed., *Caging the Bear: Containment and the Cold War*, 1974

Richard J. Kirkendall, ed., Essays by Bernstein and Ferrell, *The Truman Period as a Research Field: A Reappraisal, 1972*, 1974

Gabriel Kolko, *The Politics of War*, 1968

Francis L. Loewenheim, et al., eds., *Roosevelt and Churchill: Their Secret Wartime Correspondence*, 1975

Curtis MacDougall, *Gideon's Army*, vol. 1, 1965

Elliott Roosevelt, *As He Saw It*, 1946

Martin J. Sherwin, *A World Destroyed: The Atomic Bomb and the Grand Alliance*, 1975

Edgar Snow, "Stalin Must Have Peace," *Saturday Evening Post*, 1 March 1947

Barbara W. Tuchman, "If Mao Had Come to Washington in 1945," *Foreign Affairs,*
    October 1972
Rexford G. Tugwell, *Off Course, From Truman to Nixon,* 1971
William Appleman Williams, *The Tragedy of American Diplomacy,* 1959

1963

The United States and Vietnam—What If John F. Kennedy Had Lived?

The assassin, or assassins, could easily have missed in Dallas and John Kennedy have lived to complete two terms. We recall that Franklin Roosevelt was fired upon in a motorcade in Miami, Florida, in December 1932, and only the fact that a woman jostled the gunman's arm prevented the President-elect from being killed. If John Kennedy had not been assassinated in November 1963, much would surely have been different in American life since that time. The mind runs to many possibilities had Kennedy served out two terms. Yet there has not been much serious discussion in print of his unfulfilled presidency. For this would be speculation! Only one aspect of Kennedy's unlived presidency, from 1963 to 1968, has attracted significant attention, and that is his probable course in Vietnam.

Nothing has pained the country so badly as that war. Estimates are always tentative and are periodically revised upward. The dollar cost of the war is beyond close calculation, given the bookkeeping of our national security expenditures. The United States Department of Commerce acknowledged in 1972—when the war was not yet over—that the total would probably reach $352 billion, when all veterans' benefits and interest charges were paid up in the middle of the next century. Let us take that as a low figure. Much larger is the $676 billion estimated by an economist writing in *The Progressive* in mid-1973.

Dollars are perhaps the least of it. More than 56,000 Americans were killed in action, and 300,000 more were injured. The deaths of

Vietnamese, both South and North, have not much concerned the American public, but they add another imprecise and staggering figure, perhaps as high as 2 million if one counts only those dead due to military action and not those due to war-related starvation and disease. Other costs etch themselves in the resistant surface of the public mind. Resources were squandered there that were desperately needed by humans somewhere—money and manpower expended for 8,000 aircraft that might have been spent for schools or clinics, for 100 million pounds of herbicides that might have been used for fertilizer, for 15 million tons of munitions that might have been earmarked for medicines or books, and for oceans of petroleum that one day the nation will begrudge most bitterly.

Of course, there were also the costs of social disruption, political turmoil, generation set against generation, and the damage done to the credibility of the national government and to the military itself, which have no units of measurement. Could all this have been avoided by any American decision or any different turn in American policy that was plausibly open to the poor mortals who charted our course? Many points along the winding road to Vietnam have been designated as points of turning. In Theodore Draper's book, *The Abuse of Power* (1967), there are five such points prior to direct intervention; they are: June 1950; October 1954; December 1961; November 1963; and February 1965.

Notice that two of these came in the presidency of John F. Kennedy. It was here, in a short 34-month period, that "the situation in southeast Asia" became critical in the eyes of American leaders. That is, the revolution began to succeed in South Vietnam and Laos, threatening communist control of much if not eventually all of what was formerly called Indochina. It was in these months of the early 1960s that the American role, through a series of presidential decisions, took on a new degree of involvement.

What makes the Kennedy period in Vietnam policy so intriguing is its ambivalence, not its decisiveness. It is true that America had 800 military "advisors" in Vietnam when Kennedy was inaugurated, and that the Southeast Asian country was certainly not at the top of the list of the government's foreign-policy concerns. Three years later, the absorption with Vietnam had sharply risen, aid was increased, and the 800 advisors had become 16,500; the country was dangerously on the verge of committing combat units. Decisions had obviously been made that deepened the American involvement on the mainland of Asia. Yet only later, under another President, would the most fateful decision be made and both American air and ground power be deployed in Vietnam. This would be done between late 1964 and early 1965 under Lyndon Johnson.

Kennedy had held back. Those who recall his record of thought and decision on Vietnam tell us that he had serious doubts that a deeper involvement was correct. One has the impression, in most accounts of the

Kennedy era, that real options remained alive. This is an impression that Lyndon Johnson never gave, even though he waited a year after taking office to formally make the decision to send ground forces. So it is the Kennedy era that attracts those who search for an understanding of the paths that somehow led to war in Asia, and for a glimpse of other roads that might have been taken.

Kennedy was elected, without having taken a firm position on Vietnam during the campaign (neither had his opponent, Nixon). The South Vietnamese army was holding its own against insurgents who were reputedly communist-led. Government forces outnumbered guerrillas by perhaps 10 to 1. The "good" Vietnamese were expected to win their war, given the level of American aid that had commenced in 1950 and greatly increased when the Geneva Accords partitioned Vietnam. It was Eisenhower's government that had decided to support Ngo Dinh Diem in building an independent, anticommunist South Vietnam. American aid comprised advisors and money—some $4 billion by 1960.

But the new President's first news from Vietnam was bad in 1961, and it was worse when he turned from official channels to read the reports of American news correspondents, who did not have the Pentagon's interest in glossing over the military and social weaknesses of the Diem regime. A special task force recommended in the spring of 1961 that Kennedy dispatch combat forces from the United States to stem a deteriorating military situation. Kennedy was wary, and also preoccupied with Cuba and with the more serious Asian insurgency in Laos. He sent Vice-President Lyndon Johnson on an inspection tour. Johnson returned full of enthusiasm for President Diem and the cause of the Saigon government. He recommended increased aid, but reported that Diem did not seem to want large American troop units at that time. Kennedy bought time with a small but significant enlargement of the American effort. He authorized 400 Special Forces troops, and ordered American-trained South Vietnamese units, to undertake clandestine sabotage and harassment inside North Vietnam. Both these steps were violations of the 1954 Geneva Accords, which the United States had not signed but promised to respect.

Through the rest of 1961, the top-level civilian and military advisors continued to supply the President with memos urging the commitment of American ground forces. The Joint Chiefs of Staff, we learn from *The Pentagon Papers,* secretly told Kennedy that 40,000 United States troops could clean up the Viet Cong threat. General Maxwell Taylor suggested 6,000–8,000 troops, and Defense Secretary Robert McNamara and Secretary of State Dean Rusk agreed. Nearly everyone who was an expert in these matters told the President that United States troops would be "a shot in the arm" for the South Vietnamese, transforming their army into a marvelous counterrevolutionary machine. *Nearly* everyone. The intelligence community continued to provide memos reeking with skepticism about the Diem government, the impact of American troops, and the prospects for any kind of military victory by the American-Saigon coalition against a revolutionary enemy with a broad popular base.

The Viet Cong continued to gain strength in the South, operating in larger units, and by 1963 tripled the level of their attack over the summer and seized a provincial capital just 55 miles from Saigon in September. The Diem government was shaken and now talked of a defense treaty with the United States and the early landing of American troops. To appraise the crisis and gain time, Kennedy sent General Taylor and the hawkish State Department economist Walt Rostow to Saigon in October. They returned in a mood of spirited resistance, urging that the American role be shifted "from advice to limited partnership," and Taylor specified the figure of 6,000–8,000 American combat troops as meeting the need quite adequately.

Secretaries McNamara and Rusk, while agreeing with Taylor, worked out for Kennedy a way to broaden the American commitment in the late-1961 crisis without quite taking the critical step of direct combat involvement. Kennedy sent a letter to Diem in December, affirming the promise of American support and increasing all forms of aid. Kennedy tried to combine military support with political measures, since it was dimly understood inside American councils that the war had an important political dimension. The South Vietnamese government must somehow earn the loyalty of its own people—as apparently it had not. Kennedy was to say in his second State of the Union Address (with reference to Laos):

> . . . no one nation has the power or the wisdom to solve all the problems of the world or manage its revolutionary ideas; . . . extending our commitments does not always increase our security. . . . No free peoples can be kept free without will and energy of their own.

His strategy thus became one of escalating the American commitment of aid and advisors, while pressing Diem to institute reforms in landholding and political life, which Americans decided were the key to South Vietnamese viability against the communists. Kennedy would hold to this strategy during the 34 months of his presidency, trying to combine a military and a political emphasis in some effective mixture. At this point, the only division among his advisors was over this mix. A small minority, usually looking to Under Secretary of State Averill Harriman for leadership, thought the war primarily a political struggle and urged a politically renovated Saigon government as the main element of resistance to local revolution.

Kennedy seems to have understood the argument that land reform, broadened public participation in South Vietnamese government, and an end to official corruption would be useful in reducing the communist appeal. American cables often urged such things on the reactionary and aloof Diem government. Yet most of the American stress always fell upon military measures, since a great majority of Kennedy's advisors were either military men or people who shared their general outlook. Military measures were obviously required, since the enemy had taken up arms and, anyway, it was far easier to get the South Vietnamese army to follow American advice on tactics than to push the civilian government an inch toward what Americans thought would be an attractive democratic image in the eyes of the peasants.

The Kennedy strategy—if that is not too strong a word for a course of policy adopted so incrementally and without a clear statement of objectives—came under mounting pressure. The war continued to go badly for the South Vietnamese official forces. Another crisis came in mid-1963, again brought on by political as well as military weakness in Saigon. The Diem government was losing control of the countryside, and Buddhists, students, and other political opponents of Diem became increasingly active despite government repression. Diem was eventually ousted and killed by rebellious elements of his own army, a coup that was "authorized, sanctioned, and encouraged" by the United States, in the words of the Pentagon's own history of these events.

This was early in November 1963, the month of Kennedy's own death. As the situation in Vietnam deteriorated, the President was frequently pressed to clarify American policy, and to indicate what the future might hold if the South Vietnamese continued to weaken. In a television interview in September, he spoke with what seemed a revealing candor:

> In the first analysis, it is their war. They are the ones who have to win it or lose it. We can help them, we can give them equipment, we can send our men out there as advisers, but they have to win it, the people of Vietnam.

And in the hearing of his aides, Kennedy expressed frank skepticism about the habit of sending more and more Americans to stiffen the backs of the South Vietnamese: "It's like taking a drink. The effect wears off, and you have to take another."

His most extensive comment in a skeptical vein, this one actually promising to disengage, is reported by aide Kenneth O'Donnell. In the spring of 1963, after Senator Mike Mansfield had advised the President to stay out of Asian wars, O'Donnell reports that:

> the President told Mansfield . . . that he now agreed with . . . the need for a complete military withdrawal from Vietnam. "But I can't do it until 1965—after I'm re-elected," Kennedy told Mansfield . . . [or] there would be a wild conservative outcry. . . . After his re-election he would take the risk of unpopularity and make a complete withdrawal of American forces from Vietnam.

Some are dubious about this exchange, since it was reported in 1970 by a loyal friend who obviously would prefer to detach his chief from the disaster of Vietnam. But Mansfield has confirmed the general accuracy of the exchange, and perhaps he has not a similar interest in putting Kennedy in the best light.

Such comments have been the stuff upon which many analysts have built the possibility—and it can be no more than that—that John Kennedy would not have taken the final step to direct military involvement in Vietnam, and would instead have withdrawn. He was known to doubt the internal strength of the South Vietnamese regime and ruling classes, he had watched the French bled by a ground war against aroused Asian peasants, and he had a deep suspicion of the advice he got from his own military advisors ever since the CIA-Pentagon sponsored fiasco at the Bay of Pigs, Cuba, in 1961. He was flexible, intelligent, and young. Admittedly a cold warrior at the beginning of his presidency, he had been frightened by the Cuban missile crisis in 1962, and had made an important speech at American University in June 1963, signalling a new American interest in the lowering of Cold War tensions. When he went to Dallas in November he was on a political tour, and as his speeches carried more talk of world peace, he had been buoyed up by the rising enthusiasm of the crowds. Some have argued that Kennedy and the country were moving together, in 1963, toward a more peace-oriented and less militant American foreign policy. Perhaps, had he not been killed, he would have resisted the pressures for intervention that the older and more impetuous man, Lyndon Johnson, yielded to in 1964–65.

This speculation has engaged many students of the Kennedy and Vietnam problem. But none have followed it out very far. Let us look at Kennedy's options had he come back from Dallas and been reelected in 1964—a very strong possibility, considering not only his own political gifts but the stubborn habit of twentieth-century Americans of reelecting their Presidents to second terms no matter what they do.

We may compress Kennedy's choices down to basically three. The first alternative was the one he chose, and it was running out to its end. This was to continue economic aid and military advice, raising the levels of support as the communists gained, and to press hard for internal reforms even though it did little good. The line would be drawn short of direct military involvement by American combat forces.

Time was running out on this strategy because the revolution in Vietnam was succeeding. The Viet Cong, with assistance from the North, were beating the Saigon forces in the field and besting them in the political struggle for control of villages and provinces outside the capital. In 1964 or 1965, Kennedy would have stood where Lyndon Johnson eventually stood, hearing from his intelligence sources that the collapse of South Vietnam was imminent, and that a part of the "Free World" was about to swing into "the Red orbit." This would be described as a resounding victory for North Vietnamese communism, for the Chinese doctrine of guerrilla warfare, for world communism, and for lawless aggression.

1963: The United States and Vietnam — What If John F. Kennedy Had Lived?

169

At that point, two other broad options would remain. Kennedy could then allow it all to happen, refusing to step over the line to military engagement in Asia, as Truman had decided against it in 1947–48 when China went communist, and as Eisenhower had decided in 1954–55 when the French surrendered at Dienbienphu.

Or he could have staved off that horrible result by direct American military intervention. Within this latter option, there would have been any number of variations. The United States could join the war on an unlimited basis, with full ground and air power, including nuclear weapons perhaps, "bombed them to the Stone Age," and "come home." Or at least one could have tried that strategy, so appealing to the American with his affection for quick solutions. Senator Goldwater, or so his speeches indicated, would probably have done so.

At the other extreme, the American military involvement could have been limited to holding enclaves around urban areas in contact with the sea, and accepting a stalemated military situation with a long, tedious search for a negotiated diplomatic solution. In between these two would have been a vigorous ground effort to destroy the Viet Cong everywhere in the South, but an effort limited to conventional weapons employed within the borders of South Vietnam itself or carefully applied against the North.

The latter was Lyndon Johnson's choice within the war framework. It ruined him, and almost ruined the country (incidentally, it ruined much of South and North Vietnam, especially as continued and intensified by Nixon). Could Kennedy, if he had lived, have chosen differently and brought another result? Choosing different methods of making war would have been one thing, and we shall look at the choices here in a moment. Could Kennedy have chosen not to intervene directly at all, but to let events take their course in Vietnam, permitting in the end a communist victory? Could he, that is, have chosen the path so quietly accepted in 1974 by Gerald Ford, of "letting" South Vietnam, Cambodia, and now Laos—all of old Indochina—come under communist regimes?

Events are very close, and anyone who writes of these matters is unavoidably touched by the passions of the era of Vietnam in American life (1961–74). Yet it is difficult to imagine that the passage of time will do other than confirm the conclusion that John F. Kennedy, living and presiding over American foreign policy until 1968, could not have chosen any option other than the road to war.

He may have been "young," meaning that at age 42 (in 1961) he was the youngest person ever to be President, but he was a tested veteran of American politics, since he had entered the House of Representatives in

1947. These were the beginning Cold War years, and Kennedy was at heart and without serious reservation a cold warrior. He regarded world communism as a deadly reality and the struggle against it as the highest calling for American statesmanship. He campaigned vigorously in 1960 for a firmer line in national-security affairs, for closing the missile gap, for taking the offensive in the struggle for the hearts and minds of men, and for other ideas of similar trumpeting resonance.

Communism in Southeast Asia was to him, as to virtually everyone in public life in 1961, just one leg of the worldwide elephant. It was a "challenge" to be met by "Free World" leaders with the tested tools forged since the Second World War—military containment at every point of contact with the communist world, eternal vigilance, military superiority, and readiness to die for freedom. As a young man, Kennedy had absorbed the apparent lesson of Munich, that aggressors are deterred only by counterforce. He had written his first book to shame appeasement. When asked about the "domino theory" under which Eisenhower had operated, which held that each and every territorial advance of the communist system tended to add to the strength of world communism, Kennedy responded vigorously: "I believe it. I believe it."

Retrospect has somehow obscured the intensity of John Kennedy's anticommunism. He did work for and sign a treaty with the Soviet Union banning atmospheric testing, he did make the conciliatory, peace-oriented American University speech, and he showed every outward sign during his lifetime of being a man who was open to new perspectives and was not afraid to change his mind. Some people actually thought him "soft on communism," but this was mainly because he was a liberal Democrat. Remembering that there were people who held that view, it is a small shock to review the films made of Kennedy at Berlin, or to reread his campaign speeches and presidential addresses dealing with world affairs. The famous Inaugural Address, read today, has a harshness and bellicosity of tone that was not much remarked on in 1961 because most intelligent people thought and felt in just this way. The address, indeed, was entirely directed to the world situation, and contained nothing in it of domestic issues:

> Let the word go forth from this time and place, to friend and foe alike, that the torch has been passed to a new generation of Americans, born in this century, tempered by war, disciplined by a hard and bitter peace, proud of our ancient heritage, and unwilling to witness or permit the slow undoing of those human rights to which this nation has always been committed, and to which we are committed today at home and around the world.
>
> Let every nation know, whether it wishes us well or ill, that we shall pay any price, bear any burden, meet any hardship, support any friend, oppose any foe to assure the survival and the success of liberty.

Of course, he spoke in that address also of never fearing to negotiate, and of the need for "both sides" to curb the arms race and to cooperate. Still, the main images were combative; there were trumpets calling us "to . . . a long twilight struggle," against "the common enemies of man: tyranny, poverty, disease, and war itself." The order of these was not accidental. The first was tyranny—plainly, communism. And so the trumpet called us to "the role of defending freedom in its hour of maximum danger. . . ."

Daniel P. Moynihan, a Kennedy friend and administration official, has created a substitute Inaugural Address in his book *Coping* (1973), which sharply clarifies the Cold War ideological essence of the speech John Kennedy gave as he began his presidency. Moynihan's version, written ten years later when everybody's view of the world had changed—surely Kennedy's view would have changed, too, if he had lived—is almost hilarious:

> . . . Let every country know that we would be crazy to pay any price, bear any burden, meet any hardship, support any friend, oppose any foe to assure the survival and success of liberty. This will be especially so in countries which we haven't dealt with much. . . . Small countries attacked by big countries should go to the United Nations. When that fails they should try to get the best terms they can. The more the Communist hegemonies expand, absorbing dissident nationalisms, the more internal trouble they will have, and they are welcome to it.

But this, of course, was unthinkable, and if it had been thought of in 1961 by some speechwriter doing drafts of the Inaugural Address, it would not have been regarded as funny—even on the New Frontier, where wit was highly prized. In addition to Kennedy's vigorous and traditional view of the world struggle between the free and communist worlds, we must remember the circumstances behind his coming to power. For our purposes, these include the history of his party on the communist issue, the narrowness of his election and political base, and the activist image of his candidacy which had contrasted so sharply—and so favorably—with the tired Eisenhower administration.

The first of these takes us back to the late 1940s and early 1950s, a good decade before Kennedy's crucial decisions on Vietnam. Yet this was a time when he, his secretary of state Dean Rusk, his Vice-President Lyndon Johnson, indeed, every Democrat who would exercise influence in the Kennedy administration, had been busy learning what happened to a Democratic administration that permitted a foreign country to "fall" to communism. Harry Truman had tried to avert a communist takeover of China through aid to another faltering conservative regime. But Truman and his astute secretary of state, Dean Acheson, finally decided that nothing more could be done about the collapse of Chiang Kai-shek's nationalist regime in China and had stood aside as the communists led by Mao Tse-tung took over. This was in 1948–49.

By 1950 one Senator Joseph McCarthy had taken the lead in pounding the Truman government for weakness and appeasement. Acheson's lucid testimony on the dangers of any course of action other than the one they chose, which one might call acquiescence in the inevitable after years of economic and military aid, seemed to convince almost none of the angry senators who interrogated him or the newspapers who howled for his repudiation. Acheson's reputation was smirched, Truman was criticized and harassed, and the Democrats suffered the unforgettable stigma of being labeled "soft on communism." It did not help that the late 1940s had seen many charges of communist infiltration of various Democratic administrations reaching back to the New Deal.

Few Democrats would ever forget the political punishment they took in the McCarthy era.* Nor, by the way, would foreign-service officers and others whose livelihood came from government employment in the area of foreign relations. Because they advised a path of accommodation with the Red Chinese, several distinguished diplomatic careerists—John Paton Davies, John Carter Vincent, O. Edmund Clubb, and John Stewart Service—were driven from their jobs and blacklisted. "It was a particularly dark chapter in American life," wrote David Halberstam about the McCarthy era and its narrowing of American imagination and of the boundaries of permissible discussion; "Our foreign policy had become locked into an all-encompassing blind and total anti-communism." Two institutions especially, Halberstam points out, "the Democratic Party and the Department of State—[were] damaged beyond easy repair." People in both institutions learned that they must never again show "weakness," or else howlers from the Right would drive them from power as they had in 1952.

This had all taken place ten years before Kennedy came into office by one of the narrowest margins in American presidential elections. He had no strong mandate, and a conservative Republican had very nearly beaten him. The lessons to be drawn were obvious. Kennedy must be vigilant lest he be outflanked from the Right, where half the voters were. He must not appear soft, uncertain, and young, or exhibit any of the other deadly sins of which he as a Democrat was automatically suspected. One sin he would certainly not commit, judging from the campaign, the personnel around him, and the early spirit of his administration: that was to be sluggish, hesitant to take the initiative, and indecisive. For this had been part of Eisenhower's image, at least as Kennedy campaigned against it. The New Frontiersmen

---

*John Kennedy would not. Ernest May, in *Lessons of History* (1973), quotes Kennedy as saying in 1963 in explanation of his expanded aid to South Vietnam: "Strongly in our mind is what happened in the case of China at the end of World War II, where China was lost. . . . We don't want that."

were energetic, spirited, confident, and eager to get the country moving. This, too, was a part of the background essential to an understanding of the new President's world of choices as the Vietnam situation worsened.

As always, Presidents handle crises by "staffing them." Clusters of advisors send around a flow of paper, collecting and sifting facts, and analyzing options. For the Vietnamese issue, we have a unique recording of this process in *The Pentagon Papers,* the Defense Department's own inside and secret (until Daniel Ellsberg released it) history of the decision-making process as it dealt with that Asian country.

We know that when John Kennedy asked for expert advice on Vietnam, he found—with only two recorded exceptions in nearly three years of incessant meetings and memos*—that the best and the brightest, in Halberstam's phrase, were telling him that he must stay and win in Vietnam. Whether they tried to give political warfare equal stress with military tactics or, as was more often the case, told the President to increase the firepower of the army of South Vietnam, the advisors presented their President only with varying forms of escalation of the American effort. As John P. Roche reminded us, drawing upon his memories as a White House aide and presidential advisor, "all hands were gung ho" as Kennedy considered what he ought to do in Vietnam.

Perhaps this would have changed? They were the best and the brightest, graduates of the top schools, able to work long hours, and splendid technicians in crisis management. Their government gathered more information than any in the world. And at its head was a bright and flexible President. Might he not have learned from the months of failure of our efforts in Vietnam and, when the South Vietnamese regime collapsed in 1965, held back?

This reasoning places enormous weight on one man, Kennedy.† Lyndon Johnson came to his bombing and troop-commitment decisions of 1964–65 when advised by the same men who had worked for his predecessor. In our political folklore, we make too much of presidential decision as an individual

---

*We learn from *The Pentagon Papers* that a 39-year-old diplomat, Paul Kattenburg, spoke up for disengagement at a National Security Council (NSC) meeting in August 1963 (the President was not in attendance), just as the Diem government staggered toward collapse. Attorney General Robert F. Kennedy discussed the possibility of withdrawal briefly at another NSC meeting in September. On neither occasion, apparently, was the idea pursued at all.

†This David Halberstam does, harshly, in his *The Best and the Brightest* (1972). "He had deepened the commitment there . . . always known better. He had preached, both in his book and in his speeches, about the importance of political courage, but his administration had been reasonably free from acts of courage, such as turning around the irrationality of the China policy. In this most crucial area the record was largely one of timidity."

act,* and too little of the process, in which many men are involved. Remember that virtually every fact and every interpretation of facts about the Vietnam situation (or any other) that came to the President's eye came up through what Richard J. Barnet has called the system of National Security Managers. This structure for providing foreign-policy advice produces a remarkably narrow selection of ideas from all those available in the society at large. The social background of the members of this small but influential system is quite homogeneous. When we examine the diplomats, foreign-service officers, State Department personnel, and military officers who make up the National Security Managerial class, we find them to be white males of middle age, with upper-middle- to upper-class backgrounds, university educations, legal or business training and experience, and overall a rather conservative outlook upon the world. They are not in favor of change, and are especially opposed to violent revolution. Their interest in domestic problems is slight, since by economic class they are able to rise above them and by career they are dedicated to what they see as larger challenges, principally managing the worldwide struggle against communism.

When Kennedy asked this system for advice, it consisted of men of certain basic assumptions that only today are coming widely into question. These assumptions may be found strewn across the formerly secret record of administration discussion of Vietnam policy. They might be summarized as follows:

1. There is a worldwide struggle between the Free World and the Communist Bloc; this is the single most important development of our time.
2. Every territorial gain for communism adds to the strength of that Bloc, and undermines the American world position; this is not only because of the loss of land, resources, and population, but also because of the reduction in American prestige.
3. Therefore, America must contain communism everywhere in the world; Munich taught that small concessions only encourage and strengthen aggressors.

---

*John Kennedy encouraged this old habit. He talked often about the lonely task of decision, rather enjoying the grand role this implied. In a foreword to Theodore Sorensen's *Decision-Making in the White House* (1963), Kennedy wrote: "To govern, as wise men have said, is to choose. . . . For an American President, choice is charged with a peculiar and daunting responsibility for the safety and welfare of the nation. . . . The heart of the Presidency is therefore informed, prudent, and resolute choice." Of course. But if he had lived to write memoirs explaining his occasional errors, he might well have appreciated and stressed the structured channels of information and interpretation which immeasurably limited the President's real choices. And there were other limits that Kennedy, in power, experienced fully but did not like to dwell upon.

1963: The United States and Vietnam — What If John F. Kennedy Had Lived?

175

4. The struggle between South Vietnam and the Viet Cong is merely one aspect of this worldwide struggle.

Where Vietnam was concerned, we find in the thinking of the National Security Managers of the early 1960s two errors that are only now seen as such. One was their misunderstanding of the revolution in Vietnam, and thus their underestimation of the Viet Cong and the North Vietnamese. To Kennedy's advisors, and to Kennedy himself, communism could never be popular, for it was a tyranny unredeemed by any social virtues, as was easily discerned in the record of Stalinism, which was best known to Americans. Communism could hardly blend with a nationalistic movement, since it was internationally controlled from the Kremlin, or perhaps from Peking. The United States government never understood the attachment of the Vietnamese peasant to the revolution—it correctly pointed out that many peasants shunned communism—and accounted for the Viet Cong's success in recruitment by stressing terrorism. Daniel Ellsberg, in his book *Papers on the War* (1972), makes this striking statement:

> Americans in office read very few books, and none in French; and . . . there has never been an officer of Deputy Assistant Secretary rank or higher (including myself) who could have passed in office a midterm freshman exam in modern Vietnamese history, if such a course existed in this country. . . .

Most studies of the Vietnamese revolution were written in French, as Ellsberg learned when he became interested. The first American study to offer a perceptive insight into the revolution was perhaps John T. McAlister's *Vietnam: Origins of Revolution,* published in 1969. "I've just been reading John McAlister's book," said former McNamara aide and Secretary of the Army Cyrus Vance to Ellsberg. "If only we had had it in the mid-sixties!"

McAlister's book, and others by Frances Fitzgerald, Bernard Fall, Paul Mus, and a lengthening list of authors either writing in or translated into English, tell us what was not at all realized in the early 1960s—that the revolution was political, and that the communists offered an alternative to the South Vietnamese social structure and government which was considerably more appealing than we suspected and was impossible for Americans, let alone the reactionary elite whom Diem represented, to duplicate. This insight would have had a chastening effect. As they misunderstood and underrated the social power of Vietnamese communism, so the National Security Managers continually overestimated what Americans could accomplish halfway around the world in cultures thoroughly different from our own. The Managers had the "can-do" spirit; they told their President that if a few more Americans were sent into some muddy little country, they could show the natives how to handle their problems. In this attitude there was something that must be admired, a sort of reckless urge to social service. But there was much more in it to deplore—parochialism, arrogance, and not a little racism.

These misunderstandings, as we now see them, were of course shared in the early 1960s by most Americans, to some degree. Yet there were always other views in the country, other values and interests that, if represented, would have held up the decision for war. The intellectual community was fast losing its faith in Cold War attitudes. Urban dwellers who faced rising crime rates, congestion, ugliness, and pollution had other uses to which national resources could be put. So did artists, scientists, clergymen, minorities, and environmentalists, even if most of them were slow to see that a foreign-policy decision might subtract from the resources available to them. We must remember that social interests that were harmed by the decision to wage war in Vietnam were not well mobilized in the early 1960s, and lacked a keen appreciation of the extent to which decisions reached at the Pentagon and ratified in the White House impacted upon themselves. If they had been alert and determined to counter military claims on the budget with claims of their own, the process of foreign-policy decision-making would have screened out the opposition.

For national-security policy is preeminently the preserve of the imperial presidency. It is thought to be constitutionally the President's responsibility and is expected to be formulated in secret, with very minimal congressional participation or basic objection. The agencies belonging to the NSC circle gather their own data, circulate papers, and decide what to tell the President. These institutions are the military, the Department of State, the intelligence community, and White House staff chiefly under the national-security advisor. It is a remarkably closed system, isolated from interests and perspectives that might introduce extraneous considerations. The NSC was the forum where presidential decisions were analyzed, discussed (such as it was), and made final. The secretary of the treasury was not there to caution about the effect of war costs upon the deficit. The secretary of housing and urban development was not there to complain that bombing raids cost money that might have been spent on urban transportation. The chairman of the federal reserve board was not there to warn of the inflationary aspects of defense expenditures not paid for out of taxation. No congressmen or senators were there, and it was a long time before they learned of executive-branch decisions or their implications.

Thus national-security policy was then and is now made in a setting that excludes interests and perspectives that will be indirectly but powerfully affected. This is not to mention other groups who were most certainly not asked to participate—mothers whose sons would be expected to die in rice

1963: The United States and Vietnam — What If John F. Kennedy Had Lived?

177

paddies, university presidents whose campuses would be paralyzed by dissent, and newspaper reporters whose view of Vietnamese reality was vastly different from that of the government's diplomatic and military sources.

Perhaps it is preferable that no mothers, reporters, ghetto dwellers, environmentalists, or secretaries of the treasury be deeply involved in the making of national-security policy. The fact is that John Kennedy's policy-making apparatus screened out these and other sources of what might have been anti-interventionist, antimilitary views. Thus he received advice to stay, pay, and win. This would remain the advice of the policy-making establishment under Lyndon Johnson. Whoever was President would have to opt for war or, as Johnson himself tellingly framed the alternative in 1961, "throw in the towel" and "pull back our defenses to San Francisco." As this was then unthinkable, America would, regardless of who was President, go to war against an adversary that was, like its geographical and cultural terrain, misunderstood and greatly underestimated. And we would carry to war a technology and a set of military-political ideas whose efficacy was stunningly overrated.

Now we think we know better. Costs turned out to be higher than anyone anticipated, and also more varied. The enemy would push us to a major effort, taking more than 50,000 American lives, distorting the national budget, producing an insidious inflationary surge, and injecting turmoil and division deep into our domestic life. These truths were unimagined in 1961, in 1963, or in 1965. Now we have reason to believe that the "loss" of all Vietnam to communism was an exaggerated misfortune. China did not automatically add to her strength when Saigon surrendered. Vietnamese communism was intensely nationalistic and may yet prove to be a balancing weight against Chinese power. The alleged damage to American "credibility" due to a withdrawal has not been tested, since we did not withdraw without taking a terrible toll of Vietnamese life. We will never know whether "throwing in the towel" in 1965 would have damaged the American reputation and thus undermined in some psychological or geopolitical way the foundations of freedom. Most people now doubt it, and think themselves much wiser than the men of 1961–63.

But all of this insight came from three rending years of war. Not logic, nor reading of scholarly books in French and English, but three years of frustrating war and domestic upheaval were finally sufficent to bring presidential advisors to a change of heart—and then only a few, and not a complete change. In 1968, Clark Clifford, who had advised Harry Truman in the 1940s, told Lyndon Johnson that he must stop trying to save Vietnam from communism and negotiate a withdrawal; he was joined by a few top men, such as George Ball and Townsend Hoopes. But without these years of war, the seemingly endless casualty lists, the disaffection of the young, and the intolerable domestic divisions with no end in sight, what top-level official would have counseled John Kennedy to "withdraw," "disengage," or "throw in the towel"? These were words to gag upon in those days. And so no such person did. And if Kennedy had lived longer, none would. War was required to put that kind of advice in a better light.

There are those who say that a decision for war need not have led to the misfortunes that America suffered. (They do not mention the suffering of the people of Vietnam, Laos, and Cambodia, who endured incalculably more pain than the visitors from America who would save them.) Kennedy had, it is said, interesting options within the war decision. He might have committed American air and ground power more moderately than Lyndon Johnson did, perhaps accepting Maxwell Taylor's "enclave strategy" whereby coastal zones would be held and no large battles would take place. Johnson went for victory on the ground, urging the troops to "hang that coonskin on the wall." Kennedy might well have fought, but aimed at less. Of course, one may not rule out the possibility that he would order a full-scale air and ground attack upon all communists in the Indochina theater.

It would require a longer essay to pursue these options as they would have appeared to whoever was President from 1965 to 1968. It is our view that they are not as important as they seem. The limited-warfare, enclave strategy would have pitted American patience against Asian patience. Casualties and costs would have been lower in the short run, but the entire Vietnamese enterprise would have stretched out much longer. Such a policy would not have spared American society the bitter debates over the war, and perhaps would only have reduced their intensity while prolonging their duration. The end result seems hardly much more attractive.

As for the unlimited bombing that was advocated by some civilians and many military men, its risks were widely appreciated in Kennedy's day and they are real. America had experienced Chinese intervention once before, when the military forces of the United States struck too close to the Chinese mainland. Johnson turned away from this risk, as Kennedy very likely would have done. If one of them had chosen unlimited war, we would surely be less happy today than we are permitted to be in the aftermath of our limited resort to force.

We conclude that the United States had to make war upon the Vietnamese revolutionaries in the 1960s—insofar as one may conclude in such murky terrain, squinting at paths taken and not taken. We had to make war, even if led by a young man brighter than most and in many ways bent upon finding new and better paths. For the roots of foreign-policy error run deep. In this essay we have briefly examined the mind of a President who stood at a pivotal moment in the American relation to Vietnam; a historical record

1963: The United States and Vietnam — What If John F. Kennedy Had Lived?

179

that made his party deeply reluctant to lose another country to communism; and the policy-making structure that served all who sit in the Oval Office. Vietnam was an event in the Cold War, and any analysis of the roots of that larger conflict would eventually have to take into account the influence of the military-industrial complex in reinforcing Cold War stereotypes, the economic opportunities in underdeveloped countries as perceived by developed countries, American racial attitudes, and the constitutional imbalance between the executive and legislative branches in the American system. Exploration of the roots of the Vietnamese intervention tends quickly to become a book-length scrutiny of American society.

What was most fundamental to the string of disastrous decisions? We would offer two sources. At every point of escalation, one hears a persistent note, often subdued, never fully examined, but always dominant—the idea that to let the revolution succeed in Vietnam would bring upon the President, the party, and the bureaucracy that happened to be in power at the time a fatal punishment from the American public: ouster from office! This threat was not, of course, put in such terms; when discussed at all, it was called "loss of opportunity to be of service." If we lose another Asian country, the Right-wing patriots will arouse the American public to an unforgiving fury, and there will be trouble that no one who loves his country would want.

One catches many glimpses of this fundamental fear. Rusk and McNamara, in a memo to Kennedy on November 11, 1961, wrote that "loss of South Viet-Nam would stimulate bitter domestic controversies in the U. S. and would be seized upon by extreme elements to divide the country and harass the Administration. . . ." No President—and this includes Richard Nixon right up to August 1974 when he was forced from office—would take the political risks at home of having the loss of a country from "our" side to "their" side blamed upon his administration.

If the American people, given the chance, had in fact labeled as fools and traitors any administration that stood back while distant Vietnam changed its form of government through guerrilla action, and drove that administration from power, then one would have deep sympathy for those beleaguered leaders of an emotional people: Eisenhower, Kennedy, Johnson, and Nixon. Were the American people so unforgiving, so dedicated in any circumstances to the role of world policeman, and so determined that the world struggle against communism go forward without regard to costs and sacrifices? We do not and will not know. John Kennedy, like all other American Presidents, did not run the risks required to find out.

A second fundamental element working to cloud American policy was brilliantly exposed in a series of articles by Jonathan Schell in *The New Yorker* in 1975. At virtually every point of decision in the Cold War, Schell notes, there is in the American rationale for policy an overriding determination to ensure the credibility of American power. One easily pulls a few examples from the 1960s: We must "avoid humiliation," wrote an assistant secretary of defense in 1966; shore up "the confidence factor," an assistant secretary of state said in 1967; and prevent any development that encourages the idea that "no nation can ever again have the same confidence in American promise or in American protection," as President Johnson said in 1965. These sentiments are fundamental to the reasoning of American officials. They are expressions of the Doctrine of Credibility, which, as Schell writes, "was a coldly reasoned strategic theory that was designed to supply the U. S. with effective instruments of influence in an age dominated by nuclear weapons."

It was a theory articulated best in two books at the end of the 1950s: Henry Kissinger's *Nuclear Weapons and Foreign Policy* (1957) and General Maxwell Taylor's *The Uncertain Trumpet* (1960). The nuclear arsenal of the great powers had made war unthinkable; its ends would be destroyed by the means. Yet if the bomb made war unthinkable, America would be rendered powerless, and *that* was unthinkable too. If we allowed ourselves to be paralyzed by thoughts of the costs of nuclear war even to the victor, this would virtually be giving the Russians "a blank check," in Kissinger's words. They would know that America shunned the risks of war at every point where military power might legitimately be considered as an instrument of policy.

In these circumstances, Kissinger and Taylor saw limited war as a vital and necessary opportunity to prove American "credibility" to the Soviet Union. Limited war would presumably have its strategic ends, but its psychological function was perhaps more important. It would allow us to demonstrate that we were not paralyzed by the nuclear dilemma, but still retained abundant supplies of "will," "determination," "resolve," and "toughness." These were key words to the Doctrine of Credibility, and they were key words in the lexicon of John F. Kennedy (as well as Lyndon B. Johnson and Richard M. Nixon). Once in Vietnam even as an advisor, to "throw in the towel" would encourage the image of paralysis and reduce the image of will and toughness.

Thus, as Schell summarizes, "the war was not being fought only for the tangible objectives. It was being fought also for the psychological objective of maintaining American credibility—an aim that was bound up in the strategists' thinking with the prevention of nuclear war and the prevention of global totalitarianism." As Dean Rusk wrote to a group of student leaders in 1967: "We are involved because the nation's word has been given that we would be involved." Appearances. Reputation. Image. Whatever happens in Southeast Asia is not so important, an aide wrote to McNamara, as that "the US emerge as a 'good doctor.' We must have kept promises, been tough, taken risks, gotten bloodied, and hurt the enemy very badly." Then our nuclear power will be credible, rather than an expensive pile of unusable doomsday weapons that bring powerlessness and not power to their creators.

Thus at the very core of American foreign policy, informing every decision and, especially, requiring a war in Vietnam, was the awful weapon of 1945 and Hiroshima, which still exacted its terrible price from the nation that had devised it.

South Vietnam fell to the communists in early 1975, Viet Cong troops and Red flags moving triumphantly through the streets of Saigon. The American stock market went *up*. Laos fell to the communist-led Pathet Lao in August 1975, but there was little notice of it, no angry editorials, no word from the White House, and no speeches from a recessed Congress. After all that sacrifice and death, there was so little stir over the arrival of the dreaded event. Perhaps the factors that led to American involvement have been altered, and a future President may have choices that Kennedy, for one, did not have. The public, clearly, will not howl for the blood of a President who decides to allow a civil war in a faraway country to run its course without sending American boys. All the old clichés about the "Free World" and "the Communist Bloc" have been reexamined. The costs of counterinsurgency by an American expeditionary force have been reevaluated upward, and the effectiveness of American intervention on behalf of reactionary regimes battling popular revolts has been found to have humbling limits.

Fighting in Vietnam did not "save" Vietnam, but it shattered the force of many assumptions that were virtually irresistible in the 1960s. From this review of Kennedy's choices, we may take some comfort for the future, perhaps. But war draws encouragement from many other sources, and nothing that happened in Vietnam has resolved the dilemma of nuclear warfare with its premium upon the credibility of American power. Vietnam, as Jonathan Schell notes, was an episode. "What will not come to an end is the nuclear dilemma itself."

SUGGESTED READINGS

Richard J. Barnet, *The Roots of War,* 1972

Henry Brandon, *The Anatomy of Error,* 1969

Theodore Draper, *The Abuse of Power,* 1967

Daniel Ellsberg, *Papers on the War,* 1972

Leslie Gelb, "Vietnam: The System Worked," *Foreign Policy,* Summer 1971

Richard Goodwin, *Vietnam: Triumph or Tragedy,* 1966

David Halberstam, *The Best and the Brightest,* 1972

Henry Kissinger, *Nuclear Weapons and Foreign Policy,* 1957

Gabriel Kolko, *The Roots of American Foreign Policy,* 1969

Ernest May, *The Lessons of History,* 1973

Richard M. Pfeffer, ed., *No More Vietnams,* 1968

Jonathan Schell, "Reflections: The Nixon Years," *The New Yorker,* June 2–July 7, 1975

Arthur M. Schlesinger, Jr., *The Bitter Heritage,* 1967

Arthur M. Schlesinger, Jr., *A Thousand Days,* 1965

Neil Sheehan et al., *Pentagon Papers: As Published by the New York Times,* 1971

Maxwell Taylor, *The Uncertain Trumpet,* 1960

James C. Thompson, Jr., "How Could Vietnam Happen?" *Atlantic Monthly 221,* 1968

What If There Had Been No Watergate?

Not long after midnight on June 17, 1972, security guard Frank Wills noticed tape across the lock of one of the entrances to the Democratic National Committee headquarters in the Watergate apartment complex in Washington. Having noticed and removed a similar tape earlier in the day, Wills became suspicious and called police. They arrested five men inside the Democratic offices, and later two others. The investigation of the break-in was to lead to Richard M. Nixon and to topple him from office.

The series of events from a 1972 burglary to Nixon's 1974 resignation—generally referred to as Watergate—remains the most dramatic, far-reaching, and improbable political development in modern American history. One must stress how frequently the string of events that we now know so well and that have taken on a certain logic of inevitability was almost interrupted at several points. The burglars were professionals with CIA experience and with several undetected break-ins behind them. It is astonishing how inept they were. Darker masking tape or tape run vertically would probably have avoided Wills' eye and the scrutiny of history. When the burglars pled guilty and refused to talk, the affair seemed over. However, Democratic presidential candidate George McGovern could claim that something very much bigger was involved than a "third-rate burglary," since one of the men was general counsel for the Committee to Reelect the President. But Justice Department investigators could find no evidence tying the break-in to anyone in the administration. Only the persistence of a handful of people kept the case alive—Judge John Sirica, who thought that important truths were being concealed; and a pair of reporters for *The Washington Post,* backed by their editors and publisher. Sirica set stiff sentences and pressed the defendants to turn state's evidence.

In early 1973 one of them did, a former FBI and CIA agent named James McCord. He went before both a federal grand jury and a Senate investigating committee to implicate administration officials up to former Attorney General John Mitchell. Gradually, agonizingly, the story came unraveled, connecting the Watergate break-in with a series of illegal burglaries, campaign disruptions, wiretaps, and bugs, most of these carried out by a special unit in the White House called "the Plumbers." This group had been established at President Nixon's order and was supervised by his immediate staff and his attorney general.

The administration denied every element of the story as it unfolded, and pressed both the FBI and the CIA to obstruct the investigation. The President claimed no knowledge of illegal activities, and when his two top staff assistants, Robert Haldeman and John Ehrlichman, were forced to resign in April 1973 (along with Acting Attorney General Richard Kleindienst), Nixon insisted upon his own innocence while admitting bad judgment in permitting a climate of overzealousness. The case seemed stalled at this point, having already produced a stunning series of blows to the administration's credibility and reputation for high-minded public service.

Then a minor official mentioned the existence of a taping system that had recorded all conversations in the President's office; in a complicated series of struggles between the Senate investigating body and the grand jury on the one hand and the White House on the other, Nixon began to release transcripts of the tapes. Crucial tapes were withheld under the doctrine of executive privilege, but were ordered released to the federal prosecutor in a 8 to 0 Supreme Court decision in July 1974 (*U.S.* v. *Richard Nixon*). The administration did not destroy the tapes nor, after pondering the option, did it defy the Court. The tapes were released and were found to contain conclusive evidence of presidential involvement in both the planning and the coverup of illegal activities, and of lying about both. It did not help the protective mystique of the White House to find the President exceptionally, if unimaginatively, profane. An incredible 22 months ended with the exhausted President's resignation on August 8, under threat of certain impeachment.

What is perhaps most astonishing about Watergate is its precarious concatenation of events, from bungled burglary to presidential resignation, which reversed the electoral landslide of two years before. At half a dozen.

points, at the very least, the investigation could easily have been inconclusively stalled. Any of the following would have been sufficient to break the chain of events—less careless burglars, assignment of a less stubborn judge, a less relentless set of journalists at *The Washington Post,* neglecting to ask Alexander Butterfield the lucky question that revealed the existence of the tapes, or a decision at the White House to destroy the tapes before pressure built up. Then the Nixon presidency would have carried through to January 1977. Especially if the Watergate scandal had been squelched at a very early stage, that presidency would have been vigorous, untainted, and free to unfold as fully as its leader's political strength and astuteness allowed. That is the road not taken, yet worth some attention from a generation that so narrowly missed traveling along it.

Where did it lead? There are, broadly speaking, two views on this. One is generally favorable to the overall direction of the Nixon presidency; the other is implacably hostile.

At this writing, Richard Nixon is working on his memoirs at his villa in San Clemente. One supposes that he will put the best face upon his presidency, while admitting some errors, as he did in his farewell remarks to the public on August 8, 1974. Others from his administration have already sketched out the favorable view, even while expressing great disappointment at the leader's mismanagement of a series of small crimes of which Watergate was one. Such an account is found in William Safire's *Before the Fall* (1975). In *The Plot That Failed: Nixon and the Administrative Presidency* (1975) by Richard P. Nathan (who served in Nixon's administration in both the Office of Management and Budget and the Department of Health, Education, and Welfare), one finds a perceptive and plausible explanation of the principal thrust of the Nixon presidency in domestic affairs.

Nathan reminds us that Nixon faced large Democratic majorities in Congress, which even his 1972 landslide had not altered or intimidated. The public had voted for divided government, electing a President bent upon conservative reforms and a Congress controlled by the other party with more or less liberal commitments. Nixon wanted change—specifically, to reduce the size and power of the federal government (with certain activities such as "law and order" excepted), returning power to local governments. This he called The New Federalism or, in another elevated phrase, The New American Revolution. Congress, in Democratic hands, resisted most of Nixon's program, seeing it as an abdication of national responsibility for social problem-solving.

A near deadlock was the result. Nixon's reform of the welfare system was turned back, his revenue-sharing proposals were minimized and altered, and his proposed cuts in domestic spending were resisted. But Nixon's frustrations did not come only from Congress. Like other Presidents before him, he found that he could not control the federal bureaucracy that he nominally headed. It was liberal in political leaning and entrenched in expensive programs. He could not force the bureaucracy to alter course or cut budgets significantly. Another problem was his own inherited decision-making apparatus. Here the central difficulty lay in the cabinet, his only deliberate body for policy formulation, yet a group on the whole more loyal to departmental staff and interest-group constituencies than to the President.

Like every President before him reaching back at least to Herbert Hoover, Richard Nixon searched for ways to strengthen the chief executive's capacity to formulate coherent policy and then carry it through despite the various obstacles between himself and the common folk of Peoria who had voted him into office. In this search, Nixon was more inventive and determined than any President since FDR. He centralized power in an expanded and very aggressive White House staff, devised a new Domestic Council for central policy formulation, proposed a radical executive branch reorganization, and set up a tight inner circle of aides and special counselors between himself and his cabinet secretaries. To an unprecedented degree, the executive branch under Nixon was run from the White House.

All these changes, which had their precursors in earlier administrations, aimed in Nathan's view at a new system—the "Administrative Presidency." Nathan, a gifted public administrator, does not disguise his preference for this system over the old. Functions of government that could be performed at lower levels would be decentralized; those retained in Washington would be closely managed by a chief executive who, for the first time, had adequate staff and institutional support and a rationalized bureaucracy. "If there had been no Watergate and assuming that Richard Nixon had adhered to higher campaign and personnel standards," writes Nathan, "are there not serious reasons for concluding that . . . he was right about the Administrative Presidency?" Agreement comes from a surprising source, Franklin D. Roosevelt's brain truster, Rexford Tugwell, who wrote in 1975:

> I conjecture that if Nixon had not been caught with a household of crooks, he might have made the presidency what it was trying to become. His crooks will now set back the evolution of the institution for maybe a generation.

This is one version of the direction of the Nixon presidency. As far as it goes, it is persuasive. Watergate interrupted a series of presidential reforms in the functioning of the presidency, reforms that grew out of and directly addressed the long history of the weakness of that office in domestic management. Most students of American government have applauded every successive step toward a more centralized presidency, and Richard Nixon had made more progress than any single President since FDR.

A second broad perspective absorbs this view, and goes beyond it to a thoroughly alarming projection. Nixon was engaged not only in altering the presidency, enabling it to cope with the executive branch bureaucracy and the inherent difficulties of policy formulation and review. He had launched a full-scale effort to alter both the balance of powers between the three branches of the national government and the political system upon which they rest.

Arthur M. Schlesinger, Jr., published in 1973 a book titled *The Imperial Presidency,* tracing the rapid transformation of the presidential office from FDR to Nixon—years of transition from the traditional presidency to the imperial one. The backdrop was the Cold War, and the architects were a bipartisan group of Presidents, both liberal and conservative. So long as the expanding power of the President came under liberal leadership, most intellectuals—Schlesinger confessed himself one of them—had endorsed the trend. Nixon's continuation of the development of an activist, strong presidency, accomplished with his own special emphases and innovations, forced a painful reappraisal. What was the presidency becoming?

Part of the alarm came from objectionable alterations in governing style. As late as Truman and Eisenhower, the President had managed to appear to live somewhat modestly amid the trappings of power. But this tradition, that the President was merely the first citizen and never *royalty,* could not survive in the era of world power. Presidents after World War II were surrounded by servants, swimming pools, retreats in the mountains, yachts on the Potomac, and buffers of courtiers to isolate them from contact with unpleasant or irrelevant people. Assassinations of public figures, and of one President, by the late 1960s brought about an almost total physical isolation of the chief executive. He was coddled, transported from one Shangri-la to another, waited upon by yes-men, and reminded daily of his leadership of something called the Free World. That this isolation from daily reality was not good for the character or the judgment of Presidents became especially clear when presidential press secretary George Reedy published his disquieting *The Twilight of the Presidency* in 1970 (it was a book about Lyndon Johnson), and when in the same year Richard Nixon dressed the White House police in Prussian-type uniforms with tall hats and gold braid. He removed the uniforms after some critical press comment, but continued to relish the grandeur of his two villas, one in Key Biscayne where the government had spent $1.8 million in improvements, the other in San Clemente where $2.4 million of public money had purchased every comfort for the leader of the Free World.

Yet much more than isolation and regal pretensions signaled the emergence of the imperial presidency. There was a marked shift of power—one uses the word *shift* to avoid choosing between *taking* on the part of the President and *surrendering* on the part of Congress—from legislative to executive branches during Nixon's six years. There was also a complementary thrust toward domination by the presidency of the processes of electoral democracy and public information.

Let us take these in order. Congress found the Nixon years a time of sustained confrontation. When laws were passed that the President did not like and could not block with a sustainable veto, or that he chose for political reasons not to veto, he seized upon an ancient privilege of Presidents and would not spend the funds appropriated. Presidents had been impounding funds from the beginning of the republic, but almost always the impoundment was brief and was done for administrative convenience rather than to cancel the operation of a valid statute. But Nixon, writes Arthur Schlesinger, Jr., in *The Imperial Presidency* (1973), "embarked in his first term on an impoundment trip unprecedented in American history." By 1973 he had nullified congressional intent by impounding a total of $15 billion from one hundred programs, or 17–20 percent of controllable funds. Asked whether his impoundment policies were constitutional, Nixon asserted an almost unlimited constitutional right to use that "inherent power."

The presidential usurpation of powers beyond the claims of any of his predecessors went beyond aggressive impoundment. Nixon selectively enforced the law, announcing on one occasion that the administration would not enforce Title VII of the Civil Rights Act of 1964 and, in another instance, dismantling the Office of Economic Opportunity when Congress had explicitly voted its continuation. Neither act had any constitutional sanction, and Nixon made little claim to one. But in the area of executive privilege, he radically expanded both the practice and the rationale.

Executive privilege was a concept undefined in the Constitution but so obviously implicit in the chief executive's role that it had been successfully exercised from Washington's day forward. The separation of powers, it was assumed, implied the President's right to withhold from Congress both information and the opportunity to interrogate presidential advisors—under compelling circumstances! What these circumstances were had never been specified in any statute, nor had litigation clarified the matter. Presidents usually complied with congressional requests for information. When, on rare occasions, they had not, courts had always upheld the executive. Executive privilege was a large grey area in American law, exploited by some Presidents more bravely than others.

Eisenhower, for example, out of dislike for the congressional witch-hunts launched by Senator Joe McCarthy and others of that sort, instructed administration officials to refuse testimony before Congress forty-four times in the period 1955–60. This was a more frequent resort to the refuge of executive privilege than had occurred in the previous 100 years. John Kennedy had been one of the senators irked by Ike's refusal to honor requests for information, and he invoked executive privilege very rarely and made it clear that he thought the practice should be restrained. Johnson was equally cautious, invoking executive privilege four times.

Nixon cast aside this habit of restraint. Not only did he personally invoke the privilege four times in the first term, and high-ranking members of his administration refused to testify on twenty-three occasions, but Nixon's attorney general told Congress that Presidents had the right to refuse congressional access to any of the 2.5 million federal employees. There were, in other words, no limits to executive privilege and, if Congress did not like that doctrine, then the remedy was impeachment. A constitutional arrangement that had developed in order to permit necessary confidentiality in federal administration and that survived because of executive restraint had been boldly pushed to the status of an unlimited authority.

In view of a presidential invasion of congressional power across a broad front, some observers concluded that the Nixon presidency was not pursuing the usual incremental encroachment characteristic of Presidents, but rather an entirely new theory of the balance of powers. While Nixon did not directly repudiate the constitutional doctrines of the Founders, he was known to view himself, especially after his overwhelming 1972 reelection, as the tribune of the people who was frustrated by a legislature of parochial political barons who could only obstruct. (FDR, of course, had felt this way about "the nine old men" in 1937.) Nixon advisor Kevin Phillips wrote in 1973 that modern technology required a government more swift in decision-making than our divided system, and he urged that the separation of powers be replaced by a fusion of powers under a powerful chief executive. As Arthur Schlesinger, Jr., pointed out in his excellent study, *The Imperial Presidency* (1973), this was to propose a parliamentary system with President and legislature standing or falling together. This may have been Phillips's idea, but Nixon himself seemed to be aiming at a plebiscitary rather than a parliamentary presidency. In the former system, modeled more on de Gaulle's France than on any part of the American experience, the people would periodically elect their champion, and neither party nor legislature would be allowed to stand in his way.

If Nixon leaned in this direction, Congress would not be the only limiting institution against which he would move. Logic required that he exert pressure upon the media, shrug off the weak bonds of political party, and finally systematically attempt to gain satisfactory control over the electoral process. All of these lines of effort were to be pursued. Like earlier Presidents, Nixon disliked the press and thought of it as an adversary. Other Presidents had mixed this attitude with an acceptance of the press ranging from the stoical to the good-natured, but Nixon's dislike of the media came rather pure. He inherited a long tradition of presidential manipulation of the media, an art that no President after FDR could afford not to practice. Press conferences and presidential addresses were used to reach the public on grounds most favorable to the executive and at no cost to him or his party. Presidents rewarded friendly reporters with stories, excluded critics from easy access to sources, wined and dined publishers, and even occasionally—as with John F. Kennedy and *The New York Times*—asked a publisher to kill a story in the interest of "national security," which meant to avoid embarrassing the administration.

These practices confined press and media freedom somewhat, but did so in subtle ways that left the media considerable independence and a formidable critic's role. Nixon was not satisfied with the situation. His administration went to court to establish the right of prior restraint when it sued *The New York Times* over publication of *The Pentagon Papers.* It wiretapped the telephones of irritating reporters and unleashed Vice-President Agnew in a campaign of denunciation of the larger networks and Eastern newspapers. It threatened radio and television stations with loss of broadcast licenses if the content of news was not changed to reflect a more conservative outlook.

As Nixon's second term opened, the media—or a substantial part of the community of publishers, broadcasters, and reporters—was alarmed, on the defense, and scrounging for allies. It was unclear just how far and in what ways the President would press his attack. Another institution in a position to limit presidential power somewhat was Nixon's own party. Nixon saw to it that the Republican party's potential restraints upon his freedom of action were minimized by eliminating serious consultation with party leaders and running his 1972 campaign through an organization entirely separate from the Republican National Committee. What other impediments to presidential power required attention? The administration compiled a list of its enemies, which included antiwar militants, liberal Democrats, novelists, reporters, and civil rights leaders. Members of the White House staff, now augmented to the impressive total of 250 ranking officials, were assigned to move against the administration's enemies on a variety of fronts.

While this use of the apparatus of governmental power seems shocking on its face, it was not so innovative a thrust as might be imagined. Presidents had been using the machinery of the executive branch to harass, intimidate, and weaken their own political opponents for at least three decades prior to Nixon. FDR had ordered the Bureau of Internal Revenue to investigate Huey Long's tax returns, and had allowed the FBI to wiretap those it suspected of subversive potential. From the Second World War onward, the FBI kept secret files on the private lives of congressmen, senators, and other public officials to provide incriminating material to Presidents when there was a chance that it would be useful.

No clear line was drawn between enemies of the administration in power and opponents of the existing social order. Long before Nixon, the FBI had used wiretaps, electronic bugging, break-ins, mail openings, and informers to keep track of citizens charged with no crime. J. Edgar Hoover had set up the Cointelpro operation within the FBI "to expose, disrupt and otherwise neutralize the activities" of the entire "New Left" in the 1960s—and to Hoover the New Left definitely included the civil rights movement. Under this program, phony letters were sent to employers of people who had committed no crime beyond dissent, and Martin Luther King's wife was sent a tape purporting to reveal his extramarital activities.

By the end of the 1960s, the CIA had joined in the domestic political-operations game, spying on antiwar activists and keeping files on more than 10,000 Americans suspected of deviant ideas. The United States army, not to be left out, maintained at Fort Holabird, Maryland, files on 80,000 nonmilitary citizens, had 770 organizations coded, and received 1,200 reports a month from undercover agents.

This was the situation when Nixon came to Washington in January 1969. The FBI, CIA, and army were deeply engaged in an unannounced, secret war against those they defined as subversives and potential troublemakers. Yet as flagrant as was this misuse of governmental power, the effort remained within certain limits. It was not coordinated from the White House, and it was not turned against the political party that lost the last presidential election.

The decision to pass beyond these limits was Nixon's. In the summer of 1970, just after college campuses had erupted against the administration's incursion into Cambodia, the President stirred his aides to creative thought about how the administration might, in White House lawyer John Dean's words, "maximize the fact of our incumbency in dealing with persons known to be active in their opposition to our Administration." Dean went on: "Stated more bluntly—how can we use the available federal machinery to screw our political enemies?" An Enemies List was the first step. The Department of Justice, headed by John Mitchell, conducted a series of political trials against opponents of the war in Vietnam. The Post Office and Treasury both offered help in the surveillance of suspected radicals. This was a heartening response from the departments, but Nixon was not satisfied. He wanted better domestic intelligence, and to know everything he could about radicals and about certain Democrats.

He called a meeting of the FBI, the CIA, the Defense Intelligence Agency, and the National Security Agency to discuss the problem. A task force was set up under White House aide Tom Huston, and they proposed a series of activities that included several known to be illegal—breaking and entering, spies on university campuses, expanded wiretapping, opening and copying letters, and the spread of misinformation within opposition organizations. J. Edgar Hoover opposed the plan, feeling that the FBI was doing very well as things stood. So Nixon took a step that was ultimately fatal to his presidency. He established his own private intelligence and undercover-operations force in the White House, the Special Investigations, or "Plumbers," unit. This band of ex-CIA agents and soldiers of fortune reported to the President through John Ehrlichman, and was paid chiefly out of campaign funds. Other White House aides from time to time hired special operators for additional illegal work.

Before the Watergate arrests forced a dismantling of all these operations, men acting for the President of the United States had burglarized a doctor's office, broken into the Democratic National Committee headquarters, forged cables to injure the reputation of the late John F. Kennedy, and repeatedly disrupted the 1972 presidential campaigns of Senators Hubert Humphrey, Henry Jackson, and Edmund Muskie. While this private strike force operated directly out of the White House, the FBI continued its harassment of political radicals, and the Internal Revenue Service, under White House pressure, set up a special staff to investigate the tax returns of war protesters, civil rights activists, politicians, and writers.

This was the iceberg uncovered when the Watergate burglars were meekly captured by police in June 1972. As journalist Stewart Alsop wrote:

> Watergate has been an attempt to alter the very nature of the ancient American political system. . . . To transfer . . . secret-service techniques, on an obviously planned and organized basis, to the internal American political process is a genuinely terrifying innovation. . . . They were not practicing politics. They were making war. . . .

He wrote this before the presidential tapes were released. On them we hear the President saying to John Dean:

> This is war. We take a few shots and it will be over. We will give them a few shots and it will be over. Don't worry. I wouldn't want to be on the other side right now. Would you? . . . They are asking for it and they are going to get it. . . .

Then came Watergate, a 26-month trauma of uncovering criminality and lies, and the resignation of a President. How might things have been different if Nixon had somehow covered it all up? There would have been a Nixon administration in power until 1976, engaged without exposure or effective check in a systematic expansion of presidential power. Today not even the conservatives who voted for Richard Nixon and hoped for so much from him can feel comfortable with that alternative future. They would perhaps point out that there were redeeming features in the Nixon era. Apart from foreign affairs, which may be set aside for purposes of this analysis, the same President who presided over Watergate was also working toward Nathan's administrative presidency. Many observers of American public administration would find much to praise in this. But the gain, if we may for the moment concede the case, would have come in a package with something resembling democracy's first emperor.

In this light, Watergate appears to have made a great difference, averting the full development of a runaway presidency. Almost hopefully, we may summarize the tangible changes it forced upon the stream of events. Richard Nixon is gone from our public life, replaced through 1976 by Gerald Ford, who conducted a more open, cooperative, and conventional presidency. The Plumbers were disbanded, the IRS destroyed its 11,000 files, the army its two million files, and Director Clarence Kelley of the FBI apologized for abuses of power. Our system is perceived as fundamentally vindicated, in that it produced and enforced the decision that even a President is not above the law. Impeachment has reemerged as a credible element in the American constitutional architecture of balanced powers. Campaign spending limitations and public funding of presidential campaigns have been enacted, and a War Powers Act requires the President to secure consent of Congress within 60 days of sending armed forces into combat. Congress has passed an act to improve its own participation in the budgetary process and to regulate impoundment. It has strengthened the Freedom of Information Act. Among the important intangibles, Congress appears to have recovered some of its sense of responsibility for the oversight function, one example being the investigation of both the FBI and the CIA through Senator Frank Church's Select Committee on Intelligence. Certainly the American public between 1972 and 1974 pondered more about its laws and Constitution than at any time since the ratification debates in 1788.

These are beneficial developments, some with a rather temporary look about them, some more structural and lasting. How far do they go toward removing or neutralizing the sources of the imperial presidency? It would be rash to be optimistic. While the character flaws of the man from Whittier, California, are behind the abuses of presidential power since 1969, in a fundamental sense he inherited every tendency he carried to such bitter culmination. Watergate is best understood not as an aberration but as a logical end-product of trends long established. The problem is systemic and not a phenomenon of personalities, however important the character traits of individual Presidents.

Essentially the imperial presidency has been nurtured by the new activist State that emerged during the 1930s, and by the endless ordeal of war and national emergency that began in 1941. Especially it is war and national emergency that have legitimized secrecy, illegal means to noble ends, stretching of the Constitution, lying and deception, and the aggrandizement of executive power. When the nation has to be saved—every day, year in and year out—hard questions about constitutional rights and balances will not be asked of the organizer of our defenses, the President.

No solution to these conditions suggests itself. The managerial State is a permanent feature of every industrial society and, despite recent rhetoric, the regulatory and welfare functions of the national government will not be much reduced in the future. As for international rivalry and a sense of standing danger, those also appear to be embedded in the circumstances of America's size and affluence among the community of nations. Without a change in these circumstances, it is no solution to propose a drastic shrinking of the responsibilities of the executive.

An accountable yet strong President is the main direction of hope. But how is this to be arranged? Political theorists Rexford G. Tugwell and Leland Baldwin have proposed entirely new Constitutions, but there is little interest in such fundamental reshaping. Congress passed the Budget and Impoundment Act in 1974, and established modest oversight procedures to monitor the intelligence community. That is the extent of remedy within the legislative branch, and even now the tide of alarm and indignation recedes. Representative Otis Pike of the House committee investigating the CIA conceded to a reporter in 1976:

> The CIA and the NSA are going to be a little more careful for a while. What I am afraid of . . . is . . . [that] there will be no congressional oversight in the near future, I'm afraid. The real oversight will have to come from the executive branch. And I don't think that the executive branch will ever completely monitor itself. So, after a while, I fear, the oversight will become *pro forma* again. And the abuses, I fear, will start again.

Some express hope that the memory of Watergate and of the impeachment trauma will serve in place of those structural changes that have not emerged. Yet memories grow dim. It is said that we would not need to fear another runaway presidency if we would elect honest and honorable men and women. This is a truism that brings little comfort. Politics does not attract enough honest and honorable people, and those in politics who possess these qualities are often not also endowed with the wealth and the television manners required to seek high office. Even if our electoral processes somehow improved and citizens with less flexible ethical standards were sent to the White House, that place is designed to weaken the fibers of judgment. One need only read the recent books on the presidency by insiders George Reedy, Joseph Califano, William Safire, and John Dean to catch a sobering glimpse of the regal isolation of recent Presidents. Nothing has been done to attack that unhealthy isolation directly other than to reminisce about Thomas Jefferson in buckskin and Harry Truman outstripping the Secret Service on his daily walks.

How much of the problem is deeper yet, in the people themselves? The public, or a great part of it, holds the President not merely in esteem, but in a degree of awe and veneration that hints at monarchy. Formerly merely the chief executive, the President is now somehow a symbol of an imperial nation, his house a shrine, his personal appearance an occasion for trumpets, and his wife and children fawned over like European royalty. Citizens criticize "the government" with a democratic candor, but they do not feel comfortable with criticism of the President, especially when he draws around himself the mantle of defender of the national security. Whatever it is in contemporary culture that produces this need for a symbolic figure upon which to focus our uncritical loyalties, it has not been defined, remedied, or deflected to symbols of less dangerous potential.

These thoughts suggest that Watergate made only a temporary difference, after all. In the short run it was a convulsion of the body politic, expelling a President and dozens of men who had served him uncritically and chastening every practicing or aspiring politician in the nation. The succeeding President, Gerald Ford, was conspicuously unimperial and law-abiding. This was much change from, let us say, 1973. Yet these were changes in personalities, style, and appearances. The underlying conditions of executive aggrandizement remain—international rivalry, world preeminence, a society that longs for symbols of authority, and a technology that permits the monitoring of the thoughts and actions of millions.

These the Watergate experience left in place. It was educational and it bought us some time. After a season of presidential caution and public vigilance, the pressures toward a runaway presidency will build again. Presidents seek power, after all, for our own good—to secure us from external and internal threat, from bad ideas and wrong-headed factions, and from the burden of knowing too much! Such motives make leaders not only bold but pious, and strike a large minority of the citizenry as soundly patriotic. How different American history will be after Watergate depends upon how we use the time we have been given to strengthen the values, ideas, and institutions that would check such arrogant paternalism without paralyzing the institution from which crucial leadership must come.

SUGGESTED READINGS

Jerry J. Berman and Morton Halperin, eds., *The Abuses of the Intelligence Agencies*

Demetrios Caraley et al., "American Political Institutions After Watergate—A Discussion," *Political Science Quarterly 89*, Winter 1974–75

Richard E. Cohen, "Watergate May Alter Style but not Substance of Power," *National Journal Reports 97*, 1974

Congressional Quarterly, *Watergate: Chronology of a Crisis*, 2 vols., 1973–74

Rowland Evans and Robert Novak, *Nixon in the White House*, 1971

J. Anthony Lukas, *Nightmare: the Underside of the Nixon Years*, 1975

Clark Mollenhoff, *Game Plan to Disaster*, 1975

Richard P. Nathan, *The Plot That Failed: Nixon and the Administrative Presidency*, 1975

New York Times, *The White House Transcripts,* 1974

William E. Porter, *Assault on the Media: The Nixon Years,* 1975

George Reedy, *The Twilight of the Presidency,* 1970

William Safire, *Before the Fall,* 1975

Arthur M. Schlesinger, Jr., *The Imperial Presidency,* 1973

Rexford G. Tugwell and Thomas Cronin, eds., *The Presidency Reappraised,* 1975

U.S. Senate, Select Committee on Intelligence Activities, *Intelligence Activities and the Rights of Americans,* April 1976

Theodore White, *Breach of Faith: The Fall of Richard Nixon,* 1975

David Wise, *The Politics of Lying,* 1973

Index

Adair v. *United States,* 38
Adams, Abigail, 17, 50
Adams, John, 34, 44, 48, 53, 116
Adams, John Quincy, 47
Adams, Samuel, 11
Agnew, Spiro T., 190
Alsop, Stewart, 192
American Liberty League, 124
Articles of Confederation
  attempts to amend, 33
  committee system, 36–37
  declarations of war, 37–38
  defended by Anti-Federalists, 30–31
  federal judiciary, 39–40
  loyalty to, 32–33
  powers of, 31
Atomic bomb, 144, 153–54, 181

Baker, Newton D., 119–20
  philosophy of, 125–26, 128–29
Bank of the United States
  first, 34
  second, 57–70
Barnet, Richard J., 174
Baruch, Bernard, 124, 157
Bayard, James A., 45–46
Beatty, John, 19
Bell, Peter, 78, 80
Benton, Thomas H., 60, 66, 72–74
Biddle, Charles, 50
Biddle, Nicholas, 57–59, 67–69
Blacks; *see also* Slavery
  migration to north during World War I,
    111
Bougainville, Col. Louis-Antoine de, 9
Bowers, Claude, 60
Branch, John, 57
Brant, Joseph, 52
Brebner, John, 11
Brown et al. v. *Board of Education,* 39
Brown, John, 77–78
Brown, Sir Robert, 5
Brownlee, W. Elliot, 65
Bryan, William Jennings, 114, 124
Bureau of Indian Affairs (BIA), 88–89, 98
Bureau of Internal Revenue, 190
Burr, Aaron
  compared to Jefferson, 55
  desire for Louisiana, 53–54
  duel with Hamilton, 52
  family background, 47
  Hamilton's opposition to, 44

  and judiciary, 49–50
  knowledge of West, 52
  in New York election, 43
  political ability and strategy, 50–51
  Republican fears, 44
  secessionist approach, 51
  support by Federalists, 44–45
Butterfield, Alexander, 185

Calhoun, John C., 63, 81
Campbell, John A., 81
Canada
  attitude of Americans toward, 11ff.
  battle of Quebec, 4
  under British rule, 12–14
  chosen by England, 5
  French plans for, 10–11
Central Intelligence Agency, 190–93
Chastellux, Marquis de, 18
Chesapeake and Delaware Canal
    Company, 64
China, "fall of," in 1949–50, 171
Christian Constitutional Society, 49
Christie, Gabriel, 45
Churchill, Winston, 142–43, 148
Clark, John M., 104
Clay, Henry, 58–59, 73–76
Clayton, James L., 139
Clemens, Diane, 148
Clinton, George, 31, 44
Cobb, Howell, 62
Cohen, Henry, 69
Cold War
  costs of, 139
  origins of, 140–60, 179
Coles, Edward, 19–20
Collier, John, 89, 91–92, 97, 101–102
Conrad, Charles, 78
Constitution
  based upon compromise, 71–72
  defects, 37
  judiciary system, 38
  opposition arguments, 30–31
  presidential powers, 35–36
  proposals to change, 29–30
  ratification, 31–32
Cooke, Jay, 69
Coombs, Walter, 30
Cooper, William, 46
Corcoran, William W., 69, 77
Cornbury, Lord, 5
Coughlin, Father Charles C., 132
Cramer, C. H., 126
Crawford, George W., 78
Crawford, William, 62
Crockett, Davy, 67

Croghan, George, 12n.
Crystal Palace Exhibition, 82
Cultural pluralism, 94–95

Dallas, Alexander J., 50
Davis, Allen, 107
Davis, Jefferson, 74
Davis, Matthew, 43
Dawes, Sen. Henry L., 86
  quoted, 97, 99
Dawes Act, 87–102
Dawson, John, 43
Dean, John, 191
Declaration on Liberated Europe, 147
Democratic party
  convention of 1932, 119, 125
  nature of, in 1930s, 123–24
Deponceau, Peter S., 50
Depression, Great (1930s), 110, 120ff.
Dexter, Samuel, 62
Dickinson, John, 35
Diem, Ngo Dinh, 165–67
Divine, Robert, 149
Donelson, Andrew, 59
Douglas, Stephen A., 77
Douglass, Frederick, 26, 79
Draper, Theodore, 164
Duane, William J., 59

Ehrlichman, John, 184
Eisenhower, Dwight D., 15, 90, 165,
  171, 188
Election of
  1800, 43ff.
  1824, 47
  1828, 57–58
  1860, 79
Ellicott, Thomas, 68
Ellsberg, Daniel, 173, 175
Emancipation Proclamation, 83
Emerson, Ralph W., 80
Erie Canal, 63
Ezell, John, 127

Federal Bureau of Investigation, 140,
  190–91, 193
Feis, Herbert, 155–56, 160
Fischer, Fritz, 112
Foote, Henry, 73
Ford, Gerald, 193, 195
Forsyth, John, 67
Forten, James, 24
Franklin, Benjamin, 6–8, 31, 34
Franklin, John, 40
Freneau, Peter, 44
Friedrich, Carl, 34

Galissonière, Michel La, 10–11
Gallatin, Albert, 43, 46
Garner, John Nance, 119–20, 124

  philosophy of, 126–29
Garrison, William Lloyd, 24
Gilmer, Thomas, 58
Gore-McLemore Bill, 116
Gouge, James, 62
Gouge, William, 62
Greeley, Horace, 75
Green, Constance, 111
Gregg, William, 26
Gunn, James, 53

Halberstam, David, 172–73
Haldeman, Robert, 184
Hamilton, Alexander, 31, 35, 40, 47, 62
  on Burr and Jefferson, 44
  national bank, 34
  New York ratifying convention, 32
  on presidency, 37
  relations with Burr, 47–55
Hammer v. Dagenhart, 38
Hammond, Bray, 60–62, 64–65
Hammond, James H., 21
Harper, Robert Goodloe, 45
Harriman, Averill, 151, 166
Harrington, James, 5
Harrison, William Henry, 19
Heady, Morrison, 35
Hearst, William Randolph, 119, 127
Henry, Patrick, 6, 18, 32
Hichborn, Benjamin, 45
Hillhouse, James, 51
Hilliard, Henry, 78
Hitchcock, Sen. Gilbert, 115
Hoadly, Bishop, 38
Hofstadter, Richard, 107
Homestead Act of 1862, 85
Hoover, Herbert, 120–21, 123
Hoover, J. Edgar, 191
Hopkins, Harry, 129, 145
Horsman, Reginald, 94
House, Col. Edward M., 115
Huntington, Samuel, 35
Hutchinson, Thomas, 5

Indian Reorganization Act of 1934, 89

Jackson, Andrew, 39, 47, 54, 81
  and Bank war, 57–70
Jackson, Helen Hunt, 86, 99
Jay, John, 11
Jefferson, Thomas, 14, 27, 34
  on Andrew Jackson, 57–58
  on Articles of Confederation, 33
  on cities, 26
  election of 1800, 43–55
  on Indians, 93, 116
  on slavery, 18–19
Johnson, Lyndon B., 165, 169, 173,
  177–78
Johnson, Richard "Tecumseh," 68

Kaiser Wilhelm, 116
Kallen, Horace M., 95
Kalm, Peter, 9–10, 13
Kemble, Fanny, 22
Kendall, Amos, 59
Kennedy, John F., 69, 163–81, 190
King, Martin Luther, Jr., 140
King, Rufus, 48

La Galissonière, Michel, 10–11
La Hontan, Baron, 9
Lansing, John, 50
Lawrence, Cornelius W., 68
League of Nations, 109, 114, 119, 125
Ledyard, Isaac, 48
Lenox, Robert, 67
Lerner, Max, 30
Leuchtenburg, William, 111, 123
Lewis, Morgan, 50
Lincoln, Abraham, 18, 20, 37, 78–83
Linn, James, 45
Livingston, Robert R., 40
Long, Huey, 132, 134–36
Lovejoy, Owen, 20
Lusitania sinking, 113–14
Lyon, Matthew, 45

MacArthur, Gen. Douglas, 134
Madison, James, 20, 31, 35, 40, 43, 47
   balancing of factions, 71
   veto of Bonus Bill, 63
Mangum, Willie, 59
Mansfield, Sen. Mike, 167
Marcy, William L., 67–68
Marshall, Humphrey, 78
Marshall, John, 39, 48
Mason, Stevens T., 44
Matter of Heff, 38
May, Ernest R., 147
McAlister, John T., 175
McCall, George A., 74
McCarthy, Sen. Joseph, 139, 172
McCloskey, Robert, 34
McCord, James, 184
McCormick, Cyrus, 65
McCullough v. *Maryland,* 58
McDuffie, George, 67
McGovern, George, 183
McKean, Thomas, Jr., 50
McLane, Louis, 59
McNamara, Robert, 165, 180
Meacham, A. B., 95
Melting-Pot theory, 94
Merry, Anthony, 52
Miranda, Francisco, 53
Mitchell, Broadus, 52
Mitchell, Atty. Gen. John, 184, 191
Moley, Raymond, 127
Monroe, James, 35, 43
Montcalm, Marquis de, 3–4, 7–8
Morris, Gouverneur, 50

Morris, Robert, 35
Mowry, George, 108
Moynihan, Daniel Patrick, 171
Munitions, ban on, 115–16

Naegele, Kaspar, 12
Nashville convention of 1850, 72, 80–81
Nathan, Richard P., 185
National Security Managers, 174–77
Native American Indians, 85–102
   passim
Newbold, George, 68
New Deal, 122–31
Nixon, Richard M., 36
   on Indian affairs, 88, 90, 101
   Watergate, 183–95

O'Donnell, Kenneth, 167
Olson, Gov. Floyd, 132
Otis, Harrison G., 53
Otis, James, 6

Panic
   of 1837, 60–61
   of 1857, 62–63
Parkman, Francis, 5
Parton, James, 60
Passenger ban, 116
Peckham, Howard H., 9
Pentagon Papers, The, 173
Perry, Ralph B., 15
Persia sinking, 116
Pichon, M., 54
Pickering, Timothy, 40, 51
Pike, James S., 75–77
Pike, Otis, 194
Pinckney, Charles C., 44
Plumer, William, 50
Poinsett, Joel R., 80–81
Polk, James K., 35
Pontiac, 12*n*.
Potsdam Conference, 153
Presidency, imperial, 35–36, 187–89,
   194–95
Preston, William B., 80
Priest, Loring, 96
Progressivism in America
   pre–World War I, 106–107, 117

Quitman, John A., 80

Radicalism, in the 1930s, 131–33
Radisson, Pierre, 10
Randolph, Thomas Jefferson, 22
Reedy, George, 187
Riggs, Elisha, 69
Roche, John P., 173
Roosevelt, Elliott, 141–42
Roosevelt, Franklin D., 60
   and Cold War, 139–60, 189
   in 1930s, 119–37

Roosevelt, Theodore, 113
Rosen, Elliot, 125
Ross, George, 39
Rusk, Dean, 165, 171, 180

Safety Fund System, 65
Saunders, Adm. Charles, 4
Schell, Jonathan, 179
Schlesinger, Arthur M., Jr., 60, 62, 68, 187–89
Sedgwick, Theodore, 60
Selkirk, Earl of, 52
Seward, William H., 73
Shepherd, W. B., 67
Shirley, William, 6
Sinclair, Upton, 132
Sioux Indians
    and General Custer, 86
Sirica, Judge John, 184
Slavery
    British emancipation, 17
    Compromise of 1850, 73–77
    economic value, 18, 21–23
    first attack upon, 17–18
    in Brazil, 23–24
    in cities, 26–27
    in the West, 19–20, 72
    Jefferson's bill, 19
    Lincoln on, 18–20, 79, 82–83
    Missouri Compromise, 72
    three-fifths clause, 37
    treatment of, 23
    Wilmot Proviso, 72
Smith, Al, 123–24
Smith, Gen. Samuel, 45
Smith, Walter B., 63
Snow, Edgar, 150
Soule, George, 110
Stalin, Joseph, 141, 145–60
Stephens, Alexander H., 26, 78, 80
Stimson, Henry S., 155–56
Suffolk System, 65

Taney, Roger, 59, 68
Taylor, Maxwell, 166, 178, 180
Taylor, Zachary, 73–83
Teller, Sen. Henry M., 95
Thomas, Norman, 132–33
Tocqueville, Alexis de, 14
Toombs, Robert, 78
Townsend, Dr. Francis E., 132
Tracy, Uriah, 45
Tredegar Iron Works, 25
Trist, Nicholas, 60

Troup, Robert, 48
Truman, Harry S., 141, 147–60
Trumbull, Lyman, 20
Truxtun, Thomas, 50
Tuchman, Barbara, 29–30
Tugwell, Rexford G., 130, 141, 186
Twelfth Amendment, 44

Union Party of 1936, 133

Van Buren, Martin, 60
Van Gaasbeck, Peter, 48
Verplanck, Gulian, 67
Versailles Treaty, 109
Viet Cong, 166, 168
Vietnam War, 37, 108, 163ff.

Walker, Quork, 18
Wallace, Henry A., 141
Waller, William, 111
War; see also Vietnam War
    Civil, 78–83, 85, 103, 120
    Mexican, 12, 35–36, 72–73
    of 1812, 37–38
    World War I, 104–17
        domestic impact of, 103, 139–40
Ward, John, 69
Washburn, Wilcomb, 86
Washington, George, 11, 15, 22, 24, 31, 34–35
Watergate, 183–95
Watson, James, 48
Webster, Daniel, 58, 67, 73–74, 77–78
Weems, Mason, 35
Whitney, Reuben M., 68
Wilburn, Jean, 66
Williams, T. Harry, 135
Williams, William A., 151, 153
Wilmot Proviso, 72, 75
Wilson, James, 34
Wilson, Woodrow
    and New Freedom, 106–109, 112–17, 124, 141
Wolcott, Oliver, 51
Wolfe, Gen. James, 3–4, 7
Women in World War I, 111
Woodbury, Levi, 59, 62
Worcester v. Georgia, 39

Yalta Conference, 145–47, 149

Zangara, Joseph, 120